VOLUME I

A PICTORIAL HISTORY OF

ARCHITECTURE IN AMERICA

by G. E. KIDDER SMITH

Fellow, American Institute of Architects

Chapter Introductions by

MARSHALL B. DAVIDSON

Editor in Charge

AMERICAN HERITAGE PUBLISHING CO., INC.

BONANZA BOOKS

NEW YORK

EDITOR IN CHARGE
Marshall B. Davidson

ART DIRECTOR
Murray Belsky

MANAGING EDITOR
Beverley Hilowitz

COPY EDITOR
Brenda Savard

EDITORIAL ASSISTANT
Donna F. Whiteman

CONSULTANT LIBRARIAN
Laura L. Masters

This edition is published by Bonanza Books, dis-
tributed by Crown Publishers, Inc., by arrangement with American Heritage Publishing Co., Inc.

h g f e d c b a
1981 EDITION

Library of Congress Cataloging in Publication Data

Smith, G. E. Kidder (George Everard Kidder),
    1913-
    A pictorial history of architecture in America.

    Originally published in 2 v.: New York :
American Heritage Pub. Co. c1976.
    Includes index.
    1. Architecture—United States—Pictorial
works.
I. Title.
NA705.S58   1981   720'.973   81-16773
ISBN 0-517-36237-6   AACR2

Volume I, title pages: Detail, Orange
County Government Center, Goshen, New
York. Volume II, title pages: Detail, San
Francisco de Asis, Ranchos de Taos, New
Mexico. Page 417: Detail, Congregational
Church, Middlebury, Vermont. Page 421:
North Christian Church, Columbus, Indi-
ana.

CONTENTS

EDITORIAL FOREWORD

The pages that follow present what we believe to be the most comprehensive pictorial review of the American architectural scene in all its many phases that has yet been attempted. As he indicates in his introduction, in addition to taking all the superb photographs that are reproduced in these two volumes, G. E. Kidder Smith has documented each subject by, among other measures, copious field notes taken at the site, with the assistance of his wife Dorothea. He has generously made this information available to the editors at American Heritage who have adapted it to prepare the texts and captions accompanying the illustrations. Although they often differ in form from his copy, largely because of the exigencies of space, in substance these texts conform as closely as possible to the essential facts and observations recorded by Mr. Smith. Occasionally, to explain certain combinations and sequences that evolved as the design of the two volumes progressed, the editors have added further information, particularly historical data, and changed points of emphasis. At every stage in the preparation of the work, Kidder Smith has contributed his informed advice and his sympathetic understanding of the problems of design and production, for which the editors are most grateful.

As Mr. Smith also indicates in his subsequent remarks, America has a very large number of distinguished and interesting buildings, old and new, which deserve our attention. Over the years this country has probably produced more different styles of buildings than any other nation in the same span of time. In part this is testimony to the many different strands of tradition, native or brought here sometimes from far places, that have been woven into the rich fabric of American life. It is testimony as well to the innovative aspects of American experience. Finally, it is testimony to the enormous diversity of this wide land and to the large variety of its resources, which have led builders and planners, especially in earlier days, to meet the demands of local and regional circumstances in special ways in special places. To help elucidate that important point the material in these two volumes has been arranged in seven sections, each dealing with a separate large region of the country, where such factors as climate, available building materials, and variant cultural traditions have often led to particular and unique expressions in architecture.

During the Depression years the Historic American Buildings Survey of the National Park Service listed some twelve thousand structures in the United States worthy of notice and preservation. Within hardly more than a quarter of a century almost half of these buildings had been destroyed from one cause or another. This dismal story is unfortunately all too characteristic of American experience. The importance of Kidder Smith's documentation as here presented is underlined by the fact that as these books were being prepared for the press, it has been reported that the Novelty Building in Helena, Montana, has recently collapsed. Others may have been demolished or otherwise destroyed, but such information is not immediately available. The fate of still others remains in some doubt; this at a time when the preservation and reconstitution of significant buildings has become a profoundly influential factor in the environmental and economic well-being of America.   **M.B.D.**

AUTHOR'S INTRODUCTION

The United States possesses an impressive number of great structures from most periods of the nation's history, plus many little-known but rewarding examples of regional and vernacular architecture. These two books seek to capture the spirit of such works; sometimes their primitive cleverness, often their substantial elegance, occasionally their daring, and, once in a while, their pure poetry. Besides interesting the reader and reassuring him of the nation's extraordinary contribution to the art and science of architecture over the centuries, it is hoped that the following pages may lead him to explore the wonderful world of buildings that abound in all fifty states. These volumes constitute primarily a visual panorama of architectural developments in America, beginning with the ingenious shelters of the southwest Indians of the twelfth century and concluding with the often awesome projects of our own time.

The selection of examples shown here is a personal one, but one made only after critical on-the-spot assessments—always with my wife's aid—of some three thousand structures. Aside from an initial ground rule that every building here included be personally evaluated, with no secondhand impressions blurring conclusions, it was of course essential that each have architectural merit or historical significance. Virtually all those here presented are open to the public at least part of the time, and those who are so inclined may visit them and enjoy what they have to offer, both inside and out. The exteriors of several private buildings are so rewarding just from the sidewalk that, although their interiors are closed to the public, some of them are also included, along with a pleasant street or two lined with such dwellings.

Obviously it was not feasible to make an inventory of all this country's outstanding buildings. But after motoring some 130,000 miles in all fifty states and the District of Columbia, I believe that those here illustrated highlight our rich architectural heritage, from Columbia Falls, Maine, to the Kona Coast of Hawaii, and from Key West, Florida, to Anchorage, Alaska, and represent a cross section of virtually all periods and styles. Some styles may not appeal to all readers—several hold distinctly minor interest for me—but all major developments are shown, together with descriptive texts in each instance.

I have been asked how I established a procedure for tracking down so many buildings spread over so many miles. The first necessity was to devise a cross-indexed field sheet with space for the name of each building, its address, the architect and date when known, followed by a series of pertinent points to be checked and written up on location. These sheets would then be filled in with the requisite information and filed by state in outsized manila envelopes. For preliminary selection of the contemporary buildings, I relied basically on my extensive architectural file of selected clippings and tear sheets about important buildings from professional journals and other relevant publications of the last thirty-five years. It was then a simple matter to winnow and collate more than a thousand references and separate them by state, making of course a field sheet in each case. Interviews with architects as we traveled kept developments up to date.

Data on historic buildings were somewhat more elusive. *An American Heritage*

Guide, Historic Houses of America proved invaluable, and there are a number of books about selected older structures of the United States. Although there is no single satisfactory, complete history of the architecture of this country, there are many extremely useful studies dealing with various periods of American architecture and with individual architects. These have been most helpful. (It should be observed that little of this literature is directed to the layman.) Hugh Morrison's *Early American Architecture* (Oxford, 1952) is superb—my own copy is in shreds from repeated usage—but it covers the subject only up to about 1800. Among other prominent authors dealing primarily with historical developments were the late Fiske Kimball and Talbot Hamlin; in our own time Henry-Russell Hitchcock stands out as the dean of our architectural historians, but he is closely followed by a score of other experts in the field. Many state historical societies, university historians, fellow architects, curators, and custodians of historic buildings were of great help with suggestions and data—more than I can possibly list, although I deeply appreciate their many contributions. There are also a number of dedicated and informed journalists who cover architectural developments in the daily press and to whose writings I have profitably referred.

When, from such various sources of information, several thousand field sheets covering both historic and contemporary buildings were filled in and arranged by state, then chronologically within a city or other prescribed area, I assembled a country-wide set of road maps, circled each spot to be visited, and with my wife took off on a series of forays. Some of these, it must be admitted, were taxing: for instance, after staying at forty-seven motels in sixty days of traveling, we may have found the prospect of visiting one or two more distant buildings too much to contemplate. However, we hope there are but few lacunae in our over-all coverage.

With his extraordinary perspective of the American historical scene, my editor, Marshall B. Davidson, with the very considerable help of his associate, Beverley Hilowitz, has extracted data from my field sheets and produced the informed and pithy text which accompanies the illustrations. His introductions to the various sectional chapters, with their historical background, add appreciably to an understanding of the architectural setting that is illustrated. As art director, Murray Belsky combined text and photographs with imagination and felicity that enhances every page. I am grateful to them and to others listed in the masthead.

This project was originally suggested by John Entenza, then director (now emeritus) of the Graham Foundation for Advanced Studies in the Arts, as a guide to be called *New Architecture U.S.A.* (a companion to my *New Architecture of Europe*, Meridian-World, 1961). The Graham Foundation and the National Endowment for the Arts gave generous matching grants to finance the necessary research and travel. However, work on documenting the contemporary scene was scarcely begun when it was realized that comprehensive coverage of significant American architecture of *all* periods would make a more valuable contribution than one limited to postwar work. As a consequence, instead of taking two years, the period covered by the initial grants, the project has taken almost eight. The extra research, travel, and updating were again supported by the National Endowment for the Arts and by the Ford Foundation, the latter with two grants at critical moments, which were deeply appreciated.

Not being an architectural historian by profession, I undertook critical commentary on the great variety of historic American buildings with some hesitation. I was indeed advised against doing so by several historian friends. However, as an architect, critic, and author of five books on contemporary European architecture—and having been fortunate enough to have seen many of the world's greatest buildings, old and new—I hoped broader interest would result if I included, and even stressed, our own distinguished historic buildings along with those of the present. For in our democratic society, unless our voters, and through them our legislators, develop a sharper awareness of our man-made environment and keener judgments of what is being built (or torn down), the future of architecture and of our cities will be left to the financial interests, primarily the banks and insurance companies, whose record has so far not been encouraging.

Look closely at the man-made chaos which surrounds so many of us so much of the time. Then examine the structures shown on these pages, for in addition to rewarding as any work of art rewards, they can hone our appreciation of the elements of quality in our environment. We need more of that quality.   **G.E.K.S.**

A NOTE ON THE PHOTOGRAPHS

The greater part of the pictures used here were taken with a tripod-mounted Swiss Sinar "Expert" camera (alas, no longer made), using 4" x 5" filmpacks. The most commonly employed lenses were a 180mm Symmar and, for interiors, a 90mm Super Angulon. Most of the rest were shot with a well-loved Rolleiflex. A medium-yellow filter was used for all outdoor pictures, and the unique Metrastar exposure meter was called on for interiors. No artificial lights—other, of course, than those existing—were used for the inside shots for the simple reason that I do not have any and would not know what to do with them if I did. Moreover, although I am not a professional photographer, as an architect I feel that most largescale rooms should be happy with their own illumination. A straight, no-prop approach was sought, with, if possible, a revealing three-dimensionality as brought out by a play of light and shade. Many of the buildings had to be photographed on the run, as it were, because of demanding logistics, hence could have profited by more time, study, and better weather. However, the two recent "updating" grants earlier mentioned, which were vital in making all coverage topical (the project having started in 1967), also enabled me to reshoot under better lighting conditions many of the structures that had been indifferently taken some years earlier. The negatives were beautifully developed by Axel Grosser, who also made many enlargements; the majority of the latter, however, were made by myself.   **G.E.K.S.**

NEW ENGLAND

CONNECTICUT
MAINE
MASSACHUSETTS
NEW HAMPSHIRE
RHODE ISLAND
VERMONT

From the beginning of colonization and for scores of years to follow, the men and women who peopled New England formed a remarkably homogeneous society—for America, that is. The population was not altogether English in origin, to be sure. One of the earliest Boston silversmiths, William Rouse, was a Dutchman who emigrated from Wessel in the Rhineland. The Wendells also came from Holland, and there were others of different stock whose family names rank high in the "Yankee" hierarchy. The Crowninshields came from Germany, for instance, the Faneuils and the Reveres from France, and still others from Ireland, Wales, and Scotland. Nevertheless, in spite of these variant strains, the New England community had a firm English Puritan base and a greater cultural unity than was known in colonies to the south. That distinctive northern culture, wrote the French-born observer Michel Guillaume Jean de Crèvecoeur in 1782, exhibited "a most conspicuous figure in this great and variegated picture" of the New World.

The first permanent structures raised by the early New England settlers owed their essential character to the particular origins of their builders and owners. In many parts of the world—in India, Central and South America, East Africa, and other places —Europeans settled in regions where the native population had long since developed a relatively sophisticated culture with traditional building techniques adapted to the local climate and other conditions. However, in the arts of building, or the amenities of civilized living in general, the American aborigines had nothing to teach these newcomers to an alien and often hostile world. (To gain a foothold in the wilderness the white man did have to learn from the red man methods of cultivation and harvesting adapted to American soil and to those plants that would flourish in it; but that was living at a subsistence level.)

Like other colonists in times past and in times yet to come, in their new surroundings these pioneer settlers tended to re-create as faithfully as circumstances permitted, the world they had left behind—those aspects of it, at least, that they most favorably recalled. In this they succeeded so well that, aside from the wilderness setting, there was little to distinguish their homes in the New World from those they had quit to cross the Atlantic. A large number among the first Puritan contingents not only came from England, but from a rather limited area of southeastern England where traditions of building were relatively uniform. There most of them had lived in small towns and rural villages that lingered in the fading glow of the Middle Ages, hardly aware of those transforming forces in design and conception, originally born of the Italian Renaissance, that in the seventeenth century were radically changing the appearance of the courts, capitals, and larger cities of Europe. Then, and for long years afterward, there was no such thing as a trained architect in New England or elsewhere in the colonies. It is altogether unlikely that such words as *architecture* and *style* were even in the vocabulary of the settlers, no less in common usage. Their houses and other structures were planned and undertaken in accordance with habits and methods that were all but timeless and matters of common knowledge.

The first arrivals in America, and later generations who moved westward, were confronted by dense forests on a scale Europe had not known for centuries past. With such an overwhelming abundance of timber to work with, the early builders naturally turned to wood as a principal building material. (To this day most American houses, outside urban limits at least, are still wooden.) Despite the quantity of granite, sandstone, marble, and other stone that was stored in the rocky countryside, fewer than a handful of stone houses are known to have existed in seventeenth-century New England and fewer than that have survived.

In *The House of the Seven Gables*, written two centuries after the first foundations of that storied house were laid, Nathaniel Hawthorne suggested that, to escape the dead hand of the past with all its restrictive conditions, each generation should build its houses and public structures anew. The House of the Seven Gables still stands, of course, with the additions that have accrued to it over the years. Like other such structures of its time and place it was laboriously raised by communal effort to last through generations of daily use. However, fire, hurricanes, wreckers' tools, and sheer neglect have all played their parts in the destruction of most of such early dwellings over the course of the last three hundred years. Before the end of the eighteenth century surviving examples had already become something of a curiosity, as the Reverend William Bentley of Salem, Massachusetts, noted in his diary one day in 1796, after having examined the house of a recently deceased neighbor whose family had occupied it for generations past without altering its form or texture. The windows of the house, Bentley wrote, were "of the small glass with lead in diamonds & open upon hinges." (During the American Revolution the lead from some such casement windows had at times been melted into bullets.) "The Doors open with wooden latches. . . . The large fire places . . . ," and so on, the diarist noted, down a list of what seemed to him strangely archaic features. Although Bentley does not mention it, the rooms of the house were undoubtedly clustered about a massive central chimney, with a second story overhanging the first; and it may never have been painted on the outside, a practice that was becoming widespread only in Bentley's own day. The ubiquitous white-painted clapboards we associate with the traditional New England village scene were more characteristic of a later time.

In spite of the attrition that has so drastically diminished the number of such venerable buildings (including some that were larger and more pretentious than any that have survived, such as the Old College at Harvard), several dozen of them remain standing, scattered about the New England countryside. Most of these have experienced some alteration of their original fabric; windows and chimneys have been replaced and changed, and additions have been made. (By the time Hawthorne wrote his book, the House of the Seven Gables had been changed so often that even the author was confused; at one point, at least, the house, originally a simple two-room structure, had as many as eight gables.) Many of such houses have lost the immediate surroundings that once significantly contributed to the character of their sites. Some have been lovingly restored to their earlier state; others that had completely disappeared have been meticulously reconstructed. In any event, as the illustrations on the following pages make very clear, enough evidence remains for us to glean a fair impression of the physical appearance of seventeenth-century New England buildings and of how they functioned. Reflecting on such matters, the same William Bentley of Salem already quoted concluded that "the arts were better understood in the first generation . . . than in any succeeding. The first settlers were from old countries & were men of enterprise. In a new Country they had only the necessities of life to provide for. . . . An ingenious Carpenter made rakes, a good mason laid cellar rocks & bricks in clay. A good painter became a glazier of glass windows set in lead. They taught what they practiced not what they knew." In the meaning given to the word in those days, these men were artists.

There is a strong tinge of nostalgia in those observations. Long before Bentley set them down in his informative diary, the New England scene had taken on radically new aspects. In 1675 and 1676 New England suffered a war—King Philip's War, as it was called after Metacom, or Philip, sachem of the Wampanoags, the Indians who started the conflict. With that gory business concluded and, particularly, with the recall of the Massachusetts Bay charter in 1684 and the appointment of a royal governor, forces that had been latent in the colonies for some years past came to active life. With the reign of William of Orange following the "Glorious Revolution," the colonies were brought not only into the orbit of world politics but into the main current of world thought as well.

Some years earlier than these developments, in 1666, a great fire had virtually wiped out medieval London and opened the way to a massive modernization of the city's architecture. The new buildings that replaced the charred ruins of London were formally designed structures that owed their basic character and their ornamental detail to Renaissance formulas as these had been interpreted by English architects and builders. The most influential practitioner of the new order in England was Sir Christopher Wren, whose plan—never consummated—for re-creating the stricken capitol of London inspired the one developed more than a century later for Washington, D.C., by Pierre Charles L'Enfant, a French veteran of the American Revolution. Among the many new buildings that Wren designed were fifty-two London churches which, with their tall graceful spires rising high above low-pitched roofs, set a general pattern for Georgian churches in the years to come, in America as well as in England. Wren is mistakenly given credit for having designed a number of colonial meetinghouses. However, many of them do owe some distant debt to his original creations, seen through the interpretations of Wren's followers. In any case, the spires that rose from the very center of early New England community life became an elementary, lasting American symbol, even for those who came to America later from distant lands and who settled in remote parts of the country. Towering above each village they stood as a witness to the stability, the order, and the high purpose of the society below.

The prestige of London culture was high in America. In many important ways the colonies had much closer ties to England than they had to one another. London set a common standard in matters of dress, literature, art, and architecture. To some degree, no doubt, the large-scale rebuilding of London in the new style accelerated its acceptance and its popularity in the New World. As one English observer wrote of Boston in 1686, "when any new houses are built they are made conformable to our new buildings in London after the fire." "A Gentleman from *London*," wrote another visitor at the turn of the century, "would almost think himself at home at *Boston*. . . . There is no Fashion in *London*, but in three or four Months is to be seen at *Boston*."

There is hyperbole in both those statements. London was then a metropolis, Boston but a little "city in the wilderness." Nevertheless, both observations truly indicate the changes in style that would set standards in American architecture in general for the rest of the colonial period.

The fashionable house of the new order was distinguished from its predecessors by its emphasis on symmetry and formal plan and by its use of classical motifs and detail. In the seventeenth century, windows, doorways, and fireplaces were simple, unadorned openings cut in the fabric of a house; structural elements inside and out were frankly stated, left exposed and undecorated. Now such elements were considered as features of a studied design. Windows—double-hung sash instead of hinged casements—were set in molded frames and arranged rhythmically on the façade, whose central feature was a more or less elaborate doorway. Within, beams and corner posts that had earlier been frankly revealed were paneled or otherwise encased or plastered over altogether. To keep a larger number of rooms as warm as possible during the winter months, chimneys were built at either end of a structure and fireplaces were smaller and more efficient. More than mere formality of planning and designing was involved in such orderly arrangements. They reflected new concepts of living, attitudes that called for specialized functions of interior spaces and pointed toward modern standards of convenience and of comfort.

Broadly speaking, the term "Georgian style" is applied to the wide variety of eighteenth-century structures, public and private, built in this new manner. In their plans and designs all follow, more or less strictly, certain rules of architecture that had their origin in ancient Rome and that filtered down through the ages in a succession of manuals and pattern books, constantly adapted to local circumstance, ultimately to provide guidelines for the builders of colonial America, up and down the Atlantic seaboard. In the beginning there was the first-century Roman architect Vitruvius, whose ten-volume treatise, *De architectura*, happened to be the only writing on the subject to survive from antiquity. Fifteen hundred years later the Italian Andrea Palladio issued his "modern" interpretations of classical styles, owning his debt to Vitruvius, "my sole master and guide." Palladio's publications continued to fire the imagination of builders and architects throughout the Western world for the next several centuries. They may well have been the most influential works on architecture ever written. "Dear Impeccable Palladio's rule," as Lord Bristol referred to these prescriptions, swept England in the seventeenth and eighteenth centuries. A pocket version of his *Book I*, first published in England in 1663, raced through twelve editions in the next two generations. Thence it was but a short and logical step to the publication of handbooks presenting individual and creative variations on these basic themes. And it was largely these English interpretations, more than several times removed from their classical source, that served the colonial American builders and their clients—such popular publications as *A Book of Architecture* by James Gibbs, *Palladio Londonensis: or The London Art of Building* by William Salmon, and *British Architect* by Abraham Swan; and there were others, most of which could be found in the colonies.

Throughout the colonies, particularly in New England, local craftsmen, with bold vigor and with complete freedom from any academic restraints, translated the plates of these books in native woods, often naively carved and painted to simulate the stonework for which the designs were originally prepared. The most flexible, the most masterly, and perhaps the most prolific of colonial New England practitioners in the Georgian style was Peter Harrison of Newport, Rhode Island, a sometime ship captain and self-taught master builder who has been called the "first American architect," which he was not, and the most "masterly architect in the colonies," which he very probably was. At one time or another Harrison oversaw the construction of everything from forts and lighthouses to public markets, churches, synagogues, libraries, and private dwellings. Illustrations of several of his most notable buildings appear on the pages that follow. Born of Quaker parents, Harrison had converted to the Anglican Church. He was a Tory. Following his death in 1775 at the age of fifty-nine, a mob of patriots misguidedly and tragically burned his papers and library, including his drawings and his numerous books on architecture.

The successful conclusion of the War of Independence hardly lessened America's old reliance upon England either for manufactures or cultural guidance. Such doughty chauvinists as Noah Webster called for a fresh start toward a purely American way of life. America must be "as famous for arts as for arms," Webster insisted. They must stop "mimicking the follies of other nations and basking in the sunshine of foreign glory." However, a large part of the American public, among the fashionable at least, found nothing incompatible between an "inveterate enmity" toward Britain and a respect for the manners and customs of Britons.

During the troubled years of the Revolutionary period a separate and peaceful revolution had been brewing in the British Isles—a revolution that within roughly a score of years remarkably changed architectural fashions (as well as fashions in furnishings and decoration). Essentially the new ruling taste was another classical revival, but one that instead of finding its precepts in Palladian versions of antiquity rather looked directly for inspiration among the ruins and remains of ancient Rome itself. The startling revelations that came with excavations of the long-buried cities of Herculaneum and Pompeii led to further examinations of the ruins at Rome itself and of Athens, Palmyra, Baalbek, Split, and other ancient sites. And, in the last decades of the eighteenth century, all these discoveries in turn spawned a large shelfful of books, published in Italian, German, French, and English, describing and illustrating the finds and the studies of them that had resulted. The range of this literature brought about a greater uniformity of style throughout western Europe (although with national and regional accents) than had ever before prevailed, a uniformity that was in time and to a degree shared by America.

But America had to wait until its quarrel with Great Britain was settled before feeling the impact of the new vogue. Robert Adam was the leading exponent of that style in England. He was a Scottish architect who had toured Italy and Dalmatia and studied at first hand their classical remains. Just before the Revolution, in 1773, the first volume of *The Works of Robert and James Adam, Esquires* was issued in London. (James Adam was Robert's brother.) With this publication the Adam brothers not only won the patronage of numerous wealthy and aristocratic clients but, with their adaptations of the light and graceful later Roman forms and ornament, provided other architects and designers with material they could and did copy and further adapt to their specific needs. Some years later in a lecture before students of the Royal Academy of Arts, Sir John Soane spoke of "the electric power of this Revolution in Art" that had been sparked by the Adams' neoclassical innovations.

By the time the influence of these developments reached America the young nation was in direct contact with the European continent, where much the same classical "revolution" had taken place, as well as with England. Americans, as part of the Atlantic community, shared its common preoccupation with the new forms and designs that had taken over architectural fashion. In every part of the land the structures that were rising reflected in one way or another the classical spirit of the day. There had been relatively little building during the Revolutionary War, but in the early years of the republic construction boomed in every state of the federal union. Not only were more houses needed to accommodate the increasing population, but public buildings as well to serve the new state and national governments. The ex-colonists were attempting the awesome project of establishing, for the first time since ancient Rome, a large republican nation, and the new classicism became a national idiom, freely and easily enough used by men who saw in ancient Rome, and Greece, the models for their own experiment in government—the building blocks of achievements that it was earnestly hoped and believed would quickly come about. In other words, the style was not only an architectural fashion, it was also an expression of social and political purpose.

No city has ever been to the United States what Rome, Paris, and London so long have been to their respective countries; the main center, not only of government, but of wealth, fashion, and culture as well. Each of the burgeoning urban centers of the new republic had been born of widely different circumstances; each had been shaped differently by its separate colonial experience; and the particular inheritance of each was marked in the character of its population, the nature of its enterprise, and its physical appearance. In and about a number of these little cities there developed regional expressions in architecture that, although rooted in the classical spirit, were distinctly different in their own ways.

In naturalizing the new style, in giving it what could be termed a national character —a Federal style, as it has been labeled—individuals played much more prominent roles than in the colonial period. During the last ten or twenty years of the eighteenth century, men of truly professional training in architecture now took their place at the head of the distinguished laymen and amateurs and the practical builders who had for so long set standards in the field. The earliest of this new caste came from overseas, from England, Ireland, France, among other places, bringing with them ideas, and ways of realizing them, that broke sharply with colonial precedents. And by their example they stimulated native talents to unexpected achievements.

For a generation following the Revolution, Salem, Massachusetts, was one of the most celebrated seaports of the world. (In some remote parts of the world where its sleek little ships journeyed for such exotic cargoes as pepper and spice, it was believed that Salem *was* the United States—an immensely rich and important country.) Whether or not he was aware of the emigrants' work, Samuel McIntire, a carpenter (among other things) of Salem, applied his native skills to the design and construction of a number of buildings in and about his home town and produced personal versions of the Adam style that gave additional and special grace and dignity to the local scene. The houses that he designed, built, and decorated (he was also a master carver), for the contemporary merchant princes, a number of whose dwellings are still standing, are among the finest examples of domestic architecture in the Federal style. Unfortunately, the great house he built for Elias Hasket Derby, New England's first millionaire —"more like a palace than the dwelling of an American merchant," according to a visitor to Salem from Baltimore—was destroyed shortly after it was completed.

Although he may justifiably be called an architect, this Yankee jack-of-all-trades, who worked on ships and buildings alike, was also a sculptor and musician of sorts. "His industry, usefulness and consistent virtues gave him an uncommon share of the affections of all who knew him," reported one obituary. "By his own well directed energies, he became one of the best of men." In the tradition of earlier fine craftsmen, he often tackled such modest jobs as mending fences and building pigsties. "Directed by an ear of exquisite nicety," he also performed on different musical instruments and repaired his neighbors' when they were out of order. As one Salem minister recalled on the day McIntire died: "All the Instruments we use he could understand & was the best person to be employed in correcting any defects." He further observed that there was no one left in Salem who could take the place of this versatile craftsman.

Meanwhile, in and about Boston McIntire's slightly younger contemporary Charles Bulfinch was building a towering reputation. As a young man he had made a grand tour of England, France (he saw Paris with Thomas Jefferson as a guide), and Italy, observing "particularly the wonders of Architecture" that he encountered on his travels. In 1798 he finished atop Beacon Hill the new Massachusetts State House, whose lofty gilded dome, covered with copper by Paul Revere and Son in 1802, remains one of the great architectural landmarks of the Boston area. (When it was completed a group of "southern gentlemen" pronounced it "the most magnificent building in the Union.") It has been said that during the three decades between the Constitutional Convention of 1787 and the end of the War of 1812, Bulfinch largely helped to transform his native Boston from a provincial town into an orderly and elegant New England capital. "The great number of new and elegant buildings which have been erected in this Town, within the last ten years," observed one returning visitor in 1808, "strike the eye with astonishment, and prove the rapid manner in which the people here have been acquiring wealth." All too little evidence of Bulfinch's considerable achievement still stands.

Many of his finest buildings were razed during his own lifetime, and the majority of his remaining creations were dismantled in the course of the next fifty years.

In 1817 Bulfinch was summoned to Washington by President James Monroe to complete the construction of the Capitol, a Herculean task that occupied most of his middle age until he returned to Boston and retirement. In some ways his disciple, Asher Benjamin of Greenfield, Massachusetts, had an even greater impact than his master on the architecture of New England. It was in 1796, during the Federal period, that Benjamin issued the first original architectural handbook to appear in this country, *The Country Builder's Assistant: Containing a Collection of New Designs of Carpentry and Architecture.* It was the first of seven guides that he published and which went through forty-four editions. Although English manuals continued to be a principal source for American builders, Benjamin's books were specifically intended to represent the economical use of native materials with practical plans and construction details. With such a guide at one hand, and with saw, hammer, and nails at the other, local carpenters throughout New England—or anywhere in the land for that matter—could work out their problems on the spot to their own or their clients' tastes.

Benjamin kept revising his books to keep abreast of the times. "Since my last publication," he wrote in the introduction to his 1830 edition, "the Roman school of architecture has been entirely changed for the Grecian"; and he proceeded to advise his readers in the practical and ornamental nature of what we now term the Greek Revival style, covering everything from the decoration of a fireplace to the design of a façade. It was with the Greek Revival style that classicism in architecture reached the end of its long sway—for the time being, at least. (White paint had by then become a customary coating for frame structures; the color was inseparably associated with classic precedents.) Evidence of the influence of these books can be seen in the tidy villages that are so characteristic of the New England countryside, villages that moved James Fenimore Cooper to rapture when he visited the region after a trip abroad. "New England may justly glory in its villages!" he wrote. "In space, freshness, an air of neatness and comfort, they far exceed anything I have ever seen, even in the mother country. . . . I have passed, in one day, six or seven of these beautiful, tranquil and enviable looking hamlets, for not one of which have I been able to recollect an equal in the course of all my European travelling."

Following the War of 1812 the increasing pace of the industrial revolution nurtured a new sort of community in New England—the manufacturing village—and new developments in architecture were now required. Partly because of the abundance of convenient water power, the new factories did not at first mass in existing cities but rather sought points along the swifter streams of the countryside. In contrast to the grimy, congested manufacturing centers of England, where coal supplied the power, the American counterparts had an almost idyllic aspect. In Connecticut, wrote the economist Tenche Coxe early in the nineteenth century, the traveler's eye was "charmed with the view of delightful villages, suddenly rising as it were by magic, along the banks of some meandering rivulet, flourishing by . . . the protecting arms of manufactures." Such water-powered mills initiated mass production in America.

The new factories called for a special type of architecture. Larger spaces had to be spanned; stronger floors were required to support heavy machinery; improved heating and lighting were necessary for efficient operation; greater fire resistance was demanded than in the ordinary home. In time all these conditions were met, and in further time the improvements that were developed were applied to the design and construction of domestic and public buildings as well.

In New England as elsewhere in the Western world the advance of industrialism was paced by the growth of romanticism; the one looked to the future in its aspirations, the

Hoxie House, Sandwich, Mass. (about 1637)

The Hoxie House in Sandwich, Massachusetts, not far distant from Plymouth, is the oldest dwelling on Cape Cod. According to local legend it was built in 1637, the same year the town was settled by "ten men from Saugus." Like the early houses at Plymouth, it too was constructed with vertical boarding. The town of Sandwich bought the house in 1959, and it has been restored to its condition of 1680-90, but with a renewed shingle covering. With its long, sloping roof line at the rear, in outline it resembles a medieval saltbox, whence the name given to this type of dwelling so familiar to the New England landscape. Although it is not apparent from the outside, the main room of the Hoxie House rises to the full height of the roof, a very rare feature of interest.

Ironworks Reconstruction, Saugus, Mass. (as of 1646)

Ironmaster's House, Saugus, Mass. (1646)

The earliest ironworks in the American colonies was founded by John Winthrop, Jr., at Saugus, Massachusetts, in 1646. Handicapped by high production costs, insufficient capital, and lack of skilled labor, the operation continued only for about twenty years. However, the foundation of the future nation's iron and steel industry was here laid. (A similar enterprise had been projected at Falling Creek, Virginia, in 1622, but the workmen were killed by the Indians before actual production was started.) The ancient mill had long since completely disappeared when, with funds provided by the American Iron and Steel Institute in the 1940's, it was reconstructed on the basis of meticulous archaeological research and informed conjecture by the firm of Perry, Shaw & Hepburn, Kehoe & Dean, architects of the Colonial Williamsburg restoration, and their technical consultants. Fortunately, the nearby house of the ironmaster survived the years and was continually lived in for more than two and a half centuries. In that time it had experienced alterations, but it has been restored approximately to its original condition. With its many-gabled roof, its leaded-glass casements, its second-story overhang with carved pendants, it bears a strong resemblance to the House of the Seven Gables. The Saugus buildings, America's first "company town," are now fortunately under the competent supervision of the National Park Service.

The Whipple House in Ipswich, Massachusetts, is a good example of the "growing" house so typical of early New England domestic buildings. Initially, it was a two-and-a-half-story boxlike structure with one room on the ground floor. About forty years later a slightly larger section was added and in another forty years a lean-to ell was incorporated with those two elements to produce the irregularly shaped complex we see today in its restored state. (The house was purchased by the Ipswich Historical Society in 1898, moved from its original site to its present location, and completely restored.) Ipswich was founded in 1634 by John Winthrop, Jr., the entrepreneur of the Saugus ironworks. A man well versed in "Physicke," he had transported his English garden to America in seed form, to grow plants useful for remedies, seasoning, dyes, cosmetics, and other highly practical purposes. Ipswich soon burgeoned into a "store of orchards and gardens," where families like the Whipples distilled "syrup of clove gilly flowers," angelica, mint, strawberry, and rose water. A thorough 1683 inventory of the Whipple House helped with restoration of the garden by its list of "products" then on the shelf.

John Whipple House, Ipswich, Mass.
(about 1640 and later)

Guilford, Connecticut, was an early offshoot of the colony at New Haven. In 1639 the Reverend Henry Whitfield, an Oxford graduate and a pillar of the Puritan church, led his faithful followers to the site where he almost immediately started construction of what has been called the oldest stone house in this country. Over the centuries the structure served not only as a dwelling, but also as a church and even a fort (its outer walls are two feet thick), and it suffered fire and other vicissitudes. However, it has been restored to a fair semblance of its early appearance when it was the finest residence of the village. With wood so plentiful and so easily worked and lime for fine mortar in scarce supply (except in Rhode Island), stone houses were rarely built in early New England. An entire end wall of the Eleazer Arnold House, built in Lincoln, Rhode Island, about 1687, is made of field-stone. This immensely sturdy construction rises into a tall and massive pilastered chimney. The house is a fine and characteristic example of what is called in Rhode Island a "stone-ender."

OVERLEAF: *Eleazer Arnold House, Lincoln, R.I. (about 1687).* The rest of the house, which Eleazer Arnold once ran as a tavern, is of timber construction. Its narrow, unpainted clapboards, diamond-paned casements, and nail-studded door, as restored on the front façade, create a pattern that three centuries ago was a ubiquitous ornament to the New England scene.

Eleazer Arnold House, Lincoln, R.I. (about 1687)

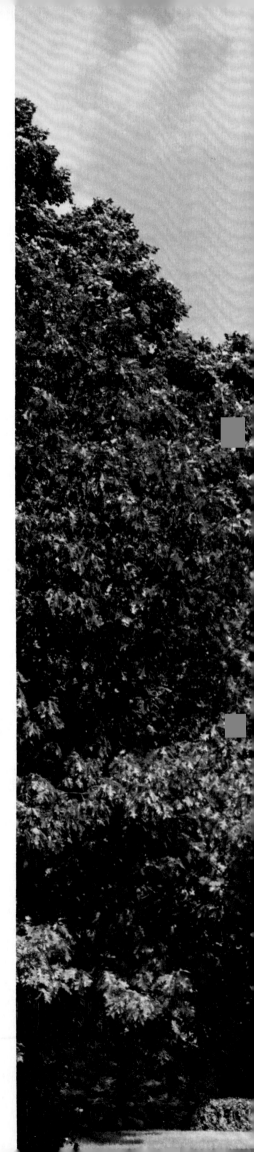

Henry Whitfield House, Guilford, Conn. (1640)

Old Ship Meetinghouse, Hingham, Mass. (1681; 1755)

Old Ship Meetinghouse at Hingham, Massachusetts, is the only surviving
example of the boxlike, frame-structured New England houses of worship
of the seventeenth century. It is also the oldest wooden church in America
and the oldest meetinghouse in continued use. (A seating plan drawn up at
the time of the building's dedication in 1681 still exists.) Such a structure,
serving both religious and secular functions, had no prototype in England;
it was an innovation of the New World. The interior of Old Ship, on the
other hand, reveals an intricate arrangement of beams, rafters, and trusses
hewn of massive oak timbers that owns a clear debt to Gothic engineering
in wood. That it also recalls an inverted ship's hull accounts for the name
Old Ship. Additions were made in the eighteenth century and the whole
structure reroofed in its present form.

The house raised in 1683 (the date June 8 of that year is gouged in one of the beams) as a parsonage for the Reverend Joseph Capen by the community at Topsfield, Massachusetts, on a twelve-acre lot of land allotted to him by the town, stands as one of the most picturesque architectural reminders of New England's Puritan past. A deep (sixteen-inch) overhang along the front and others above the second story at both gabled ends, each embellished with large, decorative pendants at the corner, enliven what would otherwise be a simple box form. They also suggest the skilled heavy carpentry that was brought to New England by craftsmen from such areas as Kent and Essex in southeastern England. The house, including its chimney stack, fancifully paneled in Tudor fashion, its clapboards, and window embrasures, has been restored and is in the custody of the Topsfield Historical Society.

Parson Capen House, Topsfield, Mass. (1683)

Stanley-Whitman House, Farmington, Conn. (about 1660)

As the four illustrations grouped together on these pages so strongly suggest, the architectural landscape of seventeenth-century New England had a sculptural quality that is of unique interest in our country's history—a quality that gradually vanished with the passage of time and with changing building styles. The profiles of the early framed dwellings, with their triangular gables and their steeply pitched roofs punctuated by prominently rising chimney stacks, have a geometrical nicety that is akin to abstract design—an unpremeditated effect that appeals to modern eyes. The color of unpainted, weathered oak clapboarding (cut from the timber of neighboring trees) adds an earthy warmth to that impression and ties the buildings to their sites in a natural intimacy. The Stanley-Whitman House at Farmington and the Buttolph-Williams House at Wethersfield, both in Connecticut, with their substantial proportions and overhanging upper stories, are classic reminders of these solid shapes of the past. Two of the oldest houses in their respective districts, both saltbox in form, are the Jethro Coffin House on Nantucket and the Richard Jackson House in Portsmouth, New Hampshire. The former was built in 1686 as a wedding gift for Coffin and his bride Mary Gardner, and legend tells that the inverted horseshoe in raised brick on the huge central chimney was designed to discourage witches from entering the home of the newlyweds. (It is well known that witches do not fly down flues that are thus protected.) This is a rare surviving example of the typical Cape Cod house—the "Cape Codder," a type of structure that later became all but universal in small New England houses. Richard Jackson was a shipbuilder who built his house about 1664 facing his shipyard on North Mill Pond. At the rear, the very steep roof line slopes to within a few feet of the house's hillside site.

Buttolph-Williams House, Wethersfield, Conn. (about 1693)

Jethro Coffin House, Nantucket, Mass. (1686)

Richard Jackson House, Portsmouth, N.H. (about 1664)

Christ Church (Old North), Boston, Mass. (1724)

It was from the handsome wooden steeple of Christ Church (later known as Old North) in Boston that Paul Revere's friend Robert Newman hung the lanterns that signaled the advance of the redcoats on Lexington and Concord. The structure, built in 1724, was Boston's second Anglican church and in its provincial way reflects the new architectural styles that had been made popular by the London churches of Christopher Wren after the great fire in that city in 1666. In the approved Church of England manner the pulpit is at the left—rather than in the center according to Puritan tradition—its height enabling both those in the balconies and in the high-walled pews to see the minister, and vice versa. At first glance, with its unpainted clapboard exterior, the Jonathan Ashley House, which stands near the head of Old Deerfield's historic main street (one of the most agreeable reminders of a colonial village scene in America), recalls seventeenth-century structures. However, its symmetrically placed sash windows, its ingenuously carved pedimented doorway, and other features are a country builder's tribute to the burgeoning Georgian style in architecture.

Jonathan Ashley House, Old Deerfield, Mass. (1732)

Stockbridge village in Massachusetts was founded in 1734 and incorporated in 1739 as a mission for the Mohican tribe of Algonquin Indians. In 1739 the Reverend John Sergeant, first of the missionaries, built the early Georgian house—like the Ashley House, a frontier expression of the style— that still stands on Main Street. The belfrey and tall, delicate spire of the Church of Christ at Farmington, Connecticut, rise from a foursquare meetinghouse that was built just before the Revolution.

OVERLEAF: *Interior, Rocky Hill Meetinghouse, Amesbury, Mass. (1785).* Although the last religious services in the meetinghouse were held more than a century ago, and the last town meeting in 1886, this structure has miraculously survived much as it was built and furnished in 1785. With its balcony ranged about three sides of the interior and with organ and choir in the central gallery facing the pulpit, it remains one of the finest and most characteristic of such houses in New England. The elevated pulpit, topped by a well-turned sounding board, and the deacon's table in front are among the best examples of their kind. Columns supporting the balcony and pilasters bordering the pulpit are painted with marbleized patterns; the unpainted pine pews have mellowed to a warm glow of subdued color that relieves the otherwise Spartan interior. Some authorities believe that one Timothy Palmer, master carpenter, was responsible for this remarkably fine construction, now carefully maintained by the Society for the Preservation of New England Antiquities.

First Church of Christ, Farmington, Conn. (1772)

Mission House, Stockbridge, Mass. (1739)

Rocky Hill Meetinghouse, Amesbury, Mass. (1785)

In its general character the post-Revolutionary Rocky Hill Meetinghouse represents a type that was common in New England throughout the eighteenth century. The boxlike mass with a gabled roof is without tower or steeple; two rows of windows correspond to the main and gallery levels within; and a two-story porch encloses a stairway to the gallery. The meetinghouse at Rockingham is the oldest in Vermont and the second to stand at this location. It reflects the straightforward architectural characteristics of its contemporaries along the Atlantic seaboard. This chaste house of worship is lifted above routine interest by its proportions and its sweeping command of the countryside.

Meetinghouse, Rockingham, Vt. (1800) —

Pownalborough Courthouse, near Dresden, Maine (1761)

The Pownalborough Courthouse, the oldest still standing in Maine, was built on the bank of the Eastern River near Dresden in 1761. It is a very well preserved example of civic architecture in the rural vernacular style of two hundred years ago. Once it was adjacent to and protected by Fort Shirley, raised a few years earlier, which has long since vanished. The architectural mood of these various buildings is suggested by the window detail, here illustrated, of Jefferd's Tavern, built in York, Maine, in 1750. With its thin mullions, the sash is framed in a formal but simple fashion to make a strong accent on the clapboards of the exterior wall.

OVERLEAF: *Meetinghouse, Danville, N.H. (1760).* The façade of the meetinghouse at Danville distinctively expresses this severe and restrained concession to Georgian classicism in the pilastered frame of its doorway and the cornices that top its windows.

Jefferd's Tavern (detail), York, Maine (1750)

Moffatt-Ladd House, Portsmouth, N.H. (1763)

Macpheadris-Warner House, Portsmouth, N.H. (1723)

)

One of the earliest Georgian houses still standing in New England was built of brick for Captain Archibald Macpheadris of Portsmouth, a wealthy Scottish-born fur trader. (The building was later occupied by the captain's daughter and her husband Colonel Jonathan Warner.) The fluted Corinthian pilasters that frame the central doorway and the arched pediment that caps it, the relatively large sash windows regularly disposed on the façade, and the horizontal string course between the first two stories reflect the influence of Georgian patterns that would predominate in colonial architecture for the rest of the century. Some forty years later those refinements of style were much more elaborately expressed in the Moffatt-Ladd House, a frame building in the same city.

OVERLEAF: *Wentworth-Gardner House, Portsmouth, N.H. (1760).* This house on the Piscataqua riverfront has been described as "one of the most nearly perfect examples of Georgian architecture in America." The façade is sheathed in wide boards cut and grooved to simulate stonework.

Redwood Library, Newport, R.I. (1750)

King's Chapel, Boston, Mass. (1754)

The versatility of Peter Harrison, earlier referred to as the "most masterly" colonial architect, is demonstrated by the three buildings here illustrated. Each was completed during the quarter century preceeding the Revolution and modeled on the basic principles of Georgian architecture; yet each was planned to serve a different function and designed in a separate, distinctive manner. The Redwood Library in Newport is made of wood painted, sanded, and grooved to resemble stone. With its pedimented, columned portico (the earliest example of this feature in the colonies), it recalls classical temple forms. About the same time, Harrison designed King's Chapel in Boston, which never has been completely finished. It was constructed around an earlier church, which was then "thrown out through the windows of the new stone building." In 1759 Harrison undertook the design and construction of the Touro Synagogue in Newport, a town then conceded to be "the receptacle of all religions." It was America's second synagogue (now the oldest still standing) and when completed in 1763 was hailed as an architectural gem. The interior displays an extraordinary richness of carved details modeled after the engraved designs of English pattern books. In 1790 George Washington visited the synagogue and presented the congregation with a letter of recognition. For a time the building was used for town meetings and for sessions of the general assembly. Restored, it still serves as a house of worship for the local community.

Touro Synagogue, Newport, R.I. (1763)

Throughout most of the eighteenth century Newport was one of the five major cities of the colonies, an active seaport for European and West Indian commerce as well as coastal trade. It was also a summer resort that attracted wealthy inhabitants of the southern colonies and the West Indies seeking health and pleasure. Although it has long since lost its prominence as a trading port, to this day Newport owns a rich architectural heritage from its colonial past. Trinity Church, a neat clapboard structure completed in 1726 after the plans of one Richard Munday, still stands. It has been said that Munday "made a copy in wood of Boston's Old North." The building's unusual double row of roundheaded windows with their dark shutters and fans outlined against white clapboards, gives the exterior walls a geometric pattern that is both spare and compelling. In contrast, Colony House, or the Old State House, by the same architect, the colony's largest building and certainly its most ambitious and unusual, was given lavish attention in every detail. It was the colony's first major building of brick construction. The frame dwelling built in 1748 for Deputy Governor Jonathan Nicholls, Jr. (and known as the Hunter House, after a later owner), with its balustraded gambrel roof, is a less pretentious but handsome example of the city's numerous surviving landmarks. Early in the nineteenth century Samuel Whitehorne, briefly a successful shipping merchant, built an elegant three-story brick house in the newly fashionable Federal style. Whitehorne went bankrupt when two of his ships were lost at sea, and the house was sadly misused in years to come. It had been serving as a multiunit tenement when restoration was undertaken in 1969.

Hunter House, Newport, R.I. (1748)

Colony House, Newport, R.I. (1742)

Samuel Whitehorne House, Newport, R.I. (1811)

Trinity Church, Newport, R.I. (1726)

Deane, Webb, and Stevens Houses, Wethersfield, Conn. (1766, 1752, 1788)

The six houses illustrated on these pages typify the regional character of early New England domestic architecture as it was expressed in four different states over a period of about sixty years. Main Street in Wethersfield, Connecticut (the earliest settled community in the state), is graced by three adjacent eighteenth-century houses (Deane, Webb, and Stevens in that order in the illustration) that have been carefully restored and that are lovingly preserved. The mansion of Colonel Jeremiah Lee, built in Marblehead, Massachusetts, in 1768, the Lady Pepperrell House, built at Kittery Point, Maine, in 1760 by the widow of Sir William Pepperrell, hero of the siege of Louisbourg, and the Governor Goodwin Mansion, built in the Federal style at Portsmouth, New Hampshire, just before the outbreak of the War of 1812, are all outstanding landmarks maintained by responsible custodians; all bear witness to a long tradition of good and ample living.

Jeremiah Lee Mansion,
Marblehead, Mass. (1768)

Lady Pepperrell House,
Kittery Point, Maine (1760)

Governor Goodwin Mansion,
Portsmouth, N.H. (1811)

Windmill, Jamestown, R.I. (1787)

The mill designed by Samuel Slater, a brilliant English immigrant, at Pawtucket, Rhode Island, might easily be mistaken for a colonial town hall. Actually, it was one of the earliest cotton mills in the country when it was established in 1793, transforming the traditional household production of hand-spun cotton into a new water-powered system of manufacture and leading to an industrial revolution in America. Slater reworked the machinery of an existing firm, reproducing the designs of Sir Richard Arkwright, inventor of the spinning frame, from plans he had memorized in England. Windmills were introduced in America by the Dutch in New Netherland. They then spread over much of the Northeast. The example at Jamestown, Rhode Island, is restored to its original design when it was built in 1787.

Old Slater Mill, Pawtucket, R.I. (1793–about 1830)

The First Baptist Church in Providence, Rhode Island, was raised just before the outbreak of the Revolution. Its design is generally attributed to Joseph Brown, a local merchant who for guidance in this architectural enterprise turned to his copy of *A Book of Architecture*, published in 1728 at London by James Gibbs, an English disciple of Palladio. The Georgian elegance of this structure sharply contrasts with the utter simplicity of the almost contemporary Shaker Meetinghouse at Sabbathday Lake in Maine— a simplicity verging on an austerity that is reflected in the long, spindled benches designed and made by Shaker craftsmen and which substituted for pews to accommodate the congregation.

Shaker Meetinghouse, Sabbathday Lake, Maine (1794)

First Baptist Church, Providence, R.I. (1775). Joseph Brown, architect

The splendid mansion built by Revolutionary leader John Langdon at Portsmouth, New Hampshire, in 1784 is one of the great Georgian houses in New England. Langdon, first president of the United States Senate, was Acting President of the United States prior to the election of George Washington. The carved pineapples atop the fenceposts were an apt symbol of hospitality, for here Governor Langdon entertained Presidents Washington and Monroe, General Lafayette, and Louis Philippe, later King of France. The elaborate exterior—with its fanciful portico, Corinthian pilasters on the corners, scrolled and pedimented dormers, and its Chippendale rail around the captain's walk—reflects the grandeur of the late Georgian period. At about this same time, master craftsman and architect Samuel McIntire was building fine houses for the merchant princes of Salem, Massachusetts. The three-story, foursquare frame dwelling he built for Jerathmiel Peirce in 1782 is one of the outstanding houses remaining from the early Federal period. Its façade is edged with bold, fluted pilasters, and it is topped by a balustraded captain's walk. In 1801 McIntire partially remodeled the house, at which time he added a fence with classical urns capping its posts.

Governor John Langdon Mansion, Portsmouth, N.H. (1784)

OVERLEAF: *Pingree House, Salem, Mass. (1804). Samuel McIntire, architect.* The various buildings that McIntire designed and worked on in and about Salem, Massachusetts, from the end of the Revolution to his death in 1811, were personal versions of the Adam style that gave a new grace and dignity to the local scene. In 1804 he designed what may well be his finest structure, the brick house commissioned by sea captain John Gardner (and now known by the name of later owners, the Pingrees). In the severe elegance of the façade, McIntire attained an architectural sophistication rarely reached in domestic design of the period. The pink brick front, divided into three horizontal elements, each a bit narrower than the one below, is set off by three rows of windows with white keystone lintels and dark shutters. The slender Corinthian columns of its semicircular portico, the slim, reeded pilasters that flank the doorway, and the delicate fanlight above the doorway recall the grace of Robert Adam's designs. McIntire has also been credited with having designed some of the furnishings of the interior.

Peirce-Nichols House, Salem, Mass. (1782; 1801). Samuel McIntire, architect

Gore Place, Waltham, Mass. (1804)

The imposing mansion that the "young, beautiful, and excellent Christopher Gore," as a female contemporary described him, built in 1804 remains one of the finest Federal country houses in New England. While Gore was living in England as a commissioner under the Jay Treaty, his country seat was destroyed by fire in 1799. He had the plans for his new mansion drawn in Europe. On his return he became the seventh governor of Massachusetts and lived in the style of an English country gentleman in the twenty-room brick Gore Place in Waltham. It consists of two long low wings recessed from the central block, which has a projecting elliptical salon as its focal point. The governor's study is located above this bowed story-and-a-half dining room. In great contrast to the sophisticated Gore Place is the simple Federal house built by Judge Thomas Ruggles in the river town of Columbia Falls, Maine. Designed by Aaron Sherman of Massachusetts, it is notable for the delicate detail of its exterior trim and for its unusually fine interior woodwork and its "flying" staircase.

Thomas Ruggles House, Columbia Falls, Maine (1818).
Aaron Sherman, architect

State Capitol, Montpelier, Vt. (1838; rebuilt 1859). Ammi B. Young, architect

State House, Boston, Mass. (1797). Charles Bulfinch, architect

For years after it was completed in 1797, Bulfinch's state house in Boston was the most important public building in the United States. (Its majestic dome was originally shingled, then sheathed in copper by Paul Revere in 1802, and covered with dazzling gold leaf in 1874.) In 1817, the year he was summoned to Washington to serve as architect for the unfinished National Capitol, Bulfinch's design for the First Church of Christ in Lancaster, Massachusetts, was brought to completion. It remains one of the finest examples of religious architecture in the Federal style. Another boldly conceived, gold-leafed dome caps the state house of Vermont at Montpelier, the nation's smallest capitol. The structure, originally raised in 1838, burned in 1857 but was soon reconstructed by T. W. Silloway and Joseph R. Richards. The columned portico is a close approximation of the Theseion built in Athens in 465 B.C., during the golden age of ancient Greek architecture.

First Church of Christ, Lancaster, Mass. (1816-17). Charles Bulfinch, architect

Both the Congregational church at Old Bennington, Vermont, and that at Middlebury in the same state were built by Lavius Fillmore, a Connecticut-born architect who quite obviously studied and used the building manuals published by Asher Benjamin. In the extensive cemetery adjacent to the Old Bennington church are marked graves dating back to the Battle of Bennington during the Revolutionary War. (The late poet Robert Frost is buried here.) The detail of the Middlebury church, here illustrated, indicates clearly enough why this is considered by many to be Fillmore's masterpiece and the finest church in Vermont. In either case these structures are a handsome tribute, not only to Fillmore's skill but to the pervasive and beneficent influence of Benjamin's printed guides. For some time the Old Bennington church was attributed to Benjamin himself.

First Congregational Church, Old Bennington, Vt.
(1806). Lavius Fillmore, architect

Congregational Church (detail), Middlebury, Vt.
(1809). Lavius Fillmore, architect

Village Green, Washington, N.H.

The village greens of the towns of Washington, New Hampshire, incorporated in 1776, and Litchfield, Connecticut, incorporated in 1719, bring to mind James Fenimore Cooper's descriptions of those "beautiful, tranquil and enviable looking hamlets" which he so much admired a century and a half ago as he journeyed through New England. Washington's town hall, school, and Congregational church facing the town's small green form a cluster of public buildings that still provide a focus for the life of the village. The trim Congregational church bordering the common, and nearby private dwellings, justify Litchfield's reputation as one of New England's few unspoiled towns.

72

Village Green, Litchfield, Conn.

OVERLEAF: *Covered Bridge (about 1852) and Church (1853), Stark, N.H.* The covered bridge at Stark, New Hampshire, was built about the middle of the last century to span the Upper Ammonoosuc River, a distance of about 150 feet. Covered bridges were roofed and enclosed to protect the structural elements from the weather. In this example the roof has sufficient overhang to shelter pedestrian walks on either side. Thus, there was no need to enclose the structure with boarding, as was commonly the case, and the functional parts of the interior are open to view. One year after the bridge was completed a very plain little country church was raised at the nearby roadside.

73

Fort McClary, Kittery Point, Maine (1690; 1814; 1844)

Barn, Hancock Shaker Village, Hancock, Mass. (1826)

Round Church, Richmond, Vt. (1813)

The three unusual structures here illustrated, though serving three entirely different functions, have in common pronounced geometric plans. Fort McClary once guarded the mouth of the Piscataqua River, which separates the tips of Maine and New Hampshire. Its formidable granite lower bastion was built by the British in the seventeenth century. The surmounting hexagonal wooden blockhouse is a restoration of a construction added in 1814. Commissioned jointly by five Protestant sects, one William Rhoades built in 1813 in Richmond, Vermont, what is known as the Round Church, but what is actually a sixteen-sided structure, crowned by an octagonal belfry, to serve as a meetinghouse. It has long since been taken over by the town for secular purposes. The barn at Hancock Shaker Village in Massachusetts is truly round (with a dodecagonal clerestory and hexagonal lantern), and remains an outstanding example of functional agricultural building. Wagons could enter the structure and reach its upper level by a ramp, deliver hay at a central deposit, and then exit by the same door. Fifty-two horses and cows occupied stalls on the floor below, beneath which was a manure pit.

Chase Mill, Fall River, Mass. (1872)

With the introduction of the turbine and then steam power around the time of the Civil War, huge mills were built in New England seacoast towns to utilize inexpensive immigrant labor and convenient transportation. Handsome individual cotton mills arose in Fall River, Massachusetts, constructed in the gray granite underlying the town. The Chase Mill of 1872, with its great stone walls, white-trimmed windows, and dark roof, is an impressive survivor from Fall River's textile manufacturing heyday. The bucolic mill village started by the Harris family in New Hampshire and taken over by the Colony family in mid-century, has never changed. The woolen mills, public buildings, and workers' houses tumble up and down the valley of Harrisville in a plan that keeps the charming landscape intact. The warm-colored brick and local stone sheathing of all the buildings ties together these structures devoted to work, living, and worship. The village's Cheshire Mill (top, opposite), which was begun in 1846 and was added on to in 1860, finally shut down in 1971.

Mill Village, Harrisville, N.H. (about 1810-60)

Old Stone House, Brownington, Vt. (1836)

Built almost single-handedly by the headmaster, the Reverend Alexander Twilight, the Old Stone House served as a dormitory for the Orleans County Grammar School. Situated at Brownington, just south of the Canadian border in Vermont, the stark granite building which once sheltered 154 boys and girls as well as providing classroom space, now houses a summer museum. Farther to the south, in Boston, another formidable granite building served as a warehouse and shipping office on Lewis Wharf, one of many such structures built to accommodate the bustling traffic of that port. Today this nineteenth-century industrial landmark has been converted into shops and restaurants and offices on the lower floors and condominium apartments on the top four floors. The thick (ranging from sixteen to thirty inches) outer granite walls and the 14-by-14-inch framework beams form the structural basis for this imaginative rehabilitation.

Lewis Wharf Rehabilitation, Boston, Mass. (about 1838; 1972). Carl Koch & Associates, architects

Amoskeag Manufacturing Complex, Manchester, N.H. (1838-1915). Samuel Shepherd and John D. Kimball, architects

Stretching in tiers for almost a mile along the Merrimack River at Manchester, New Hampshire, the Amoskeag Manufacturing Complex presents an extraordinary industrial urban scene. The town itself was laid out in 1838 as a unified complex of mills, dwellings, canals, railroads, and parks. The company housing alone covered over thirty-five acres of majestic rows of brick boardinghouses. From the multiple lines of red brick factories issued the greatest quantity of cotton textiles being manufactured in the world in the last half of the nineteenth century.

OVERLEAF: *Mystic Seaport, Mystic, Conn. (19th century).* Mystic Seaport presents another important aspect of early- and mid-nineteenth-century commercial enterprise in America —the whaling industry and the port that supported it. The thirty-seven-acre village is comprised entirely of original structures—including modest dwellings and buildings for supporting activities, such as ropewalks and sail lofts—moved to this site from nearby seaports. Among the many vessels at the waterfront is the only surviving sailing whaler, the famous *Charles W. Morgan*, whose spars may be seen in the background.

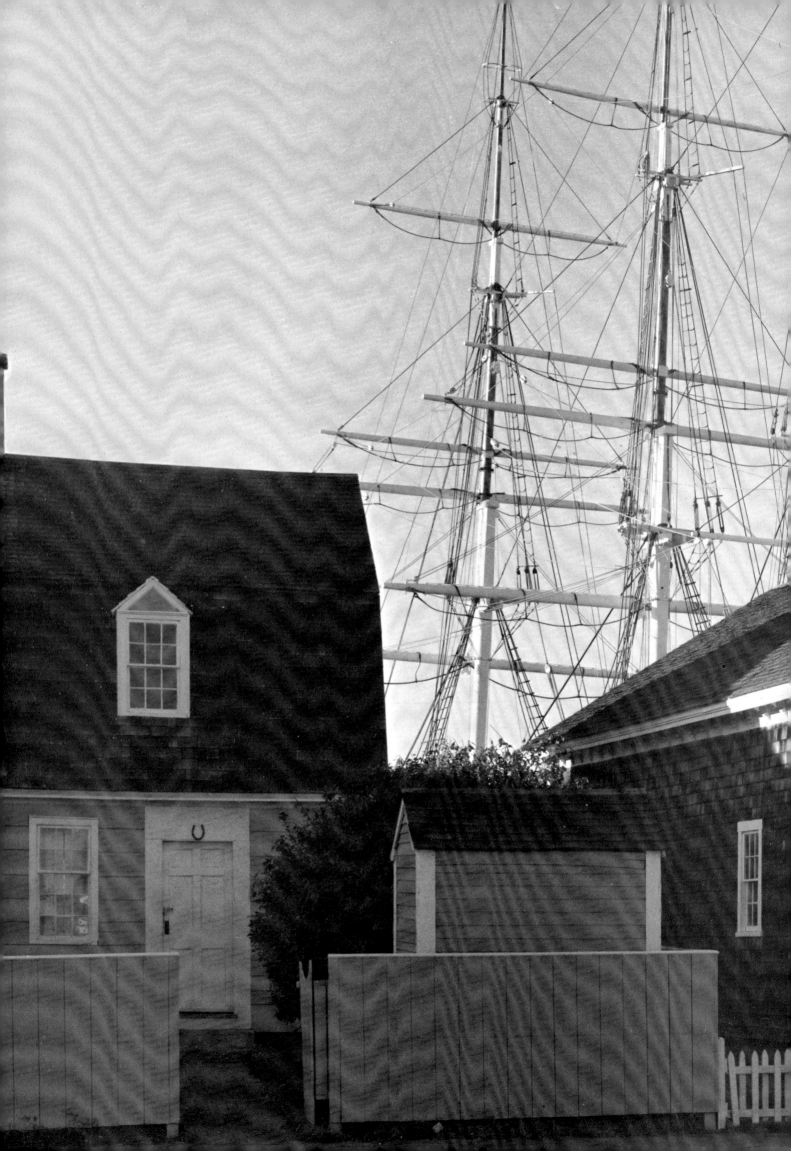

Old City Hall, Boston, Mass. (1865; 1972). Bryant & Gillman, architects (1865);
Anderson Notter Associates, rehabilitation architects (1972)

Atheneum, Nantucket, Mass. (1847)

Around the middle years of the nineteenth century, romantic nostalgia for the distant past expressed itself in architectural forms in various historical styles. The public buildings on these pages show some of the variations on classical and exotic themes that appeared in New England. The Greek Revival Atheneum on Nantucket, built entirely of wood, has a striking double-pedimented façade with two well-turned Ionic columns. In the boldly modeled Second Empire façade of the Old City Hall in Boston, the designers were inspired by the Louvre in Paris. And the red sandstone gates to the Grove Street Cemetery in New Haven own a debt to ancient Egypt for their battered pylons, lotus bud capitals, and solar disc and vulture motifs.

Gates, Grove Street Cemetery, New Haven, Conn. (1848). Henry Austin, architect

In the late nineteenth and early twentieth centuries, Newport's architectural inheritance from colonial times, earlier described, was overshadowed by the palatial "cottages" designed in a variety of revival styles for the very rich who summered there. This concentrated array of extravagant domestic architecture is unmatched in the Western world. The Marble House, designed by Richard Morris Hunt for William Kissam Vanderbilt and so named because of the profligate use of marble in its construction, typifies the unmitigated ostentation of these seashore retreats. Hunt, the first American graduate of the École des Beaux-Arts in Paris, based his exterior design for the Marble House on the Grand Trianon and the Petit Trianon at Versailles. The interiors display an indescribable opulence. It should be remembered that Hunt also designed, in 1875, one of the first skyscrapers with elevators in America, New York City's Tribune Building.

Marble House, Newport, R.I. (1892). Richard Morris Hunt, architect

Boston's new City Hall is the result of a competition that drew 256 entries, one of the few major competitions for a comparable civic building since that of 1912 for the San Francisco City Hall. (In much of northern Europe such competitions are held by law for almost all public buildings.) The building is the key element in a large-scale rehabilitation of the area where it stands, sixty acres of what has been a moribund downtown section of the city. The cantilevered upper floors with their modular window grids overhang the boldly sculptured projections of the entrance level in an exciting counterpoint of functional design. The great entrance hall with its surrounding balconies doubles as an informal auditorium.

OVERLEAF: *State Service Center, Boston, Mass. (1971-   ). Paul Rudolph, coordinating architect.* The nautilus ramps, sculptured forms, and framed vistas of Boston's Merrimac Street approach to this extraordinary complex highlight the varied but coordinated means the architects have used to shelter miscellaneous state functions and services within connected buildings. The overall plan includes a large pedestrian plaza and an extensive parking area underneath.

City Hall, Boston, Mass. (1969). Kallmann, McKinnell & Knowles, architects

Christian Science Center, Boston, Mass. (1972). I. M. Pei & Partners, architects

The colonnade illustrated at the left directly from the new administration buildings (not shown here) of Boston's Christian Science Center to the old buildings of the Mother Church erected in 1894, with an addition of 1904 that can be seen in the background. These contemporary structures were planned not only to accommodate the practical and growing needs of the religious organization, but to provide a tranquil urban retreat for Bostonians on the southwest edge of downtown. An expansive pool, benched garden enclosures, and triple rows of more than one hundred linden trees admirably serve the latter purpose. The careful orchestration of new and old buildings with a landscaped setting leads to the salutary upgrading of an entire urban area. In the small chapel of the Massachusetts Institute of Technology natural (and at times artificial) illumination pours down from a shielded roof oculus onto a reredos, a brilliant screen by Harry Bertoia, whose multiangled gold facets distribute the rays with myriad reflections. A simple cube of marble standing on a low, circular dais in front of the screen serves as altar. As intended, the chapel creates a religious atmosphere to accommodate a variety of faiths, or no specific faith. It constitutes a spiritual retreat, "a place where an individual can contemplate things larger than himself," yet with no reference to organized religion. The windowless cylinder of deep red brick, which rests on light arches in an encircling moat, walls off the busy, traffic-burdened world outside. The chapel is one of the memorable achievements of the late Eero Saarinen.

Chapel, M.I.T., Cambridge, Mass. (1955).
Eero Saarinen & Associates, architects

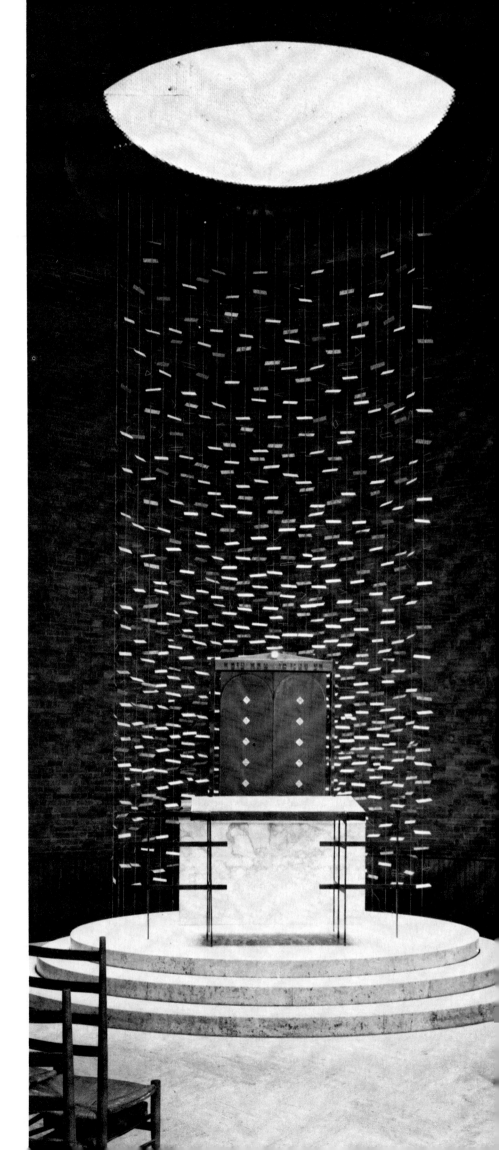

Almost the entire body of the First Presbyterian Church in Stamford, Connecticut, from floor to ridge, is composed of multicolored pieces of glass set in precast concrete panels (which also form the supporting structure). The twenty-two thousand separate glass elements are faceted on their inner faces. As the position of the sun moves during the day, some of these elements dart jeweled rays into the nave of the church, as others fade, to shine again later. Working in close cooperation with the architect, Gabriel Loire of France designed the glass using eighty-seven colors. Both inside and out the Unitarian Meetinghouse in Hartford, Connecticut, is an unusual architectural experience. Within, an inverted calix of wooden strips hovers over the roughly circular sanctuary. Twelve somewhat irregularly spaced reinforced concrete piers rise from the outer edge to form an uneven crown at the top, where they are laced together by lateral steel cables to frame and support the wooden tent of the sanctuary. Daylight filters through the wall's web of slats to supplement the natural light that also descends from the center of the roof. The unusual structural nature of the building is expressed as precisely on the exterior as on the interior.

First Presbyterian Church, Stamford, Conn. (1958). Wallace K. Harrison, architect

Unitarian Meetinghouse, Hartford, Conn. (1964). Victor A. Lundy, architect

The F. G. Peabody Terrace at Harvard University, a village for housing married students, is probably the finest of its kind in the country. This cluster of buildings consists of three-, five-, and seven-story terraced units, their heights building up from the Charles River side to maintain a residential scale along the road, combined with three twenty-two-story towers to provide 497 rental apartments, with garages for 352 cars, a small shopping center, and a smaller community room. Although the buildings vary in both height and shape, they are all based on a standardized reinforced concrete three-story unit, three bays wide—an economical module that makes it possible for the apartments to be competitively priced. The spatial relationship between low and high units is admirable; a visual play of louvers and hooded balconies enlivens the façades; and at the ground level local areas are agreeably and conveniently defined.

*F. G. Peabody Terrace, Harvard University,
Cambridge, Mass. (1964).
Sert, Jackson & Gourley, architects*

Undergraduate Science Center, Harvard University, Cambridge, Mass. (1973). Sert, Jackson & Associates, architects

George Gund Hall, Graduate School of Design, Harvard University, Cambridge, Mass. (1972). John Andrews/Anderson/Baldwin, architects

As the three buildings illustrated on these pages attest, its rich historic past has not compromised Harvard University's vision of its present and future roles. Since World War II the campus has sprouted with innovative, impressive, and serviceable architectural forms designed to meet the changing and expanding needs of the university's functions by some of the nation's leading architects, and others from overseas. (The Carpenter Center for the Visual Arts is the only structure in the United States completely designed by Le Corbusier, the Swiss-French architect.)

Carpenter Center for the Visual Arts, Harvard University, Cambridge, Mass. (1963). Le Corbusier, architect

Library, Phillips Exeter Academy, Exeter, N.H. (1971). Louis I. Kahn, architect

The U-shaped academic complex of Southeastern Massachusetts University, with its interconnected buildings, forms a boldly sculptured scene, highlighted by a vigorous play of sun and shadow. An undisturbed grass mall creates the central focus, with all parking on the periphery. The stacks and carrels of the Phillips Exeter Academy Library are grouped around a dramatically scaled, six-story-high central court crowned by X-bracing at the top, with a skylight above to flood its bold geometry. New England's venerable educational traditions are here joined with the most advanced architectural concepts.

Southeastern Massachusetts University, North Dartmouth, Mass. (1965-72).
Paul Rudolph and Desmond & Lord, architects

115

Poised on stilts along the brow of a hill, amidst a well-tended, spacious lawn that seemingly flows beneath the building, the Emhart Manufacturing Company structure is intimately married to its natural setting at Bloomfield, near Hartford, Connecticut. Concrete umbrellas support the office areas, which wrap around a two-story testing laboratory in the center part of the structure, built semi-independently so that noise and vibrations are not transmitted to adjoining areas. Windows are set back three feet to protect them from the sun—and to facilitate window washing. The elevation of the office floor permits car parking beneath. It is one of the country's more impressive corporate headquarters.

Emhart Manufacturing Company, Bloomfield, Conn. (1963). Skidmore, Owings & Merrill, architects

Like Harvard, Yale has advanced its storied past into the present with modern architecture to accommodate the changing needs of the university's activities. The Beinecke Rare Book Library is sheathed with a grid of translucent marble panels; within this outer shell, a six-story glass cage houses, protects, and handsomely displays rare volumes. At the north end of the campus the Kline Biology Tower rises high above the adjacent fifty-year-old neo-Gothic laboratories, repeating their purplish brown color. Thirty-two semicylindrical and cylindrical columns serve both as structural elements and as exhaust shafts.

Beinecke Rare Book Library, Yale University, New Haven, Conn. (1963). Skidmore, Owings & Merrill, architects

Kline Biology Tower, Yale University, New Haven, Conn. (1966). Philip Johnson Associates, architects

The Knights of Columbus Headquarters in New Haven breaks away from the traditional steel or concrete skeletal cage for skyscraper construction that almost invariably results in a geometric grid system of columns and repetitive bays of windows. Instead, this unusual structure employs great concrete cylinders (thirty feet in diameter and enclosing stairs and services) at its four corners with a concrete elevator core in the center. These five structurally separate units are connected by steel beams to support floors. All windows above the third floor consist of continuous ribbons of glass butted together and sealed with mastic. Designed by the same architects, the adjacent Veterans Memorial Coliseum is closely related in color and materials (here mostly self-rusting steel) to the Knights of Columbus Headquarters. Its exterior seems not so much a building as an articulated group of supports, most of which are concerned with carrying the massive weight of four decks of automobiles. This parking area holds twenty-four hundred cars. Concrete piers uphold gigantic trusses, which are cantilevered well beyond the supporting shafts.

Knights of Columbus Headquarters, New Haven, Conn. (1970).
Kevin Roche, John Dinkeloo & Associates, architects

Veterans Memorial Coliseum, New Haven, Conn. (1972). Kevin Roche, John Dinkeloo & Associates, architects

MID-ATLANTIC

DELAWARE
DISTRICT OF
COLUMBIA
MARYLAND
NEW JERSEY
NEW YORK
PENNSYLVANIA

In the Middle Atlantic colonies, the area now comprising New York, New Jersey, Pennsylvania, Delaware, Maryland, and the District of Columbia, there was nothing like the cultural uniformity that characterized New England. From the beginning this substantial area was settled by people from many different lands, professing different faiths and speaking different languages. As early as 1643 a French missionary passing through the Dutch settlement at New Amsterdam reported that he heard the babble of eighteen languages in and about the short streets of that infant community. "Our chiefest unhappyness here," complained one of the early residents, "is too great a mixture."

That community at the mouth of the Hudson River on the southern tip of Manhattan Island had been planted as a trading post by the Dutch West India Company in 1625. (Some dozen years earlier a tiny outpost consisting of four rude houses and a handful of fur traders had occupied the site.) It was, and always has been, polyglot at every social level; and it has always been a sailors' town. Governor Peter Stuyvesant once observed that it was "peopled by the scrapings of nationalities." Thus it was that wherever Dutch interests spread, up and down the Hudson River and into the Mohawk River Valley, across New Jersey, and along the Delaware River, society quickly took on an international aspect. In 1655, after a ten-day bloodless siege, Peter Stuyvesant took over Fort Christina on the Delaware and incorporated the Swedish colony that centered there into his short-lived colonial administration. Nine years later, "without a blow or a tear," the English in turn took over the Dutch holdings in North America.

When a small fleet of British ships arrived to assume custody of New Netherland formally in 1664 there were already numerous Englishmen among the fifteen hundred inhabitants of New Amsterdam, and others scattered about the adjoining countryside. "Doe not for beare to . . . crowd on," the governor of Connecticut had been advised in 1642, "crowding the Dutch out of those places where they have occupied, but without hostility or any act of violence." This is just what New Englanders had done, and they never stopped moving into and through New York. Two centuries later, in the 1840's, watching such emigrant Yankees swarm westward over the lands surrounding his Cooperstown estate, James Fenimore Cooper bitterly referred to the persistent intruders as those "locusts of the West."

Still other elements poured into the Middle Atlantic colonies from all directions to add variety to the extraordinary social, religious, and racial mix of the area's population. In the spring of 1634 two shiploads of emigrants from England established the first settlement in Maryland, a colony granted by an Anglican monarch to a Roman Catholic subject, Lord Baltimore, who provided a New World refuge for his coreligionists and also welcomed without distinction those of any persuasion who cared to join the enterprise. He called upon Catholics to treat Protestants "with as much mildness and favor as Justice will permitt." Here religious freedom was first established on the American continent. Fifteen years later Puritan exiles from Virginia settled at a site they named Providence, soon to be renamed Annapolis, for many years the only town of any size in Maryland.

Later in the century the earnest Quaker William Penn, in return for a large debt owed to his father by the Crown, secured a grant to what would be known as Pennsylvania for settlement by the persecuted members of his sect. It was one of the largest colonies on the continent and became more than a sanctuary for such "schismatical [and] factious" Quakers who had earlier been whipped and dragged through the streets of Boston and hanged on the Common. As Penn solemnly averred, this was a "Holy Experiment"; he was establishing a "free colony for all mankind." As such it was widely advertised abroad, and in response to Penn's summons immigrants of all stripes swarmed across the Atlantic to enjoy the promised blessings. Of great importance to the development of the colony were the large numbers of Scotch-Irish Presbyterians from Ulster and German sectarians from the Rhineland who made Pennsylvania their new homeland. Some stopped at Philadelphia; others moved into the back country.

Very briefly told, such were the complex historical origins of the Middle Atlantic region. Inevitably, each of the separate and disparate strands that were gradually woven into the social fabric of the area expressed its traditional culture in a distinctive architecture. In the beginning it was a world of startling contrasts. At New Amsterdam, visitors from other American colonies might have imagined themselves in Amsterdam, Leiden, or Hoorn, rather than in the New World. With its nestling houses of particolored brick and tile, stepped gable ends facing the street (and their insides "very white scowr'd" and "neat to admiration," as one female tourist from Boston carefully noted early in the eighteenth century), the busy little port was virtually a replica of a typical Dutch trading center—even to the "gutte," or canal, that reached into the heart of the community.

Such early city houses have virtually vanished from New York. There is not a trace left of Peter Stuyvesant's New Amsterdam, except in street and family names. (New York City telephone books still list Van Rensselaers, Schermerhorns, De Peysters, and other descendants of early Dutch settlers.) When he visited the city in 1828, James Fenimore Cooper sadly remarked on the disappearance of those venerable landmarks. "A few old Dutch dwellings yet remain," he reported, "and can easily be distinguished by their little bricks, their gables to the street, and those steps on their battlement walls. . . ." But those too would soon be gone.

Two centuries ago, in and about what is now the metropolitan area including parts of New Jersey, there could also still be seen many surviving examples of typical early New England houses of frame and clapboard construction, witness to the strong currents of Yankee tradition that infiltrated the area almost before the Dutch had firmly settled on their claims. Of more peculiar interest are those structures that appeared in rural New Netherland, a number of which do survive, that owe their design or style to no specific European or earlier colonial prototype but rather represent a composite of many different folk traditions from all over northern Europe (although they are commonly referred to as "Dutch colonial" houses). They are what might well be expected from the commingling of people from many parts of the Old World. In 1639 Jonas Bronck came from Denmark and gave his name to the present borough of the Bronx; Albert Andriesse Bradt came from Norway (and was dubbed *de Noorman*); Alexander Lindsay Glen, from Scotland, settled at Schenectady; the Englishman Thomas Chambers was the first to purchase land at Wiltwyck, which was to be renamed Kingston; and so on. Schoonmakers came from Hamburg, Kierstedes from Prussia, Hoffmans from Sweden; there were Walloons and French Huguenots in considerable numbers, and some Jews from Spain and Portugal via Brazil to add a more cosmopolitan strain to the mixture.

The most celebrated type of folk architecture in America, the log cabin, was introduced not by the Pilgrims, the Puritans, or the Dutch, but by the Swedes and Finns (and later by the Germans in Pennsylvania), who came to the Delaware Valley in the

1630's and 1640's from still heavily wooded sections of northern Europe. In a journal recording his travels from Manhattan to Maryland in 1679 one European visitor to America noted that he stayed overnight at a home "made according to the Swedish mode, and as they usually build their houses here, . . . being nothing else than entire trees, split through the middle, or squared out of the rough, and placed in the form of a square, one upon the other, as high as they wish to have the house; the ends of these timbers are let into each other, about a foot from the ends, half of one into half of the other. The whole structure is thus made without a nail or a spike. . . . These houses are quite tight and warm. . . ." Familiarity with this elementary but efficient form of construction did not spread widely until the next century—and only in the century after that, the nineteenth, did it become a symbol of pioneer simplicity and virtue which presidential candidates were eager to claim as their birthright.

So many of the hordes of Germans who were attracted to Pennsylvania came from the Palatinate, an area including much of the Rhine Valley and neighboring lands stretching from Switzerland to Holland, that the name Palatine was used as a general term for all German immigrants. Like the Puritans before them, in their new surroundings these more recent arrivals hoped to preserve and enhance a cherished way of life and to maintain the precepts and practices of their religious faith. More stubbornly—or faithfully—than the Puritans they persevered in their traditional ways, resisting the Anglicizing influences that tended to shape other non-British settlers into a common mold. Down to our own day they constitute an enclave of rural folk culture in the heart of urban and industrial eastern America.

They came in such numbers and with such steadfast purpose that by the middle of the eighteenth century even that most tolerant Philadelphian, Benjamin Franklin (himself a refugee from Boston), feared they might completely dominate the province. Why should the "Palatine Boors be suffered to swarm into our Settlements, and by herding together establish their Language and Manners to the Exclusion of ours?" he demanded. "Why should Pennsylvania, founded by the English, become a Colony of Aliens, who will shortly be so numerous as to Germanize us instead of our Anglifying them . . . ?"

Unlike their British antecedents and contemporaries, who largely followed the inland waterways to determine their place of settlement, the Germans, with the practiced eye of experienced husbandmen, took to the trail of limestone soil where tall trees flourished and good farming awaited only the clearing of the land. Here they built structures of peculiar interest, many of them recalling the medieval architecture of the Rhine Valley. The community houses of the monastic settlement at Ephrata, with their remarkably tall and steep roofs and rows of dormers, might have been modeled on the houses to be seen in engravings by the early German artist Albrecht Dürer. Also following old, traditional custom, the newly arrived German settlers built half-timber houses such as were common in the Rhineland of the medieval period. But by the eighteenth century, the Pennsylvania Germans turned readily to such thick stone walls as the abundant mineral resources of the region made possible, and these became characteristic of that countryside.

Without very much question the most impressive evidence of the Germans' enduring presence in Pennsylvania is found in the huge barns that still grace the landscape of the state. "It is pretty," observed one visitor in 1753, "to behold our back Settlements, where the barns are as large as pallaces, while the Owners live in log huts; a sign tho' of thriving Farmers." Where the stone houses tended to assume the forms of English Georgian design, the barns retained their basic German character. The most typical of these magnificent structures were built of wood and stone combined, the stone ground story topped by an overhanging level whose walls were made of vertical boards. At the end massive stone walls rose to the full height of the barn. A height of forty-five feet from foundation to ridge was not uncommon. Often the wooden surfaces were decorated with colorful symbols. Whether these had more than a decorative function can only be surmised. The possibility that they were devices to ward off the evil doings of witches and other sinister agents adds color to the folklore of German Pennsylvania.

Not all the Palatinates who came to Pennsylvania were farmers by any means. Among the almost two thousand arrivals at Philadelphia in 1709, for example, were craftsmen of virtually every kind—silversmiths, blacksmiths, brickmakers, tailors, masons, weavers, engravers, barbers, glass blowers, and the like—enough skilled workmen to sustain a diversified society. And for a good part of the eighteenth century there was no more diversified and progressive urban community in all America. The growth of Penn's "green countrie towne" was phenomenal. Less than twenty years after its founding in 1682, it had already become as populous as New York, established scores of years earlier, and before the Revolution it would surpass Boston and become one of the most consequential cities in the British Empire. Penn had laid out the city on a checkerboard plan, a scheme that well served the growing needs of the city. That regularity continued to impress visitors, as did the fact that some of the streets were numbered and others bore the names of forest trees. On his visit to Philadelphia to attend the meetings of the First Continental Congress in 1774 John Adams commented on that regularity, so different from the crooked, narrow streets of Boston—which at the time were echoing to the tramp of British soldiers' boots, its populace exasperated almost to the point of open revolt.

In 1724 a number of Philadelphia's leading housewrights, including some of the city's prominent citizens, founded a company modeled upon the Worshipful Company of Carpenters in London, chartered in 1477. The new organization, called the Carpenters' Company of the City and County of Philadelphia, was America's first builders' guild. Formed "for the purpose of obtaining instruction in the science of architecture and assisting such of their members as should by accident be in need of support, or the widows and minor children of members," it quickly issued a *Book of Prices* to assure fair charges to owners and due recompense to workmen. The company also published a manual of designs, constructional details, and other such aids to its membership.

When Benjamin Franklin was engaged with colonial affairs in London, he turned to one of the members of the company to supervise the construction of his new house in Philadelphia. Some years earlier, in 1754, the trustees of the little College of New Jersey (later renamed Princeton University) called upon Robert Smith of the company to design and see to the construction of the main college structure, Nassau Hall. This structure served its purpose so admirably that it became the model for University Hall in Providence, Rhode Island—the nucleus of what was to become Brown University— Dartmouth Hall in New Hampshire, and other college structures of later years.

Philadelphia itself was very early noted for its impressive number of brick dwellings "generally three stories high after the mode in London." In 1682 William Penn imported a young Scot, James Porteus, to build both a town house and a countryseat that would be suitable as the residences of the proprietor of the colony. This Porteus did before proceeding to plan and construct a number of other distinguished houses in and about Philadelphia. His so-called Slate House, erected about 1698 for a wealthy local merchant, was one of the city's finest dwellings of the time. Here as elsewhere in the colonies building operations were constantly changing the appearance of the urban community, but there were still housing shortages at times. Some Philadelphians had to walk "up one Pair of Stairs" to reach their quarters in multifamily arrangements. Others, to avoid the congestion and clatter of city life, moved to newly developed suburbs where several large, privately owned tracts were divided into small building lots. On the farther outskirts, gentlemen of means built their countryseats, impressive testimony to both their taste in architecture and the substantial resources which they could draw upon to indulge it. A number of these still stand, preserved and protected.

Here, as elsewhere in the colonies, those with any pretension to culture considered a knowledge of architecture an essential element of a good education and deemed English architectural books indispensable to a gentleman's library. At least eighty-seven different titles on architectural subjects were known in America before the Revolution. It is safe to say that from the 1720's to the end of the century hardly a house of any consequence was built in the colonies without reference to such manuals. (In 1737, when he was only thirty-one years old, Benjamin Franklin advertised in *The Pennsylvania Gazette*, his own newspaper, for the return of his copy of Colin Campbell's *Vitruvius Britannicus*, which he had long before lent to some forgetful or negligent person. This was one of the largest of such publications, and a very expensive volume for a young printer to own and to pass about.) The universal reliance on such guides led to a general uniformity in architectural style throughout America in the later colonial period. However, local conditions—climate, available building materials, and other particular circumstances—gave every region its own accent and idiom within the prevailing architectural language. Although their builders may have looked for guidance to very much the same manuals, no one can confuse the stone-built mansions of the Philadelphia neighborhood, for example, with the wooden dwellings of equal grace in such towns as Wethersfield, Marblehead, or Salem in New England.

The public buildings of Philadelphia were a tribute to the opulence and civic pride of the city, to an interest in the general welfare above the usual standards set in Europe, and to the enterprise and progressive spirit of its architect-builders and planners. Most renowned, of course, is the Pennsylvania State House, better known in later years as Independence Hall. Work on this brick structure was supervised by the local carpenter (and member of the Carpenters' Company) Edmund Woolley. Although clearly based on English palace types, its plan reflects the qualitative changes taking place in provincial American government, with its need for assembly rooms for representatives instead of small, royal audience chambers. In 1748 the president of the legislative group and his council met for the first time in the big room on the second floor of the building which from then on became the center of almost all important political developments in the colony. (For a time the doorkeeper and his family lived in the west wing, and occasionally Indian delegations were lodged or entertained there.)

New buildings for the Pennsylvania Hospital and the city's House of Employment and Almshouse also differed from European prototypes in their expanded facilities for separate attention to the aged, poor, insane, and sick. The hospital, aside from being one of the principal architectural ornaments of the city, with its accommodations for lunatics, its sanitary arrangements, and its liberal administration, was probably the most advanced institution of its kind in the Western world.

Across the river from Philadelphia and across another river from New York City to the northeast, New Jersey presented an architectural landscape that was a sort of recapitulation of influences from both directions. (Benjamin Franklin is said to have referred to the area as "a barrel tapped at both ends.") Here at various times were built log houses in the Swedish manner, so-called Dutch colonial dwellings, trim clapboard structures indistinguishable from contemporary houses of New England, brick buildings of the type introduced to the Delaware Valley by Philadelphia masons, and so on. (Occasionally the last of these types broke out into ornate patterns of glazed brickwork, patterns that owe their character to deep-rooted folk traditions.)

South of Philadelphia, in Maryland, architectural fashions were set in Annapolis, the social and cultural center of the colony. Even before 1700 Annapolis had presented

Billopp House (Conference House),
Tottenville, Staten Island, N.Y. (about 1680)

Jean Hasbrouck House, New Paltz, N.Y. (1694; 1712)

When in 1609 Henry Hudson sailed into New York Bay and up the majestic river that now bears his name, he opened the way for Dutch traders who came in quest of the rich furs of the region. They established permanent trading posts in the Hudson River Valley and left tidy reminders of their prosperous homeland. The Van Cortlandt manor house and gardens are all that remain of the vast estate, assembled by Stephanus Van Cortlandt, that once included eighty-seven thousand acres. The earliest part of the house, with three-foot-thick sandstone walls, was built about 1680 as a trading post at the confluence of the Hudson and Croton rivers. In the mid-eighteenth century a second floor and porch were added; here the Van Cortlandts lived for a period of 250 years. From the start men of many different lands mingled with the Dutch, and in the rural area between New Amsterdam and Albany people of diverse strains built simple houses from local materials. In New Paltz, New York, there is a rare group of five stone dwellings on what is said to be the "oldest street in America with its original houses." Built by French Huguenot refugees, the houses show a French-Rhineland-Dutch influence in their limestone walls, steep medieval roofs, and wooden gable ends. The Jean Hasbrouck House was begun in 1694 and was added to in the following years as further need required. On Staten Island, off the southern tip of Manhattan, there is an imposing seventeenth-century manor house, a two-and-a-half-story fieldstone residence built by Captain Christopher Billopp. The bold stone masonry is characteristic of the medieval influence in some of our early architecture. Now called the Conference House, in 1776 it was the scene of an abortive conference among Benjamin Franklin, John Adams, Edward Rutledge, and Lord Richard Howe, admiral of the British fleet, to end the Revolution.

Van Cortlandt Manor, Croton-on-Hudson, N.Y. (1680; 1749)

On Maryland's still-rural eastern shore in the tiny hamlet of Church Creek stands a gem of a small church set amidst an ancient cemetery. Built only forty years after the first settlement was made in Maryland, Old Trinity Protestant Episcopal Church is the oldest Protestant church still in use in this country. The quaint brick exterior is a simple rectangle topped by a steeply gabled roof and enlivened by a semicircular apse. The interior has been meticulously restored to its pristine seventeenth-century condition. The towering, natural wood pulpit on the left wall surrounded by unpainted box pews is the focal point of the congregation. The delicate brass chandelier hanging over the center aisle complements the white plastered walls and the original red square bricks of the floor. The restored church contains a silver chalice and a red velvet cushion donated by Queen Anne. At the northern end of the Delmarva Peninsula in Wilmington stands another venerable Protestant place of worship. Holy Trinity, or Old Swedes, Church was begun by the Reverend Eric Björk on the site of the graveyard near old Fort Christina. Built partly of local stone, partly of brick, the structure was consecrated on Trinity Sunday, June 4, 1699. The simple rectangular plan was buttressed by three gabled porticoes in the eighteenth century and topped by an all-brick tower in the nineteenth. An adjoining Swedish farmhouse contains a library and museum.

Holy Trinity (Old Swedes) Church, Wilmington, Del. (1699; 1802)

Old Trinity Protestant Episcopal Church, Church Creek, Md. (1674)

Interior, Old Trinity

Ephrata Cloister, Ephrata, Pa. (1735-49)

Starting late in the seventeenth century and reaching a peak in the middle of the eighteenth, numbers of German emigrants from the Rhine Valley and neighboring regions landed at Philadelphia and spread out into the hinterland of Pennsylvania. The wooden structures on these pages are a strong evocation of the medieval tradition in building brought from the German homeland. Led by Johann Conrad Beissel, a group of German Seventh-Day Baptists settled Ephrata in 1732 as a communal semimonastic religious society. The society prospered and in addition to running a successful farm, tannery, and weaving mill, founded a noted choral school and established a fine printing press. The society's buildings, known as the Ephrata Cloister, were occupied by members until 1934. The three-story Saron, or Sisters' House (1743)—with steeply pitched roof, shed dormers, and vertically lapped shakes—standing at right angles to the attached Saal, or chapel (1740), creates a fine medieval group. At about this same time in York the Golden Plough Tavern was constructed in the medieval half-timbered tradition of the Black Forest, the homeland of the innkeeper-builder.

OVERLEAF: *Graeme Park House, Horsham, Pa. (1722)*. Some twenty miles north of Philadelphia on the Delaware River stands the country gentleman's estate of Graeme Park. Sir William Keith, lieutenant governor of the colony from 1717 to 1726, originally designed the fieldstone manor for use as a malthouse, which may explain its lack of finesse in exterior detail. Dr. Thomas Graeme converted it to a residence when he married Sir William's stepdaughter in 1737. The doctor transformed the interior with rich paneling of formal Georgian design, and here he lived in the style of the English gentry.

Golden Plough Tavern (detail), York, Pa. (about 1741)

The four houses illustrated here are expressions of the local stone vernacular in several different regions of the middle colonies. The early fieldstone house, built about 1740 by the founder of Hagerstown, Maryland, was used as a combined fur-trading post and storehouse. The plain stone building, built by ironmaster Isaac Potts, served as headquarters for George Washington during the severe winter of 1777-78 when the Continental Army encamped at Valley Forge. In 1780 General Washington briefly had his headquarters in the Dutch colonial sandstone house in Hackensack, New Jersey. Confiscated from the Zabriskie family because of their Tory sympathies, the house was given to General Von Steuben, who in turn sold it back to the Zabriskies. Allentown, Pennsylvania's, first mansion was built by James Allen, son of the city's founder, as a hunting and fishing lodge. Trout Hall, constructed in limestone with rather delicate exterior detail, is a good example of eastern Pennsylvanian Georgian architecture.

Trout Hall, Allentown, Pa. (1770)

Washington's Headquarters, Valley Forge State Park, Pa. (1758)

Zabriskie-Von Steuben House, Hackensack, N.J. (1752)

Jonathan Hager House, Hagerstown, Md. (about 1740)

147

New Castle, the colonial capital of Delaware, was founded by the Dutch in 1651, surrendered to the Swedes, and was retaken by the Dutch before it was finally captured by the English in 1664. Together with the public buildings on the green, which was laid out by Peter Stuyvesant, is the brick-and-clapboard Old Dutch House, considered to be the oldest extant dwelling in the state. Its low lines accentuated by its sloping roof, broad shutters, and large chimney are characteristic of the colonial style in the Dutch tradition. In the 1740's Moravians from Bohemia and Saxony settled Bethlehem, Pennsylvania, and made it their headquarters for missionary work among the Indians. The Moravian society was divided into living units—single men, single women, and married couples—and their buildings were designed for these various groups. The earliest, the Gemeinhaus (common house), is built of square-hewn white oak logs later covered in clapboard, and has a delicate upswing to the roof.

Old Dutch House, New Castle, Del. (about 1690)

Gemeinhaus, Historic Bethlehem, Pa. (1742)

Lake-Tysen House, Richmondtown Restoration, Staten Island, N.Y. (about 1740)

Late in the seventeenth century a small village was established in the center of Staten Island. The settlement was called Cocclestown—because of the large quantity of oyster and clam shells, or cockles, found in the area—until after the Revolution, when it was officially designated as Richmondtown. It was a compact little village of houses, shops, taverns, a school, a courthouse, and a jail, and it continued to grow until 1898, when Staten Island was incorporated into Greater New York and Richmondtown was no longer the county seat. Today many of the original buildings and others brought in from nearby places are being restored to depict the evolution of an American village from the seventeenth to the nineteenth century. The Voorlezer's House, built before 1696, is believed to be the oldest extant elementary-school building in the United States. The charming clapboard Lake-Tysen House, pictured here, was built around 1740 in the nearby town of New Dorp. Its sloping roof, dormer windows, two-section door, and shutters all proclaim the influence of Dutch architectural traditions. When completed, the restoration will include thirty-six buildings.

Dey Mansion, Wayne, N.J. (about 1740)

Hope Lodge, Fort Washington, Pa. (about 1750)

John Dickinson Mansion, Dover, Del. (1740; 1804)

Trent House, Trenton, N.J. (1719)

The three manor houses and one town house shown here illustrate some of the variations of Georgian architecture in the middle colonies. The earliest is the simple red brick house built in 1719 by New Jersey's first chief justice, William Trent, after whom Trenton is named. It served as the official residence of the first royal governor and a number of state governors. The two-and-a-half-story mansion of Flemish bond brick built by Judge Samuel Dickinson in 1740 and added to in the 1750's was gutted by fire in 1804. Samuel's son, John Dickinson, the "Penman of the Revolution," rebuilt it on slightly simpler lines. The brick and brownstone manor house accented by stone quoins and steep gambrel roof was built about 1740 by a carpenter for his son Colonel Theunis Dey. In 1780 George Washington had his headquarters here; he returned later that year to escape a kidnapping plot. Hope Lodge, an elegant mansion of brick and stucco, was built about 1750 by a successful gristmill operator. During the Revolution the house was for several weeks in the midst of military operations between Washington's and Howe's armies. James Watmough, owner of the house from 1784 to 1812, named it after his guardian, Henry Hope, from whose family the celebrated Hope Diamond took its name.

Old State House, New Castle, Del. (begun about 1732)

It is almost impossible to consider Independence Hall in architectural terms. This is the nation's birthplace, a shrine and the quintessential symbol of our free destiny. Yet, inside and out, it remains also a distinguished colonial structure in its own right. The decision to raise such a building was made by Pennsylvania's legislative assembly in 1729, but work proceeded slowly. It was only in 1753 that the steepled tower was added and a "bell of about two thousand pounds weight," ordered from London, installed within it. (Prophetically, cast into the bell was the phrase "Proclaim liberty throughout all the land unto all the inhabitants thereof.") The central section of the Old State House in New Castle, Delaware, served as the first capitol of that colony.

OVERLEAF: *Nassau Hall, Princeton University, Princeton, N.J. (1756).* When it was finished in 1756 Nassau Hall (named for William of Orange and Nassau, later King William III of England) was "the largest academic building in the Colonies." A dignified, straightforward structure built of local stone, it was shelled and injured during the Revolution, it served as a barracks for a time, and then, briefly, was the capitol building of the nascent United States; it suffered a serious fire in 1802 and in 1855.

Independence Hall, Philadelphia, Pa. (1732-53)

157

Christ Church, Philadelphia, Pa. (1744; 1754)

Christ Church in Philadelphia, completed in 1744 (the tower and steeple were added a decade later), is one of the most sophisticated surviving examples of colonial religious architecture. Designed after the engraved patterns in English building manuals, it strongly resembles St. Martin-in-the-Fields in London, built about twenty years earlier. The richness of the interior, with its great Tuscan columns supporting the arches that carry the eliptical ceiling, is illuminated by the enormous Palladian window in the chancel behind the altar. By the middle of the eighteenth century it was the city's most fashionable church. (Seven signers of the Declaration of Independence are buried in its nearby graveyard.) The Old Tennent Church, in Tennent, New Jersey, is surrounded by an endless panorama of ancient gravestones, many dating from the Battle of Monmouth in 1778.

Old Tennent Church (1751) and Cemetery (1731), Tennent, N.J.

Chase-Lloyd House, Annapolis, Md. (1774)

The fastidious detail of the Hammond-Harwood House in Annapolis, Maryland, as prominently displayed in its front doorway, ranks this building among the best examples of Georgian architecture in America. As mentioned in the introduction to this chapter, the house was the culminating and finest achievement of William Buckland, the English immigrant brought to this country as an indentured servant by the Mason family of Virginia. Buckland was also responsible for much of the detail of the Chase-Lloyd House, directly across the street. The house was begun in 1769 by Samuel Chase, who ran out of money before it was completed. Colonel Edward Lloyd IV purchased the shell of a building in 1771 and brought Buckland in to finish the job.

Hammond-Harwood House, Annapolis, Md. (1774). William Buckland, architect

With its two flanking dependencies, reminiscent of southern colonial architecture, Mount Pleasant is one of the most unusual and impressive pre-Revolutionary mansions of Philadelphia. It features virtually every device of late Georgian design, including Palladian windows, pediments, pilasters, and a grooved stucco surface simulating stone masonry. Built for John MacPherson, a former privateer who had accumulated a fortune, it was purchased in 1779 by Benedict Arnold, who intended to settle there one day with the comely and wealthy Peggy Shippen, but such plans were altered by the course of events.

Mount Pleasant, Philadelphia, Pa. (1761)

Old Town Hall, Wilmington, Del. (1798). Pierre Bauduy, architect

Charles Ridgely, the wealthy builder of Hampton Mansion, may well have designed this unusual structure with the aid of a master carpenter named Jehu Howell and with ideas gleaned from English architectural manuals. In any case, the house exuberantly departs from any "correct" Georgian scheme. With its front and back porticoes—whose pediments are flanked at the roof level by projecting dormer windows and shapely, carved urns—and its tall, domed and glazed cupola, the building bears the stamp of an original designer who was undeterred by purely academic strictures. The Old Town Hall at Wilmington, Delaware, was built just before the turn of the eighteenth century. It was designed by a French-born West Indies-based painter and architect named Pierre Bauduy who had come to Delaware with his young wife in 1790 as a refugee from uprisings in what is now the Dominican Republic. This small, chaste building has been miraculously preserved amidst a welter of later commercial developments that have taken over the downtown area of the city.

Hampton Mansion, near Baltimore, Md. (1790)

The White House, Washington, D.C. (1792-1800). James Hoban, architect

The White House, or the President's House as it was originally called, was designed by James Hoban, an immigrant from Kilkenny County in Ireland. John and Abigail Adams were the first tenants. Abigail wrote her sister that the building was "twice as large as our meeting House" in Massachusetts, and was "built for ages to come." Hoban restored the structure after it was burned by the British in 1814. The Octagon House was designed for Colonel John Tayloe of Mount Airy, Virginia, by William Thornton, a West Indian-born Quaker who also designed the National Capitol. (Actually, it is in the shape of a hexagon, with a semicircular entrance tower, thus designed to fit an angular plot of land.) While Hoban was restoring the burnt-out White House, President James Madison moved into the Octagon House. The peace treaty ending the War of 1812 was signed here. The National Headquarters of the American Institute of Architects is now fittingly housed in the handsome new edifice just behind.

The Octagon House, Washington, D.C. (1800). William Thornton, architect

City Hall, New York, N.Y. (1812). John McComb, Jr., and Joseph François Mangin, architects

Octagonal Cobblestone House, Madison, N.Y. (1840's)

Buildings made of cobblestones (small, water-smoothed fieldstones) proliferated in northwestern New York State between the 1820's and 1850's. This was partly because of the natural abundance of rock and pebbles in this area and partly because the building of the Erie Canal had attracted many masons to this region. It is claimed that even today there are some sixty cobble-built houses, stores, and churches standing between Niagara Falls and Rochester. One unusual example is the octagonal house, shown above, at Madison, New York. In the school at Childs, built in 1849, small "lake-washed" stones of fairly uniform size serve as a veneer over a wooden frame.

Cobblestone School, Childs, N.Y. (1849)

Hyde Hall, near Cooperstown, N.Y. (1811-33). Philip Hooker, architect

Farmers' Museum and Village Crossroads, Cooperstown, N.Y. (1783-1861)

When the Englishman George Hyde Clarke settled in America to supervise his landholdings, he commissioned the New York architect Philip Hooker to build for him near Cooperstown a mansion, to be called Hyde Hall, be-fitting his eminent status. Begun in 1811 and finished in 1833, this was to be Hooker's masterpiece. At the nearby Farmers' Museum and Village Crossroads, a group of buildings, most of them dating before 1840, have been assembled to re-create the appearance of a typical village of that upstate area in the early nineteenth century—a well-stocked country store, a one-room schoolhouse, a blacksmith shop, a farmhouse, and so on. The church shown in the foreground of the illustration below makes a fitting terminus to this nostalgic and instructive grouping.

Rose Hill, Geneva, N.Y. (1839)

Names given to mushrooming towns of New York (and elsewhere in the country) in the first half of the nineteenth century—Athens, Attica, Sparta, Syracuse, Corinth, Carthage, Troy, and so on—suggest the awareness of ancient Greece that gave reason and meaning to the Greek Revival architecture of the time. Although it was planned to accommodate the needs of a Scottish-based faith, the First Presbyterian Church at Troy assumed the form of a hexastyle Greek temple made of stuccoed brick, accurately detailed and proportioned. Facing Seneca Lake across an ample lawn, Rose Hill remains one of the state's finest domestic adaptations of the ancient architectural formulas. The pedimented, two-story central portico is flanked by one-story wings with Ionic columns that echo the six stately ones that are placed across the main façade. William K. Strong, a retired New York City merchant, built the mansion in 1839 on land purchased from the Rose family.

First Presbyterian Church, Troy, N.Y. (1836)

On the site of New York's second City Hall, which
was renamed Federal Hall when Washington was
inaugurated there as first President in 1789, a classical revival building designed by Ithiel Town and
Alexander Jackson Davis was built in 1842 as a
United States Custom House and later served as a
Subtreasury building. The façade is directly modeled on the Parthenon. Standing on a sidewalk podium in front of the steps is a statue of Washington
by John Quincy Adams Ward. The group of five
Greek Revival temples, on Staten Island at Snug
Harbor Road, was financed by a privateer of the
Revolutionary War, Captain Robert Randall, to
house "aged, decrepit and worn out sailors." The
buildings, with their great Ionic columns of Vermont granite, are all laterally connected.

OVERLEAF: *Philadelphia Water Works, Philadelphia, Pa. (1819)*. Located on the banks of the
Schuylkill River, the water works were constructed between 1811 and 1819 and were housed
in simulated Grecian temples. Erected a century
later, the Philadelphia Art Museum towers above
the water works and is one of the world's largest
edifices in the Greek temple style.

Sailors' Snug Harbor, Staten Island, N.Y. (1833).
Martin E. Thompson, architect

Federal Hall National Memorial, New York, N.Y. (1842). Town & Davis, architects

191

Second Bank of the United States, Philadelphia, Pa. (1824). William Strickland, architect

Philadelphia was the nation's first metropolis to don the mantle of the Greek Revival. In the early 1800's this rapidly growing city attracted architects who erected public and private buildings in the new fashion. Popular enthusiasm for antiquity was generated in part by Nicholas Biddle, Philadelphia's social, cultural, and financial leader, who had traveled to Greece in 1806 and had become so enamored of its ancient structures that he confided in his diary, "The two great truths in the world are the Bible and Grecian architecture." At his Delaware River estate of Andalusia, in 1836 Biddle had a colonnaded Doric portico added to his eighteenth-century farmhouse by architect Thomas Ustick Walter. At about this same time Philadelphia-born Walter was designing Founder's Hall of Girard College with specific suggestions from Biddle. Flanked by two buildings on each side, the hall, with its robust marble columns, served as a classroom for "poor, white male orphans" for some sixty-six years. As Walter pointed out, "If architects would oftener *think* as the Greeks thought, than to *do* as the Greeks did, our columnar architecture . . . and its character and expression would gradually conform to the local circumstances of the country and the republican spirit of its institutions." The Second Bank of the United States, built 1819-24, was designed by William Strickland, who won the commission via a competition that called for a "chaste imitation of Grecian architecture." The result is a pure example of the temple style, with the two ends a literal copy of the Parthenon minus the sculpture. The white marble edifice with fluted columns served as a United States Custom House (1845-1934) after the bank failed and is now part of Independence National Historical Park. The imposing style took a while to spread from the state capital, but when in the 1840's in central Pennsylvania the successful ironmaster Elias Baker built a fine mansion he had it fashioned in the Greek Revival manner.

Andalusia, Andalusia, Pa. (1836). Thomas U. Walter, architect

Founder's Hall, Girard College, Philadelphia, Pa. (1833-47).
Thomas U. Walter, architect

Baker Mansion, Altoona, Pa. (1847). Robert C. Long, Jr., architect

The remarkable main gate house of the Green-Wood Cemetery at Brooklyn, designed by Richard Upjohn and Son in 1861, and built of brownstone with a polychrome slate roof, has justifiably been called the culmination of the Gothic Revival movement in New York. Opened in 1840, this cemetery occupies 478 acres and in the course of the years has become the final resting place for more than a half million souls, including such personages as Samuel F. B. Morse, Nathaniel Currier and James Merritt Ives, Lola Montez, "Boss" Tweed, Henry Ward Beecher, Peter Cooper, among numerous others. In the course of the nineteenth century the romantic spirit found its most poignant and liberated expression in graveyard architecture and its associated monuments. The "homes of the dead" fashioned in those years were frequently melancholy caricatures of the homes of the living—somber and sometimes extreme architectural fantasies that could be indulged in such segregated areas where reverence for the dead hushed any breath of esthetic criticism from the living. Such conspicuous memorials were a far cry from the burial sites of the first generation of Pilgrims, whose "graves were leveled and sown with grass" lest the Indians should learn of the pitiable condition of these pioneers, whose numbers had been more than halved by weakness and illness unto death. With its carefully landscaped grounds—its hills, ponds, and plantings—within distant view of New York Harbor, Green-Wood Cemetery, like others of its kind and time, provided an attractive retreat not only for the dead but for the living urbanites who came to visit the departed and who also used it as a verdant and quiet escape from the noise and congestion of city life.

Gates, Green-Wood Cemetery, Brooklyn, N.Y.
(1861). Richard Upjohn and Son, architects

Two of the most distinguished and attractive remaining structures in the Gothic Revival style in the Middle Atlantic area are St. Patrick's Cathedral in New York City and Lyndhurst in nearby Tarrytown. The former, designed by Renwick, was thought by some to be "too far out of town" when work began in 1858 on Fifth Avenue between 50th and 51st streets. However, thanks in good part to the building of Rockfeller Center directly opposite in the 1930's, the church now forms part of the core of midtown Manhattan. The 330-foot-high twin spires were added to the church's structure in 1887. Lyndhurst, standing on a magnificently landscaped slope overlooking the Hudson River, was originally planned in 1838 by Alexander Jackson Davis as a summer "villa" for General William Paulding and his son. When it was rising in 1841 it was referred to as "Paulding's folly," because of its gabled, towered, and pinnacled pretensions to magnificence. On the other hand, the leading critic of the day, Davis's friend, Alexander Jackson Downing, singing the architect's praise, thought he had not seen anything to equal it, "as I conceive it will be when finished"—a judgment broadly accepted by critics of our own day.

Lyndhurst, Tarrytown, N.Y. (1841; 1867). Alexander Jackson Davis, architect

St. Patrick's Cathedral, New York, N.Y. (1858-79; 1887). James Renwick, architect

The three greatest developments in structural achievement in the nineteenth century were the Crystal Palace in London (1851), the Brooklyn Bridge in New York (1883), and the Eiffel Tower in Paris (1889). The Palace enclosed an enormous area with its prefabricated glass and iron structure; the bridge stretched over a greater distance than any previous span; the tower rose to a height unmatched by other buildings for years to come. Construction of the bridge was undertaken by John Augustus Roebling, who came to this country from his native Germany in 1831. He died from an accident during the construction, and his talented son Washington supervised completion of the bridge, which when finished spanned a distance of 1,595 feet—more than 50 per cent longer than any other bridge of the time. The elder Roebling had developed the concept of "spinning" and tightly binding with a "jacket" the complex web of cables he used for this gigantic suspension. The double-arched Gothic towers seem dated today, but they are structurally logical. Within a day of its opening in 1883, this magnificent new highway in and out of Manhattan Island had attracted so much traffic that an urgent cry for more bridges was immediately raised. However, the scale of the Brooklyn Bridge was not substantially exceeded until the George Washington Bridge was flung across the Hudson River almost fifty years later.

Brooklyn Bridge, New York, N.Y. (1869-83).
John Augustus Roebling and
Washington Roebling, engineers

201

Haughwout Building, New York, N.Y. (1857). J. P. Gaynor, architect

The development of cast-iron architecture took place more than a century ago. This building technique presaged modern curtain-wall construction as well as much of the theory of skyscraper design. It also made possible a structure that could be prefabricated of standardized units, that could be erected "with extraordinary facility," "taken to pieces with . . . dispatch" and thus demounted, transported elsewhere as need be. (Some unassembled buildings were sent around the Cape to San Francisco during the Gold Rush.) In this country the process first flourished in New York City, but foundries to supply the necessary elements were soon busy in numerous other cities. Those elements could be manufactured in an endless series of identical forms, often with intricately contrived decorative detail. The nature of cast-iron framing, with its repetitive sections, naturally led to designs that anticipated the modular construction of today's architecture. The greatest remaining monument to this cast-iron style is what was formerly the E. V. Haughwout store on Broadway in New York. Its two façades—inconspicuously but impressively—are approximate copies of the library built in Venice by Sansovino in 1536. In the Haughwout Building, Elisha Otis installed the country's first safety elevator, an apparatus that would speed the development of the skyscraper. Lower Manhattan remains what has been called "a veritable museum of cast iron, a greater concentration than anywhere else in the world." Most of the architects who used iron for the columns and façades of buildings treated metal to resemble stone as closely as possible (as in the case of the Haughwout Building). Serious fires demonstrated that although iron structures did not burn, they crumpled under intense heat. In the light of such unhappy experiences, the enthusiasm for using the metal as an architectural material waned. Oddly, when stone was reintroduced to replace the metal, the masonry was in turn painted to simulate cast iron.

Cast-Iron Buildings, New York, N.Y. (mid-19th century)

In 1885 the Jefferson Market, which now houses a regional branch of the New York Public Library, was voted America's fifth most beautiful building. At the time it served as a courthouse complex, including a jail, which had replaced a shopping and marketing area. With its Venetian-style ornamentation, its assemblage of stained glass, and its watchtower and clock, it remains a unique, almost indescribable monument to the lusty eclecticism of its period. Local associations of private individuals salvaged it from demolition when it had remained empty for some years after 1945; it was then converted to its present use by Georgio Cavaglieri. The Maryland Institute in Baltimore is a converted railroad station that now houses the city's famous art school. Another example of inspired adaptation of an affectionately regarded old structure to the service of modern needs, it was restored in 1966 by the firm of Cochran, Stephenson & Donkervoet. In the process the exterior of the building in the Romanesque manner was left largely intact. (The old train shed occasionally serves as an effective outdoor sculpture gallery.) The New St. Mary's Church was completed at Burlington, New Jersey, in 1854 by the English-born architect Richard Upjohn, who became in this country a leading apostle of Gothic Revival religious architecture. Surrounded by the ancient burial ground of an earlier church, the lofty, pointed spire changes from a square to an octagonal shape near its peak.

OVERLEAF: *Smithsonian Institution, Washington, D.C. (1847-55). James Renwick, architect.* The Smithsonian Institution in Washington, D.C., has been called the "attic of the nation." Its main building, in a freely designed version of the Gothic Revival style, emphasizes that complete rejection of classical symmetry characteristic of the period.

Jefferson Market Library, New York, N.Y. (1876).
Calvert Vaux and Frederick Withers, architects

New St. Mary's Church, Burlington, N.J. (1854).
Richard Upjohn, architect

Maryland Institute, Baltimore, Md. (1894).
Baldwin and Pennington, architects

The massive Old Pension Building in the National Capital was designed in 1883 by General Montgomery C. Meigs as a memorial to Civil War veterans. Modeled on Rome's Farnese Palace, this famous landmark was once nicknamed "Meigs' Old Red Barn." The inside boasts a great hall more than a hundred feet high divided by eight freestanding Corinthian columns made of stucco-covered brick. A nineteenth-century architect observed that "nothing short of an inaugural ball or a thunderstorm could possibly fill the immense void." And the inaugural balls of Presidents Cleveland, Harrison, McKinley, Theodore Roosevelt, and Taft were indeed held here. The Executive Office Building, built in the 1880's to house the State, War, and Navy departments, is an impressive granite monument in the Second Empire style. With its approximately nine hundred Tuscan columns on the outside and two miles of corridors within, it is claimed that this was the largest office building in the world when Alfred B. Mullet designed it. The exuberant Second Empire City Hall of Philadelphia has been appraised by a commission of the American Institute of Architects as "perhaps the greatest single effort of late nineteenth-century American architecture." From atop the tall masonry tower a statue of William Penn surveys the legacy of his enlightened leadership.

Old Pension Building, Washington, D.C. (1883). General Montgomery C. Meigs, architect

City Hall, Philadelphia, Pa. (1872-1901). John McArthur, Jr., architect

Executive Office Building, Washington, D.C. (1871-88). Alfred B. Mullet, architect

209

Olana, Hudson, N.Y. (1874)

Perched on its hilltop site high above the Hudson River, Olana, the opulent home of Frederick Edwin Church, presents a dramatic composite of Western and Near Eastern architecture. Church had traveled to remote parts of the earth—from the Arctic to the Andes, to Europe and the Near East—in quest of subjects for his eminently successful landscape paintings. He received as much as $10,000 for a single canvas. Acting to a large extent as his own architect and decorator, and taking advantage of his ample resources, he wove into the exotic design of Olana, inside and out, ornamental forms and themes from far places and distant ages. Oriental, Islamic, and European cultures were enthusiastically combined in a grandiose Victorian manner. The exterior walls of its towers, porches, and gazebos are brightly ornamented with colored tiles and painted brick. To Church, Olana was "the Center of the World." And, he added, "I own it." In the total conception of this unique project Church enjoyed the professional guidance of the landscape architects Calvert Vaux and Frederick Law Olmsted. Built at about the same time by the brilliant Philadelphia architect Frank Furness, the Pennsylvania Academy of the Fine Arts also features exotic and eclectic designs in its polychromed façade. This highly fashionable (for its time) housing for the Academy, which is the oldest institution of its kind in the country, is Furness' greatest surviving building.

Pennsylvania Academy of the Fine Arts, Philadelphia, Pa. (1876). Frank Furness, architect

Interior, Olana

211

It would be difficult to imagine a greater contrast to Richardson's solid stone jail than the lacy woodwork that characterizes the Victorian architecture at Cape May, New Jersey, where Delaware Bay meets the Atlantic Ocean. The area was first settled in 1631, and the town had its heyday in the nineteenth century when summer visitors flocked there from Philadelphia, Wilmington, Washington, and New York, first by steamboat, then also by railroad. Cape May retains what may be the greatest concentration of Victorian wooden buildings in the East. The town claims to be "the Oldest Seashore Resort in the United States," and in recent years has undertaken to preserve and glorify its unique architectural heritage. Any proposed changes (in the central "Victorian Village") must be approved before work is undertaken.

Victorian Buildings, Cape May, N.J. (mid-19th century)

Town Office Building, Cazenovia, N.Y. (1847). Andrew Jackson Downing, architect

The Baptist church at North Salem, New York, an elaborate variation of Gothic Revival style, has been in continuous use since it was built in 1878. For many years, the Old Whalers' First Presbyterian Church at Sag Harbor on Long Island was topped with a steeple shaped like a sailor's spyglass, but this was destroyed in the hurricane of 1938. The church was built by Minard Lafever, an architect whose published guides were widely influential. The attractive Gothic Revival structure that now serves the town of Cazenovia as an office building was built as a residence by Jacob TenEyck, then given to his son upon his marriage.

Old Whalers' First Presbyterian Church, Sag Harbor, Long Island, N.Y. (1844). Minard Lafever, architect

Baptist Church, North Salem, N.Y. (1878).
J. A. Wood, architect

Pierpont Morgan Library, New York, N.Y. (1906). McKim, Mead & White, architects

Public Library, New York, N.Y. (1898–1911). Carrère & Hastings, architects

Late in the nineteenth century and on into the twentieth, classical formulas enjoyed a glorious renaissance in America, notably evident in public buildings that have survived from that period. The teachings of the École des Beaux-Arts in Paris were in good part responsible for the vogue. One critic has claimed that the New York Public Library "probably comes closer than any other [building] in America to the complete realization of Beaux-Arts design at its best." Located behind this impressive structure, Bryant Park provides a lunchtime oasis whence office dwellers of midtown Manhattan can gaze at the tall buildings they fill in workaday hours. Less ostentatious than the Public Library on the exterior, even more opulent within, the Morgan Library speaks eloquently for the same tradition.

Bryant Park, New York, N.Y.

The Capitol, "the spirit of America in stone," rises majestically from its plaza, from which radiate the great elm-lined avenues according to Pierre L'Enfant's master plan. When in 1793 George Washington laid the cornerstone for the National Capitol, it was just the beginning of a building that continued to evolve under the aegis of a series of architects over the next two centuries. Dr. William Thornton submitted the winning design in the competition held for the Capitol and under the guidance of James Hoban, winner of the President's House competition, the north wing was completed. In 1803 Benjamin Latrobe took over construction and had completed the south wing when the British burned "this harbor of Yankee democracy," during the War of 1812. Latrobe restored the Senate and House chambers before he resigned in 1817. Charles Bulfinch followed to link the two wings with the domed central portion according to Thornton's design. In 1850 Thomas U. Walter won the competition for the House and Senate extensions, which doubled the length and tripled the size of the building. To maintain proper proportions Walter replaced Bulfinch's wooden dome with a taller one consisting of two cast-iron shells, a high one for exterior effect nesting over a low one for interior scale. The canopy of the dome is decorated with a fresco entitled "The Apotheosis of George Washington" by Constantino Brumidi, who also designed the frieze depicting great events in American history that encircles the Rotunda. When in 1863 Thomas Crawford's statue of Freedom was placed atop the dome, the Capitol was finished and remained thus until 1959 when the east front was unfortunately extended. The 555-foot marble-sheathed obelisk dedicated to the Father of our Country is the tallest masonry structure in the world. The original Robert Mills design called for an obelisk rising from a classical temple at its base. Work began in 1848 and continued fitfully over the next thirty-seven years. Some changes were made, including a shift from its original site due to geological conditions and the abandonment of the temple base.

The Capitol, Washington, D.C. (1793-1863). William Thornton, Benjamin Henry Latrobe, Charles Bulfinch, Thomas U. Walter, architects

Washington Monument, Washington, D.C. (1848-85). Robert Mills, architect

Scenes in Central Park, New York, N.Y.

New York's Central Park was completed in 1876 according to the inspired plans of Frederick Law Olmsted and Calvert Vaux. More than a quarter of a century earlier such a large, verdant open space had been suggested as an "essential aid to public health"—a great breathing place for otherwise hemmed-in city dwellers—the equivalent of a brief visit to the countryside; and Olmsted thus envisioned the park, not as a mere ornament to the rapidly growing city, but as an organic element in its development. So it was when completed, has been, and continues to be. Even more than that, these superbly designed 840 acres constitute a masterpiece of environmental art in the purest and best sense of that term.

Prudential (Guaranty) Building, Buffalo, N.Y. (1895).
Louis H. Sullivan & Dankmar Adler, architects

The name of the Boston-born architect Louis Sullivan is closely identified with the steel-framed skyscrapers that were newly rising in Chicago in the last decades of the nineteenth century, and his professional career in that midwestern area will be more fully discussed in a later chapter of these books. However, his Prudential Building in Buffalo, completed in 1895 (until 1899 it was known as the Guaranty Building), will serve as advance notice of the man's special genius. This twelve-story structure possesses a unity of design equaled by few of today's even modest skyscrapers. Sullivan had set himself to the task of creating an entirely new American architecture, and his creative spirit carried him far in that direction. (It also served as a sharp spur to his young protégé Frank Lloyd Wright.) The lush, flowerlike patterns that appear in the Prudential Building, as in so many of his other constructions, are a personal and poetic expression of Sullivan's rare vision. A terra-cotta skin, required for fire protection, projects a medley of earth colors high above the city street. Never have steel and "cooked earth" been more artfully wedded. In the Prudential Building, with his partner Dankmar Adler, he left one of his finest contributions to early modern architecture.

The Fuller Building was so ingeniously fitted
to its triangular plot at the angular intersec-
tion of Broadway and Fifth Avenue at 23rd
Street that for some years after its completion in 1902 it was the world's most famous
skyscraper. Almost inevitably, because of its
shape it was nicknamed the "Flatiron Building," and so it has been known ever since.
Although it is only twenty-one stories high,
with both the exterior walls and the floors
supported at each story by the steel frame, it
hinted at much greater heights to come. Rusticated limestone uniformly detailed from
ground to roof covers the building in the
manner of an Italian Renaissance palace.
When the doors of the Woolworth Building
farther downtown in lower Manhattan
opened in 1913, it was the tallest building in
the world. It soared to a height of almost
eight hundred feet. Special foundations—
100-foot-deep caissons filled with concrete
—had to be laid to support the giant, and innovative struts and braces used to fortify
the heights against the pressure of winds.
Frank W. Woolworth, founder of the immensely profitable "five and dime" stores,
extravagantly admired the Houses of Parlia-
ment in London and commissioned his architect, Cass Gilbert, to design an office building
"in the Gothic style." The daring and incon-
gruous result, a modern engineering
triumph bedecked with psuedomedieval
trappings, astonished the world. All the details are Gothic, including gargoyles, flying
buttresses, tourelles, and the rest. (One
bemused member of the cloth referred to the
gigantic structure as a "Cathedral of Commerce.") In any case, it well served the intended purpose of advertising the ubiquitous Woolworth stores.

Woolworth Building, New York, N.Y. (1913).
Cass Gilbert, architect

Flatiron (Fuller) Building, New York, N.Y. (1902).
Daniel H. Burnham & Company, architects

The so-called "Collegiate Gothic" style in architecture, which had its beginnings in this country in the 1880's, had little or nothing to do with the Gothic Revival vogue that was so widespread somewhat earlier in the century. It was rather the outcome of a movement which sought to return to the traditions of medieval humanism and learning, where scholars could enjoy close relations with their master in a setting conducive to study and contemplation, recalling the centuries-old ambience of Oxford and Cambridge in England. The architects Walter Cope and John Stewardson were among pioneers of the style, and with Blair Hall at Princeton University they gave the movement an impetus that successfully carried it on to many other college campuses during the next generation. Aside from any consideration of the archaeological accuracy of its design, Blair opens onto a landscaped area—the west campus—whose various levels, ample spaces, and adjoining buildings all contribute to an environment that will remain stimulating beyond the life of any architectural fashions.

Dodge Gate and Blair Walk, Princeton University

Blair Hall, Princeton University, Princeton, N.J. (1897). Cope & Stewardson, architects

230

Jefferson Memorial, Washington, D.C. (1943). John Russell Pope, architect; Rudolph Evans, sculptor

When the Tidal Basin site of the Jefferson Memorial was selected in 1934, it completed a crosslike scheme for the nation's great monuments in the Capital. The White House, the Capitol, and the Mall were laid out according to L'Enfant's plan, and the three presidential memorials were added some two centuries later. The Washington Monument stands just off center, with the wide vista of the Mall to the Capitol to the east, the White House to the north, the Lincoln Memorial to the west, and the Jefferson Memorial to the south. This domed, circular, colonnaded structure, housing the bronze statue of Jefferson by Rudolph Evans, was designed by John Russell Pope and his associates to reflect Jefferson's taste for classical architecture. The exterior walls and fifty-four columns are of Vermont marble, the interior walls—inscribed with selections from Jefferson's most famous writings—are of Georgia marble, and the domed ceiling of Indiana limestone. The thirty-six Colorado marble columns of the shrine to Abraham Lincoln represent the number of states in the Union at the time of his death. On the attic walls above the frieze are inscribed the names of the forty-eight states of the Union at the time the memorial was dedicated in 1922. Henry Bacon designed two side chambers—inscribed with the Gettysburg Address and the Second Inaugural Address—off the main shrine with its majestic marble statue of Lincoln by Daniel Chester French.

Lincoln Memorial, Washington, D.C. (1922). Henry Bacon, architect; Daniel Chester French, sculptor

Rockefeller Center, with its handsome grouping of harmonious buildings composed around a central plaza, is a highly successful solution to high-density urban planning. The fourteen original buildings, built between 1931 and 1940, are all faced in gray Indiana limestone, which gives them a group identity lacking in the newer additions on adjoining sites. The complex is best approached from Fifth Avenue by a promenade running between two low buildings and landscaped with a series of fountains and seasonal plantings. This mall terminates in a group of terraces around a sunken plaza that is fringed by the bright flags of all nations and that features the famous gilded sculpture of Prometheus by Paul Manship. In winter the plaza serves as a skating rink; in summer it converts to a delightful open-air café decorated with bright umbrellas and tropical foliage. Just behind the plaza the focus shifts skyward with the vertical stripes of the seventy-floor RCA building, whose lobby is embellished with frescoes by José Maria Sert and whose observation tower offers a sweeping panoramic view of Manhattan Island and its surroundings.

Rockefeller Center, New York, N.Y. (1931-40).
Reinhardt & Hofmeister; Corbett, Harrison & MacMurray; Hood & Fouilhoux, principal architects

Chrysler Building, New York, N.Y. (1930). William Van Alen, architect

The Chrysler Building has the curious distinction of having been the tallest building in the world for a shorter time than any other claimant. Only a few months after it was completed in 1930, early in the next year it was surpassed in height by the Empire State Building. The former rises to 1,048 feet above the city streets, the latter to 1,250 feet. Both structures were planned in the booming days of the twenties; both opened their doors during the Great Depression. The decorative treatment of the Chrysler Building admirably reflects the fashion of the time—"art deco," as it has since been labeled. It was one of the first skyscrapers to sheath large surfaces with stainless steel. Every setback of the masonry walls beneath the gleaming tower displays variant designs of basket-weave patterns, "radiator-cap" gargoyles, and a band of abstract representations of automobiles. The Empire State Building was constructed on a site that had earlier been occupied, first by two mansions belonging to the Astor family, and then by the old Waldorf-Astoria Hotel. When the hotel replaced Mrs. Astor's private establishment, it in turn became a gathering place for the privileged socialites of the city. Because of the hard times, for a while after it was completed the Empire State Building remained largely vacant. However, throngs of sightseers paid to ascend to its observation decks for spectacular views of the surrounding metropolitan area, thus helping with the taxes. The dirigible mooring mast at the crown of the building was never used as such, but the television antennas at that height have since been effectively used by all New York stations. This enormous pile was constructed almost entirely of standardized machine-made parts in a remarkably short time. At peak speed, fourteen and a half stories were raised in ten working days.

OVERLEAF: *Verrazano-Narrows Bridge, Staten Island, N.Y. (1964). Othmar H. Ammann, designer.* The bridges that bind together New York's several islands and the adjacent mainlands are among the greatest spans in the nation. Longest of all—the longest suspension bridge in the world—is the Verrazano-Narrows Bridge, which stretches for 4,260 feet over the entrance to New York's harbor.

236

Empire State Building, New York, N.Y. (1931). Shreve, Lamb & Harman, architects

In 1893 Frank Lloyd Wright quit his apprenticeship to Louis Sullivan to open his own practice as an architect in Oak Park, Illinois. From then until his death sixty-six years later, he continued to astonish with a long progression of unorthodox buildings in various parts of the country. He adapted his creations to their environments as well as to the special needs of their inhabitants, using open planning, natural colors, forms, and textures in his designs, an esthetic practice he termed "organic architecture." One of his most celebrated structures is Fallingwater, or Bear Run as the family called it, the dwelling he built in 1937 for the late Edgar J. Kaufmann as a weekend retreat from Pittsburgh. The dominant elements of the house that first meet the eye are the pale ochrecolored cantilevered concrete terraces, resembling enormous shallow boxes, that jut over the tumbling waters of the falls below. Within and without, the boundaries between the man-made construction and the surrounding natural setting are purposefully minimized. With the Guggenheim Museum in New York City Wright conceived one of his most controversial buildings. Here he explored "the ultimate in flexibility—the circle." The interior, with its spiral ramp ascending to a glazed roof, gives the visitor an exciting impression that he is enwrapped in serpentine coils. One distinguished architectural critic has called this "one of the most beautiful spaces created in this century." Others find this unique, single-room, ramped plan for a museum disconcerting. At the very least, the structure demonstrates Wright's vigor in the tenth decade of his life.

Guggenheim Museum, New York, N.Y. (1944-59). Frank Lloyd Wright, arch

Fallingwater, Ohiopyle, Pa. (1937). Frank Lloyd Wright, architect

The Beth Sholom Synagogue dominates its hilltop site like some gigantic biblical tent—a translucent one, for the double-thick roof-walls that shelter the congregation are of wired glass on the exterior and plastic within. This construction rests on an angled tan concrete base with a symbolic pool at the entrance. Inside, the sanctuary confronts a vast panorama of 1,214 seats. At Holmdel, New Jersey, the Bell Laboratories forms a puzzlingly scaled rectangular box packaged in one-way mirror glass which reflects the sky, the passing clouds, and the surrounding landscape. The structure is 700 feet long, 350 feet wide, and 5 stories high. As in the case of Alice in Wonderland's mirror, these massive reflecting exterior surfaces give no suggestion of what lurks beyond on the inside of the building, where the visitor is greeted by a surprising and delightful space full of light and greenery. The Finnish-born architect Eero Saarinen, son of Eliel Saarinen, who lived in America after 1923, has produced a wide variety of significant, innovative structures.

Beth Sholom Synagogue, Elkins Park, Pa. (1959). Frank Lloyd Wright, architect

Bell Telephone Laboratories, Holmdel, N.J. (1966).
Eero Saarinen & Associates, architects

OVERLEAF: *Maryland Blue Cross Building, Towson, Md. (1972). Peterson & Brickbauer, architects.* The building that houses the Blue Cross in Towson, Maryland, is a mirrored cube measuring 134 feet in each dimension and containing eleven floors of office space. Most mechanical services are housed in a separate and smaller cube of bright red brick, forty-two feet on a side, whose image—along with that of the surrounding countryside—is clearly reflected in the glass walls of the main building in the following illustration. Combined, the two structures form an unusual sculptural composition on a large scale.

243

The thin slab of Lever House on New York's Park Avenue, resting on its stilts and with its low connecting wing, has become a major architectural landmark since its construction in 1952. Skidmore, Owings & Merrill created this first "prestige" office building by utilizing only one quarter of its square-block site. The horizontal "wing" element floats on columns one floor above the street, thus freeing the ground level for a pedestrian passage with an open-to-the-sky garden court in the center, beside which a stainless steel and green-tinted glass tower rises to a height of eighteen floors. Lever House's crystalline design was in part inspired by the work of Mies van der Rohe, whose most famous statement, the thirty-eight floor Seagram Building, stands diagonally across Park Avenue. The distiller's headquarters is set back from the street by a formal plaza—with granite paving, marble benches, trees, and fountain pools—on which there is a changing exhibit of monumental sculpture. The double height of the ground floor allows the plaza to flow visually into the lobby, while the set-back from the street allows the tower shaft to rise without breaks. (This is an interesting contrast with the Lever House's use of site.) The bronze-colored exterior of the building—brown-tinted glass between bronze metal spandrels and bronze mullions—has spawned a rash of dark skyscrapers in imitation. Directly opposite, just south of Lever House, the Italian Renaissance Racquet and Tennis Club (not open to the public), designed by McKim, Mead & White in 1918 of rusticated granite with bronze trim, provides in effect the west wall for the Seagram Building's plaza.

Seagram Building, New York, N.Y. (1958). Ludwig Mies van der Rohe and Philip Johnson, architects

Lever House, New York, N.Y. (1952). Skidmore, Owings & Merrill, architects

Morris A. Mechanic Theater, Baltimore, Md. (1966). John M. Johansen, architect

Charles Center, Baltimore, Md. (1957-69). Wallace, Kostritsky & Potts, planners

Baltimore's Charles Center represents a notable achievement in the transformation of a worn-out urban wasteland of some twenty-two acres into a lively, enterprising core of the city—an attractive, convenient area of many aspects. Two high-rise buildings containing four hundred apartments provide essential residential units in the scheme. Their upper stories survey the surrounding city. At the ground level range a tantalizing variety of shops, a restaurant, and a 510-seat cinema. An eight-hundred-room hotel, office buildings, a civic center, and a theater contribute to variety in the life of the center. The whole complex is laced with elevated pedestrian walks so that one never has to cross a street to reach an objective. Cars are housed underground. The theater, adding animation to the night life of the center, is a boldly conceived concrete structure whose complex functions are clearly manifest in the projections of the exterior. The night-and-day animation of the center has its focus in a plaza by the theater. Here, by day, office workers sit in its terraced, well-planted park at lunchtime. By night the theatergoers take over. As a whole, the center has become the focus—and pride—of Baltimore.

2 Charles Center Apartments (1967). Whittlesey & Conklin, architects

There are few large planes of unbroken exterior walls in the Orange County Government Center at Goshen, New York. Rather, the walls project and recede here and there in the manner of a massive cubist sculpture. These carefully composed planes of various dimensions create a complex pattern in reinforced concrete and sand-colored ribbed concrete blocks that gives outward expression to the thoughtfully considered spaces within that accommodate various functions. On two sides the building presents completely blank façades; on the other two, windows appear where needed. The large number of different-sized courtrooms required windowless walls, and these were placed near the center of the building with the council chambers wrapped about them. At Niagara Falls, the Brydges Library, by the same architect, Paul Rudolph, presents another exterior of geometrically composed planes and angles—a surface so seemingly arbitrary on the exterior but one which provides for spacious and quiet facilities for the library's activities. The first two floors are used by the public library, the Nioga Library System occupies the third, and mechanical services are on the fourth floor. On the second floor there is also an auditorium and meeting and conference rooms. The libraries can shelve almost a third of a million volumes.

Earl W. Brydges Library, Niagara Falls, N.Y. (1974). Paul Rudolph, architect

Orange County Government Center,
Goshen, N.Y. (1970). Paul Rudolph, architect.
Peter P. Barbone, associate

In late years at the Albright-Knox Art Gallery in Buffalo, and at the Munson-Williams-Proctor Institute in Utica, modern additions and appendages have been built to supplement much older museum structures. A one-story white marble wall of classical severity connects the original early-twentieth-century Greco-Roman building of the Buffalo gallery, and its caryatid porch, with the galleries and auditorium of recent construction. Fountain Elms at Utica, designed in 1850 by W. J. Woolett in the Tuscan style, offers a sharp foil to the honed austerity of the new museum nearby, a structure which has been termed by *Architectural Forum* "the perfect professional museum." The older building continues to play an active role in the museum's varied programs.

Albright-Knox Art Gallery (1905) and Addition (1962), Buffalo, N.Y.
Green & Wicks, architects (1905); Skidmore, Owings & Merrill, architects (1962)

Fountain Elms, Munson-Williams-Proctor Institute, Utica, N.Y. (1850). W. J. Woolett, architect

Munson-Williams-Proctor Institute, Utica, N.Y. (1960). Philip Johnson, architect

The Whitney Museum occupies a severely limited plot of land, hence its inverted, stepped-pyramid shape which provides maximum exhibition areas in the successive projections of the upper floors. For the same reason, its open, street-viewable sculpture court—an essential element in the concept of the institution—is placed a full floor below the street level across the front of the lot, with a curtain of glass separating it from the exhibition space inside. This "moat" is bridged by a partly hooded passage leading to the front entrance. The impression of the building from without is that of a functional sculptured form, while from within it offers some of the finest exhibition space in New York City. The Everson Museum in Syracuse also suggests a work of sculpture, consisting as it does of four largely windowless interrelated galleries with carefully considered spaces between. Inside, the interplay of solids and voids, animated by shafts of light from roof "windows," re-creates and intensifies the impression of sculptured form in the enclosed space. A superb spiral staircase rising from the ground floor entry hall presents an irresistible invitation to the visitor to explore the second floor of the museum.

Whitney Museum, New York, N.Y. (1966).
Marcel Breuer and Hamilton Smith, architects

Everson Museum of Art, Syracuse, N.Y. (1968).
I. M. Pei & Partners, architects

OVERLEAF: *Keystone Generating Station, near Shelocta, Pa. (1968). Gilbert Associates, engineers.* The Keystone plant is a major component of an interrelated power development program in western Pennsylvania. This four-station complex was constructed by seven companies representing four eastern states and the District of Columbia to provide, inexpensively and in a socially responsible manner, adequate electric power over this large area. It is the largest coalburning steam generating station in North America. Located at the mouth of a coal mine, it burns more than five million tons of the fuel annually when the plant is fully operational. Statistically, the construction is very impressive. Its stacks reach 800 feet into the sky; its four cooling towers are each 325 feet high; it contains a boiler structure the size of a major music hall.

A. N. Richards Medical Research Building (1960) and Biology Laboratory (1964), Philadelphia, Pa. Louis I. Kahn, architect

First Unitarian Church, Rochester, N.Y. (1962).
Louis I. Kahn, architect

The Richards Research Building and the adjacent Biology Laboratory number among the very influential buildings in the development of mid-twentieth-century American architecture. In 1961 the Museum of Modern Art termed the former "probably the single most consequential building constructed in the United States since the war." It is unequivocally a brilliant demonstration of the conversion of awkward utilitarian requirements into logical and vital elements of design—one based on the fact that scientists and professors who work here use noisome gases and fumes. Instead of treating the need to introduce fresh air and to dissipate the noxious as an embarrassing nuisance, the architect, Louis I. Kahn, seized upon that need as a rationale of the whole building, achieving both functional and esthetic ends. In Kahn's Unitarian Church building, the congregation occupies the central area, which is surrounded by two floors of classrooms—fittingly expressing for Unitarians the contention that education must precede intelligent worship. This division of function within is clearly manifest in the red-brick exterior. The four towers that project upward to form a commanding silhouette serve to admit natural light from above into the house of worship.

U. S. Steel Building, Pittsburgh, Pa. (1970). Harrison & Abramovitz and Abbe, architects

1 Liberty Plaza, New York, N.Y. (1972). Skidmore, Owings & Merrill, architects

Building codes concerned with fire prevention have long dictated that the steel frames of multistory structures must be encased in concrete, masonry, or asbestos to prevent the steel from buckling in the event of a conflagration. The exoskeletal, hollow-box framing columns of the United States Steel Building in Pittsburgh are, rather, filled with water and antifreeze to achieve this purpose, thus leaving the steel exposed. At 1 Liberty Plaza in New York fire protection is achieved by the extended projection of the steel spandrel girders, whose flanges are covered with flame shields. These projections also help to protect the strips of windows behind from excessive glare from the sun.

Sculpture Garden, Museum of Modern Art, New York, N.Y. (1953; 1964). Philip Johnson, architect

The gardens, reflecting pools and fountain, sculpture, and waterfall illustrated here provide islands of serenity and escape from the crowded and noisy urban scene of midtown Manhattan. In the very limited area (110 by 200 feet) of the Sculpture Garden of the Museum of Modern Art there are spatial surprises and delights in the delicate balance of stone, plantings, water, and great contemporary sculpture. When Philip Johnson remodeled the garden in 1964, he provided from the garden's upper level an excellent view of the museum and its surrounding towers. In a formal pool at Lincoln Center, a Henry Moore sculpture is silhouetted against the glass-enclosed lobby of the repertory theater, designed by Eero Saarinen & Associates in 1965. William S. Paley, the head of CBS, presented the city with a "pocket" park (42 by 100 feet) in memory of his father Samuel. The walls of gray brick and the honey locust trees are set off by the minipark's focal point—a twenty-foot-high waterfall cascading into a six-foot-wide pool, the rushing waters damping the traffic noises outside to make a delightful aural and visual retreat.

Vivian Beaumont Theater, Lincoln Center, New York, N.Y. (1965).
Eero Saarinen & Associates, architects; Henry Moore, sculptor

Samuel Paley Park, New York, N.Y. (1967). Zion & Breen Associates, landscape architects

The Chase Manhattan Building and the twin towers of the World Trade Center have altered the appearance of lower Manhattan, interrupting its long-familiar filigreed, many-spired skyline with boxlike masses. The sixty stories of the glass and aluminum Chase Building rise aside a terrace with a sunken circular "garden," the first open plaza to be built in the financial district. The plaza is further enlivened by a forty-two-foot-high sculpture of fiberglass and aluminum entitled "Four Trees" by Jean Dubuffet. The 110-story World Trade Center towers are one hundred feet higher than the Empire State Building, but still not so high as Chicago's Sears Tower. Its plaza, with its four surrounding eight-story units, still under construction, is larger than the Piazza San Marco in Venice and slightly reminiscent of this famous Old World square because of the Venetian Gothic arches where the towers meet the plaza. The observatory atop the south tower offers a view as from an airplane.

Chase Manhattan Building, New York, N.Y. (1960). Skidmore, Owings & Merrill, architects

World Trade Center, New York, N.Y. (1972-   ).
Minoru Yamasaki & Associates, and Emery Roth & Sons, architects

SOUTH

ALABAMA

FLORIDA

GEORGIA

KENTUCKY

MISSISSIPPI

NORTH CAROLINA

SOUTH CAROLINA

TENNESSEE

VIRGINIA

WEST VIRGINIA

The South covers a very large section of the United States. As the term is used here it includes the ten states lying between the Atlantic Ocean and the Gulf of Mexico. In the northeast this territory reaches to the borders of Pennsylvania, Maryland, and Delaware. This is a somewhat arbitrary delineation, but political boundaries, regional cultures, and distinctive geographical characteristics rarely neatly coincide. One of the most distinguishing aspects of this area of almost a half million square miles is indeed its great diversity—diversity of land, of people, and of historical circumstance. Climate and topography vary widely within these prescribed limits; from the subtropical glades of Florida to the hard-worked mountains of West Virginia, from the sea-lashed coasts of North Carolina's Outer Banks to the distant, inland banks of the Mississippi.

Men and women from many distant parts of the world have from early times settled here and left the imprints of their disparate cultures and traditions on the face of the countryside, and they have all contributed to the new patterns of civilization whose development can be traced in architectural forms and styles.

For some years after the conclusion of the American Revolution, Spain continued to claim jurisdiction over some parts of the South, as France also had in earlier times. In April, 1513, Juan Ponce de León landed near the mouth of the St. John's River, claimed what he thought to be an island, and named it Florida, probably because it was then the Easter season (*Pascua florida*). It was more than three centuries later, in 1819, that the peninsula was finally acquired by the United States; it was organized as a territory the next year. During much of that long time St. Augustine, established in 1565, was the capital of a territory stretching, it was claimed, north to Labrador and west to the Mississippi, although it received little attention from Spain's government. However, today it is the oldest permanent white settlement in the United States.

Very few buildings in Florida date from the period of the Spanish occupation, and by themselves they have had little direct influence on architectural developments in the state. However, the presence of Spanish tradition together with the fact that the climate of Florida is comparable to that of large areas of Spain have led architects over the years to look to Spanish origins for their inspiration. At its best this revival of Spanish styles of building, freely interpreted and varied to later-day tastes and convenience, is well adapted to the nature of the land and the climate and suggests the tranquility popularly associated with the Spain of old legend. As one critic observed in 1920, "Here, for obvious reasons, the Spanish style has had a tremendous vogue. The modern buildings run through all phases of Spanish, from baroque to comparative academic corrections, from elaboration and great scale to the simplest and most picturesque informal tiny dwellings."

Directly north of Florida, from Georgia through the Carolinas and on up to Virginia, buildings of the colonial period abound in great variety. By the end of the seventeenth century English colonies had been planted or acquired practically everywhere along the Atlantic coast, from the St. Croix River in the North to the Ashley in the South. During the early years of the next century Georgia was added at the southern end of the stretch, primarily to serve as a buffer against the Spanish and the Indians still farther to the south and to the west. At each point of settlement in the South, as in the North, separate circumstances conditioned life in a different manner. Each colony presented its own situation and history; and, until a later day of diminishing sectional differences, each evolved more or less distinctive architectural features.

Early reports of the American shores fired Michael Drayton, the Elizabethan poet, to rhapsodize about "*Virginia*, Earth's only paradise," a "delicious land" of "luscious smells" where cedars reached up to kiss the skies, and where harvests were all greater than might be wished for. Riches there were in abundance, but bitter experience proved that for the most part they had to be patiently earned by toil and sweat. Very few among the first settlers at Jamestown were accustomed to the hard labor required for such pioneer beginnings. For the most they were, as Captain John Smith complained, "ten times more fit to spoil a commonwealth than either begin one, or but help to maintain one." Under such circumstances, he wrote, "a plaine soldier that can use a pickaxe and a spade is better than five knights." The true "first families of Virginia" were not the cavaliers of old fable, but hard-working yeomen. As early as 1656 one reporter wrote, "such preferment hath this country rewarded the industrious with, that some, from being wool-hoppers and of as mean or meaner employment in England, have there grown great merchants and attained to the most eminent advances the country afforded." Such were the tribulations of these first settlers, however, that at one point, to survive at all, they were reduced to devouring their horses, the snakes of the forest, their leather boots, and ultimately the carcasses of their dead comrades.

But there were survivors from that "Starving Time" (only sixty of five hundred) and from Indian massacres, and in good season the Virginia colony flourished and developed its particular cultural patterns. Although Virginians and their close neighbors in the southern colonies, like New Englanders, came almost entirely from England, they came from almost all parts of the mother country rather than, as the early New Englanders so largely did, from one relatively limited area. The houses they built in the New World expressed that varied regional inheritance in the different forms they took. There is nothing like a standard type of seventeenth-century southern house. No seventeenth-century frame houses have survived. Often built of unseasoned timber, they commonly decayed in the damp climate. Others, replaced by more pretentious dwellings as their owners prospered, were converted into slave quarters and allowed to fall into ruin. In any event, like the Dutch settlers to the north, the Virginians showed a preference for brick construction, and there were competent bricklayers among those first colonists in this area.

The original sponsors of the Virginia colony, London merchants had blithely envisioned a series of urban trading centers, with Jamestown, the capital of this tidewater domain, a commercial emporium in the image of a small-scale London. Such a dream was, of course, never to be realized. Within a few generations Jamestown was a dilapidated hamlet with less than a score of houses occupied by barely a dozen families "getting their liveings by keeping ordnaries, at extreordnary rates." Meanwhile, colonists had advanced up the navigable waterways establishing farms and plantations along their banks. The destiny of the colony was set by the soil and the genial climate, not by the visions of London merchants and the king's advisors. Tobacco became the staple commodity that dictated the economic, social, and political order of a wide region.

Then, in 1698, Jamestown burned, and it was decided to move the capital to Middle Plantation, or Williamsburg. In the years immediately following, there sprang up from that flat and empty countryside a planned city of imposing civic buildings and trim dwellings. As today's restoration so dramatically reveals, it was one of the most deliberate accomplishments in colonial town planning, and almost the only "urban" center in

Virginia. Architecturally, it was in many ways the most impressive community in America. William and Mary College, the Capitol, the Governor's Palace, and other "modern" buildings that looked over Duke of Gloucester Street—all so well known to today's tourists—embodied the most advanced and fashionable styles of their time.

Within visiting range of Williamsburg spread the plantations, large and small, where the labor of slaves produced the tobacco on the sale of which the colony's prosperity so largely depended. Before the beginning of the eighteenth century, Virginia's history was being shaped by a relatively few planters whose holdings were large and whose slaves were many, even though small landholders far outnumbered those with big estates and worked more total acreage. As early as 1653 Captain Adam Thoroughgood had acquired 5,350 acres of land, holdings that were dwarfed by the 300,000 acres amassed by "King" Carter before his death in 1732. These more successful proprietors, reported one observer, "live more like country gentlemen of fortune than any other settlers in America . . . [they] live in a state of emulation with one another in building (many of their houses would make no slight figure in the English counties). . . . In most articles of life, a great Virginia planter makes a greater show and lives more luxuriously than a country gentleman in England. . . ." So it was that at Stratford Hall, birthplace of two signers of the Declaration of Independence and of Robert E. Lee; at Westover, ancestral seat of the Byrds; at Carter's Grove, where Rebecca Burwell declined courtship of Thomas Jefferson—at these and other historic homes the landed aristocrats set a pattern of life that had no true parallel in the colonies.

In Virginia as in other parts of the country some of the largest and finest houses of the colonial period have disappeared or fallen into ruin. No surviving seventeenth-century house, for example, is comparable to the great "wilderness palace" known as Green Spring that was built about 1650 in Jamestown as a countryseat for Sir William Berkeley, governor of the colony. This mansion, Berkeley's widow maintained, was "the finest seat in America & the only tollerable place for a Governour." Across the York River from Williamsburg stand the pathetic and picturesque ruins of Rosewell Hall, built in 1726, once among the most elegant and pretentious of all colonial mansions and the seat of the Mann Page family. No contemporary records have thus far been discovered to identify the designer of this unique and magnificent structure, and possibly of others in the general neighborhood that are related in style. Shortly before the Revolution, Britain's royal governor, William Tryon, built a great palace at New Bern, North Carolina, to serve as his official residence. With its forty-five rooms, twenty-seven fireplaces, lavish appointments, auxiliary buildings, and large gardens, it was a most extravagant establishment. Its imported accessories (and its unique plumbing system) were costly enough to provoke an armed rebellion by overtaxed yeomen. But in a relatively few years the mansion burned to the ground. (It has since been meticulously reconstructed.)

As earlier stated, cultured gentlemen of the eighteenth century studied and understood the principles of architecture, an accomplishment they not only used in their own interest but occasionally put to the service of their neighbors. Thomas Jefferson is the outstanding American example of such cultivated pursuits. He not only designed, and redesigned, Monticello; he altered, redesigned, or planned changes in every house he ever lived in, including his residence in Paris and the White House. "Architecture is my delight," he once wrote, "and putting up, and pulling down, one of my favorite amusements." (However, it is doubtful whether there was time in life for him to have designed for friends and acquaintances all the houses he has been credited with.)

One of the few identified Virginia architects whose names emerge from the records of the time was the native-born Virginian Richard Taliaferro (pronounced and sometimes written "Toliver"), who was referred to by the acting governor of the colony as "our most skillful architect." If, as has been claimed, he taught Jefferson the elements of architecture, he had an indirect but far-reaching influence on the development of American architecture. And if, as has also been claimed, he himself designed such exceptional structures as Westover and Carter's Grove, his reputation was well deserved.

Throughout the colonial period Charleston was the social, cultural, and business center of the Carolina low country. From its founding in 1670 (the first settlement was across the Ashley River from the present city) it attracted no less a mixture of people than New York or Philadelphia—English dissenters, French Calvinists, Scotch Covenanters, Barbadians, Dutchmen from Holland and New York, New England Baptists, Quakers, Irish Catholics, and Jews—among others. In that benign climate those diverse faiths and traditions fused into a civilization that was leisurely, cosmopolitan, and aristocratic. Shortly before the Revolution, Josiah Quincy, Jr., a visitor from Boston, found that in "grandeur, splendour of buildings, decorations, equipages, numbers, commerce, shipping, and indeed in almost everything," Charleston surpassed all he had seen or hoped to see in America.

At the request of the proprietors of the Carolina colony the philosopher John Locke drew up a constitution consisting of 120 articles, composed in the quiet of his Oxford study and designed to regulate the degrees of nobility and dependency that would be observed in the forests of the New World. It was a fabulous blueprint for life in America, and it never worked. An aristocracy as impressive as any envisioned by Locke did develop in South Carolina, but it grew out of the raw, primeval swamps and the hot seasons of the lowlands, not out of tempered, storied Oxford: it was built on rice and "black gold," not on theory. Those productive lowlands where rice could be cultivated and where the Negro could survive the work necessary to grow and gather the crops, did find their way into the hands of a relatively small group of landholders. But the oligarchy was composed of active, resident planters, not of distant peers of the realm.

Virtually every family of importance maintained houses in both city and country. Seasonally, the rice aristocracy would flee the malarial marshes of their plantations and retreat to their town houses. Here the climate conditioned the art of building in special ways. The first floors of these mansions were raised several feet above the level of the ground to counter the penetrating dampness, encouraging the ironmaster to forge curving stair rails and elaborate gates. Some stood sideways to the street with high-ceilinged, spacious rooms opening on porches and piazzas that faced gardens, in the manner of houses of the West Indies, whence had come many of the city's residents, and so designed to mitigate the sultriness of the atmosphere and to catch every trace of a refreshing breeze. Here, wrote La Rochefoucauld-Liancourt, "persons vie with one another, not who shall have the finest, but who the coolest house."

The British statesman Edmund Burke compared the Virginia and Carolina aristocrats to Polish counterparts (and he might have added Hungarians), who enjoyed a high sense of liberty made more pronounced by the slavery surrounding them, but there was an essential difference. Not only were there many smaller landowning families in the South who owned no slaves, there were many in the back country who, having recently moved in from Pennsylvania, Ireland, or Germany, had not accepted a view of life in which slavery seemed essential. Also, in spite of occasional class conflicts between these countrymen and the tidewater aristocrats, in such a new country there was, among the whites, no sense of immemorial class separation and no feeling of the inseparable hereditary apartness that characterized life in Eastern and Central Europe. The architecture of this hinterland, it goes without saying, bore small resemblance to that of the formal dwellings just described.

One of the most distinctive of the back-country settlements was at Salem (now Winston-Salem) in North Carolina's piedmont. Hereabout, hard-working, pious Moravians from Pennsylvania (originally from Germany and what is now Czechoslovakia) bought a tract of almost a hundred thousand acres and in 1766 established the town they called Salem, meaning peace. Both the strictly regulated plan of the community and its buildings reflected the Continental traditions the brotherhood had clung to during the long emigration from their homelands. Through enlightened and persistent local efforts, in recent years a substantial number of the old buildings have been preserved, restored, and reconstructed. The Single Brothers' House, the first part of which was finished in 1769, remains probably the best example of German half-timber-and-brick architecture in this country.

At the close of the Revolution few Americans had any clear idea of what lay beyond the Alleghenies, but that did not deter a growing number of easterners from pushing westward. To preserve the profitable fur trade, to keep the Indians relatively quiet, and to minimize trouble at the border, the British government had officially forbidden the colonists from making any purchases or settlements in that region, at least until some plan for orderly expansion could be devised. However, as Lord Dartmouth averred, no authority on earth could effectively restrain "that dangerous spirit of unlicensed emigration" which had already carried the first pioneers over the mountains. If Hell lay to the west, ran a proverb, Americans would cross Heaven to reach it. Early fur traders did know the richness of the western country, an understanding quickly shared by colonial land speculators. George Washington himself had been over the crest of the mountains on the king's business, and the urgency of his official mission did not blind him to the "exceedingly beautiful and agreeable" land he there saw. Like others before and after him, he bought tracts for speculation.

The Indians had never intended men, white or red, to settle in their hunting grounds south of the Ohio River—the "Dark and Bloody Ground," as Chief Dragging Canoe called it. Before the Indian menace in that area was neutralized by Daniel Boone and other intrepid backwoodsmen an awesome price in human life had to be paid. Of the 256 men who in 1780 drew up the first government in what was to become Tennessee, hardly a dozen were living in 1790, and only one had died a natural death. One elderly woman remarked that the most beautiful sight she had ever seen in Kentucky was a young man dying peacefully in his bed.

In spite of those perils, before the peace treaty with England was signed in 1783, thousands of families had already crossed the ridge into the new West. Henry Clay is said to have stood at Cumberland Gap, the mountain passage through which Daniel Boone had earlier led pioneering settlers, listening "to the tread of the coming millions," a vision that proved to be far from exaggerated. (Modern highways follow the same route.) Little of architectural distinction survives from pioneering occupation of these lands. Much of the earliest building was of log construction, subject to attack and to the ravages of time. (Fort Harrod, or Harrod's Fort, in Harrodsburg, Kentucky, has been reconstructed in replica of that state's first permanent settlement.) Yet, before the end of the eighteenth century, all three of these "border states"—West Virginia, Kentucky, and Tennessee—could boast of handsome clapboard, brick, and stone houses, generally conforming to the late Georgian and Federal styles, on ground that so recently had been bloodstained. Jonesboro, the oldest town in Tennessee, was a planned community, and the owner of each lot was required to build "one brick, stone, or well-framed house" of specified dimensions. (Andrew Jackson began his law practice here in 1788.) At Harrodsburg, the fine Georgian mansion that was built in 1797 and that served as the official residence of thirty-three Kentucky governors between 1798 and 1914, at different times was visited by Louis Philippe, later king of France, the Marquis de Lafayette, and a number of presidents of the United States. Today it is the official residence of the state's lieutenant governors. Most memorable of such early for-

clear and large profits is open." In many areas of the region during the years that followed, northern capital made greater conquests and transformations than northern armies had ever done.

Architecturally, in the post-colonial period, there were few developments that did not reflect somewhat earlier changes in style and technique that had characterized building in the North, a trend that was noticeable even before the Civil War. On the very eve of the conflict the cotton planter Haller Nutt commissioned the Philadelphia architect Samuel Sloan to design a remarkable house to be built on the Natchez bluffs, a house that was to have been "a remembrance of Eastern magnificence which few will judge misplaced as it looms up against the mellowed azure of a Southern sky." The house, which will be mentioned later in further detail, was an octagonal Moorish castle called "Longwood," an extravaganza best remembered as "Nutt's Folly," which was raised by a small army of Pennsylvania craftsmen imported for the purpose. Because of the outbreak of the war it was never completed, but its exotic shell still stands as a remembrance of an enchanting byway of American experience, of great and thwarted expectations to which the South was then heir.

Between the end of the Civil War and World War II many different industries, such as cotton-goods manufacturing and logging and mining enterprises, took root in the South, but for various reasons they did little to improve the economy of the region. In many cases the wealth generated by such operations was siphoned off into the coffers of distant corporation headquarters, mostly in the North. "The New South" is a term that was invented by an eloquent young editor in 1880 and has been repeated over the years by numerous prophets and optimists, but only in relatively recent years has it taken on truly significant meaning.

A monumental announcement of a new era came in 1933 with the inception of the Tennessee Valley Authority. By that time the Tennessee River Valley, cutting for nine hundred miles through parts of seven states, had, by the negligence of man combined with the assaults of nature, become one of the most emaciated regions of the country, and one of the most depressed in terms of human life. The project was underwritten by people participating with a huge government agency on a level of intimacy not usually associated with such large-scale planning. Like a chain reaction in physics, each simple element of this program was related to others until all became part of a widespread complex that included an area as large as England and Scotland combined. As a beginning, a long series of dams, some of them among the largest in America, were constructed to tame the unruly river and utilize its enormous power. In the ramifications of the project the destiny of the land, water, forests, cities, countryside, and people has been considered as a single problem. Reforestation and conservation, flood control, navigation, power production, civic planning, and public health, recreation, and education have been woven into a "seamless web" of common purposes. It is the most comprehensive, intensive, and successful of such regional undertakings and has become established as a world-wide inspiration.

Meanwhile, situated on Georgia's piedmont plateau in the middle part of the state, Atlanta has become the largest, richest, and most progressive city in the Deep South — a city with one of the most rapidly changing skylines in the United States. It could be the model for any large, growing, modern American city, as it is for most of the burgeoning urban communities within the range of its influence. In the 1960's, within less than a decade scores of new office buildings sprang up in Atlanta, along with more than a hundred manufacturing plants, numerous apartment buildings, hotels, hospitals, and other up-to-date structures whose proliferation and whose architectural character testify to the city's advance and dynamic outlook and enterprise.

Since World War II a wide variety of outstanding buildings of strictly contemporary character have risen throughout much of the South. As is true elsewhere in the nation, some of these have been designed by local architectural firms or individuals, some by distinguished architects based in other regions of the country. There has been a renascence of architectural schooling in the South which has been dedicated to a new architecture—a schooling that has for the last several decades acknowledged the fact that the architectural heritage of the past, precious as it is, no longer provides an idiom that can sensibly be repeated if society is to be well served. Like the rest of the country the South is becoming progressively more urban under the impact of industrialization. Here as elsewhere, climatic and other local circumstances that once basically conditioned building traditions have by technological developments become relatively unimportant factors in the design of modern structures. Today's architect—in the South as elsewhere—is faced with the problem of accommodating his projects to the wires, ducts, pipes, and other mechanical paraphernalia that are necessary for the artificial human environment so increasingly in demand today, especially in public, commercial, and industrial architecture where, as in the past, such needs have been most quickly recognized and most effectively accommodated. A modern office building, factory, apartment building, or hotel, for example, has become a complex machine, like the ocean-going liners of passing memory, rather than just an architectural enterprise.

In the meantime, amidst these numerous signs of architectural developments, the South has by no means altogether ignored its invaluable heritage from the past. There is no more notable example of this concern for historic surroundings, without which a community risks the loss of its basic identity, than the efforts that have been made in Savannah over the past several decades to salvage and rehabilitate its distinguished old buildings from neglect and destruction. No other city in the country can match this accomplishment. Thanks to the intelligent enterprise of the Historic Savannah Foundation, Inc., first entirely underwritten by private funds, then aided by federal contributions, the city has succeeded in transforming its present and future by references to its past. Perhaps a thousand houses of historic merit (plus a wedge of commercial structures) have been directly or indirectly resuscitated by these efforts, largely by nonprofit revolving funds whereby a house, purchased by the foundation, is sold under strict conditions for rehabilitation. The citizens of Savannah are turning back to the city instead of turning their backs on it, as so many other communities unfortunately have done. On a purely practical level, as one by-product of this enlightened activity the city tax collector is delighted by the results. Charleston has had its own success in such matters; New Orleans appears to be wasting its heritage to an unfortunate degree.

OVERLEAF: *Castillo de San Marcos, St. Augustine, Fla. (1672-96).* The Castillo remains the finest and oldest example of military architecture in the United States. Designed to guard the northern flank of the Gulf routes of the semiannual passage of treasure-laden galleons from Mexico and Central America to Spain, this formidable stone structure was raised over a period of almost twenty-five years, starting in 1672, after earlier wooden forts had proved ineffectual and short-lived. It was built on the edge of Matanzas Bay, around a square courtyard with four-sided spearlike bastions projecting diagonally at each corner, in typical seventeenth-century style. Constructed of coquina, a local stone consisting essentially of shell and coral fragments, with outer walls sixteen feet thick at the base tapering to five feet at the top of the parapet, and surrounded by a forty-foot-wide moat, the fortress proved impregnable, although often besieged. It is today one of the most impressive reminders of the Spanish occupation of what is now the United States.

Earth Lodge, Ocmulgee National Monument, near Macon, Ga. (900-1100)

286

Houses and Church, Jamestown Festival Park, Jamestown, Va. (as of 1614)

About A.D. 900, groups of Mississippian culture Indians dispossessed the agrarian Woodland culture Indians in the central plateau region of Georgia around present-day Macon. The Mississippians built the fortified town of Ocmulgee with huge mounds that supported ceremonial temples on their flat tops, burial mounds, and earth lodges (circular ceremonial buildings heavily framed and covered with earth, such as the restored one at left). When the Mississippian culture disappeared from Ocmulgee about A.D. 1100, descendants of the Woodland Indians—who are the direct ancestors of the Creek nation—returned once more to this region. Farther to the north, in Virginia, the colonists who established the first permanent English settlement in America landed and began building Jamestown in May of 1607. After sustaining the initial hardships of colonizing a wilderness, the settlers introduced tobacco as a cash crop and the tidewater region began to prosper. Jamestown served as the capital of the colony of Virginia from 1607 through 1698. The only part of the original settlement remaining above ground is the Old Church Tower of 1640. At the nearby Jamestown Festival Park are careful reconstructions of the palisaded fort, the wood-framed houses with mud-daubed reed walls, and the thatch-roofed and wood-framed church of the early settlement.

Here in Virginia as in New England, the colonists took as their models structures they were familiar with in England—structures that were essentially medieval in character. And so, in consequence, were their New World offshoots. The most picturesque reminder of that archaic strain in colonial life is St. Luke's Church, built in Isle of Wight County in 1632, twenty-five years after the founding of Jamestown. With its pointed-arch windows and brick tracery, its buttressed walls, and its steeply pitched roof, St. Luke's is a small, remote, but direct descendant of the great Gothic cathedrals of England. Over the centuries alterations were made to this oldest of Gothic churches in America—another story and quoins were added to the tower and the medieval ceiling was plastered over. In the 1960's the church was meticulously restored to its original condition, with the exception of nineteenth-century stained glass, and the interior once more reveals its medieval timber trusswork, tie beams, and rood screen.

St. Luke's Church, near Smithfield, Va. (1632)

Adam Thoroughgood House, near Norfolk, Va. (1636)

Only a short distance from Chesapeake Bay stands the oldest surviving brick house in America. Adam Thoroughgood came to Virginia in 1621 as an indentured servant, gained his liberty soon thereafter, and by 1629 had been elected to the House of Burgesses. As a reward for bringing 105 settlers to the colony, Thoroughgood was granted ten square miles of land, on which he erected a dwelling in 1636. The small brick house girdled by two T-shaped chimneys and with a steeply pitched gable roof illustrates the adaptation of English medieval traditions in our earliest domestic architecture. In about 1655 another immigrant, Arthur Allen, displayed his affluence in a more pretentious manor, of cruciform plan, which featured elaborately curved gables, a design of Flemish origin that had been fashionable in England during the reign of James I. The dwelling, with its three square, angled chimneys at each gable end, has been termed by the National Trust "the sole surviving high Jacobean manor house in America." In 1676, when Nathaniel Bacon and his followers tried to overthrow Virginia's corrupt Governor Berkeley, they garrisoned themselves in this house—hence the name it has assumed, Bacon's Castle.

OVERLEAF: *Historic Restoration District, St. Augustine, Fla. (1565-1821).* Forty-two years before the English landed at Jamestown, the first permanent European settlement in the United States was established in Florida. The Spanish controlled St. Augustine from 1565 to 1763 and again from 1783 to 1821. Thus the street plan in the now carefully restored historic district is that of a typical sixteenth-century Spanish colonial town.

Bacon's Castle, Bacon's Castle, Va. (about 1655)

Originally settled in 1632 as Middle Plantation, Williamsburg was renamed in 1699, when it succeeded Jamestown as capital of the colony of Virginia. Restoration of this historic city to the period when it was a bustling colonial capital began in 1927 when Dr. William A. R. Goodwin of Bruton Parish Church persuaded John D. Rockefeller, Jr., to finance the vast project. The original plan of the town was precisely followed, with the Wren Building of William and Mary College at one end of its spinal avenue, Duke of Gloucester Street, and the Capitol at the other end. Designed by Sir Christopher Wren, the university hall, though several times altered, is the original building, while the H-shaped Capitol is a complete reconstruction on the excavated foundation of the original. The work was greatly facilitated when a perspective engraving of several buildings of Colonial Williamsburg, including the Capitol and the Governor's Palace, was found in the Bodleian Library at Oxford University, where it had been filed away over the years.

The Capitol, Williamsburg, Va. (as of 1705)

Wren Building, William and Mary College, Williamsburg, Va. (1702)

At right angle to and abutting Duke of Gloucester Street is a broad green which forms the cross axis of Williamsburg's T-shaped plan. Lesser streets developed off the two main arms with ground rules for the placement of houses and gardens on their half-acre lots. On the Palace Green the Governor's Palace is rebuilt on the foundation of the original, and its façade designed according to the details of the Bodleian engraving. The five-bay brick Georgian mansion, whose dormered roof is flanked by paneled chimneys and topped by a high cupola, has dependencies on either side behind a curved brick wall. The interior was finished and furnished according to extensive surviving inventories. Also on the green is the powder magazine raided by the colonials during events leading up to July 4, 1776. Duke of Gloucester Street, with its craft shops, general stores, and taverns, presents a three-dimensional perspective of brick, clapboard, and trees.

Duke of Gloucester Street, Williamsburg, Va.

Governor's Palace, Williamsburg, Va. (as of 1720)

Powder Magazine, Williamsburg, Va. (as of 1715)

St. James Church, Goose Creek, S.C. (about 1713)

At Goose Creek, about fifteen miles north of Charleston, South Carolina, stands a venerable colonial church in a primitive country setting. Many of the early settlers in Charleston and its environs were Englishmen from the Bahamas and Barbados—one of the first clergymen was titled "Bishop of London's Commissary for North Carolina, South Carolina, and the Bahama Islands." Prior to 1680 both sides of Goose Creek were settled by wealthy planters from Barbados. When about 1713 the "Goose Creek Men" erected the church of St. James, the pastel-colored, stucco masonry structure was reminiscent of the churches they had attended in the West Indies. Set in a walled graveyard overhung with live oaks, the pink exterior is highlighted by white quoins and woodwork and a jerkin-head roof; graceful arched windows are on either side of the large-scale portal, in whose pediment is the symbol of the Society for the Propagation of the Gospel—a pelican nourishing its young. During the Revolution the church was spared destruction by the British because the coat of arms of George I hung, and still hangs, behind the freestanding pulpit. The interior is dominated by the elaborate chancel, whose sanctuary wall of brightly painted stucco is carved in the baroque manner.

In eastern Virginia during the early part of the eighteenth century, the wealth reaped by southern planters contributed to the formation of an affluent society. Along the eastern seaboard a new class of "first families" began erecting public buildings and mansions in the fashionable Georgian mode, a style that in America actually appeared in the late Stuart period and prevailed until the Revolution. In 1725 a T-shaped courthouse was built at King William, Virginia—both the county and village were named for William III—and has been in continuous use for over 250 years. The brick courthouse, with its five-arched arcade across the façade and a well-pitched hip roof, stands behind a low brick wall built to keep out curious, intrusive cows. In 1732 Robert "King" Carter, a leading public official of the colony of Virginia, donated funds and land in Kilmarnock for Christ Church, one of the finest churches in the colonies. The details of the handsome exterior — Greek-cross plan topped by four hip roofs, keystoned windows, pedimented doorway, and fine masonry—give an impression of understated elegance.

OVERLEAF: *Stratford Hall, Stratford, Va. (1730).* Thomas Lee, who rose from an aspiring merchant to governor of Virginia, surmounted his countryseat, Stratford Hall, with chimneys enclosing roof decks, from which he could watch his ships on the distant Potomac. This H-shaped, early Georgian brick mansion was the birthplace of Richard Henry Lee and Francis Lightfoot Lee, both signers of the Declaration of Independence, and of the great Confederate general Robert E. Lee.

Courthouse, King William, Va. (1725)

Christ Church, Kilmarnock, Va. (1732)

Westover, Westover, Va. (about 1734)

Built by William Byrd II about 1734, Westover has been called the most famous Georgian mansion in the country. When botanist John Bartram visited there, he wrote: "Col. Byrd is very prodigalle . . . in short he hath the finest seat in Virginia." Byrd, a cultured gentleman, no doubt referred to his extensive architectural library when he commissioned his red brick mansion with flanking dependencies—these were connected by passages to the main house in the early 1900's. In fact, the stone doorway, with its broken-scroll pediment and pineapple finial, is an almost exact copy of a plate published in *Palladio Londonensis* by the Englishman William Salmon. The south façade, facing the James River and shaded by ancient tulip poplars, has a perfection of proportion and a nicety of detail, particularly in the fenestration, unmatched in early Georgian architecture in America. In front of the north façade, also with a fine stone doorway, stand English wrought-iron gates of great beauty guarded by two stone birds, proud symbols of the family. Engraved on his tombstone in the garden is the flowery epitaph composed by William Byrd for himself. The gardens and grounds of Westover, a privately owned estate, are open to the public, but not the mansion itself.

Wrought-iron Gates, Westover

Berkeley Plantation, Berkeley, Va. (1726)

Shirley Plantation, Shirley, Va. (about 1740)

Berkeley and nearby Shirley are the least altered of the eighteenth-century James River plantation houses. Berkeley, on the site of the nation's first Thanksgiving in 1619, is a sturdy, red brick rectangle devoid of embellishment with flanking dependencies covered in stucco. It was the birthplace of Benjamin Harrison, a signer of the Declaration of Independence, and of William Henry Harrison, ninth President of the United States, as well as the ancestral home of Benjamin Harrison, the twenty-third President. There has been a working plantation on the site of Shirley ever since 1613, and the ninth generation of the Carter family is now in residence. The square, three-story tidewater mansion, with a double-hip roof topped by a single pineapple finial, dates from about 1740. The two-tiered porticoes on front and back, similar to those on several South Carolina houses of the period (see Drayton Hall on the next page), date from the 1830's. A carefully composed grouping of four dependencies form a courtyard suggestive of the plan of a French château on the land side of the dwelling. In 1793 Shirley Plantation was the scene of the wedding of Ann Hill Carter and "Light-Horse Harry" Lee.

Drayton Hall, near Charleston, S.C. (1738)

In the sixteenth century Andrea Palladio published a treatise describing and illustrating his "modern" interpretations of classical styles—a publication that influenced architects throughout the Western world. After a complete English edition of Palladio's work was published in 1715, many books followed that presented individual, creative variations on the themes. In the 1730's John Drayton erected his plantation house on the banks of the Ashley River: the Tuscan and Ionic orders supporting the porch and balcony, respectively, on the façade of Drayton Hall derive directly from Palladio's pages. Inside the mansion all the rooms are fully paneled, and all have very rich fireplaces taken in general from the designs in eighteenth-century English handbooks. In the 1750's George Mason, author of the Virginia Constitution and Declaration of Rights, brought William Buckland over from England as an indentured servant to complete the interiors in his house, Gunston Hall, overlooking the Potomac River in Virginia. The Palladian drawing room and Chinese Chippendale dining room were very innovative in domestic design in the colonies. Buckland also designed the two porches on the exterior; the fanciful pergola-shaped one can be seen from the superb boxwood gardens.

OVERLEAF: *Carter's Grove Plantation, Carter's Grove, Va. (1755).* With its classical lines and harmonious relationship to its James River setting, Carter's Grove represents the culmination of early Georgian plantation architecture. Begun in 1750 for Carter Burwell, grandson of the wealthy "King" Carter, from whom the estate inherited its name, the red brick mansion and its flanking dependencies, which were joined to the main house in the 1920's, were reputedly designed by Richard Taliaferro, an amateur architect from nearby Williamsburg.

Gunston Hall, Gunston Hall, Va. (1759)

St. Michael's in Charleston is one of the greatest surviving American colonial churches. Who designed the building is not known, although he was surely guided by one or another of the eighteenth-century English building manuals that were so widely used as reference throughout the colonies. It could have been Peter Harrison of Rhode Island, who, as earlier told, was responsible for a number of outstanding New England structures and who as a sea captain was a frequent visitor to Charleston. Some authorities, however, name Samuel Cardy as possibly the designer and certainly the builder. The original monumental Doric portico of St. Michael's, the first of such size in the colonies, was destroyed in the earthquake of 1886 and replaced by the present copy. From directly behind the portico, flush with the front wall of the church, a well-proportioned steeple rises to a height of 186 feet. The columns and walls are of brick covered with stucco and painted white.

OVERLEAF: *Barker House, Edenton, N.C. (about 1782).* With its twin chimneys and double porches, the Barker House is typical of the late-eighteenth-century coastal dwellings of North Carolina. In 1952 the house was moved to its present picturesque site overlooking Albemarle Sound and was restored. It was Mrs. Barker, incidentally, who organized the memorable "Edenton Tea Party," at which on October 25, 1774, the patriotic ladies of that community, in protest against British taxes, pledged to drink no more tea.

St. Michael's Episcopal Church, Charleston, S.C. (1752-61)

St. Paul's Episcopal Church, Edenton, N.C. (1760)

The site of Edenton, on Albemarle Sound, protected from the brunt of Atlantic storms, was explored by an expedition from Jamestown, Virginia, in 1622; it was settled in 1660; it was incorporated in 1722 and remains one of the oldest towns in North Carolina. Some of the state's earliest buildings were erected here, and fortunately several that are two hundred years and older still survive. The so-called Cupola House is one of these. It takes its name, obviously, from the disproportionately scaled cupola that surmounts and dominates the structure, a feature influenced by the buildings at Williamsburg, but one of the earliest domestic examples in the colonies. The framed bracketed overhang is a reminder of the much earlier style of Jacobean England. Its double-hung windows, on the other hand, are thought to be the earliest of this "modern" type in the state. St. Paul's Episcopal Church, set in its own cemetery, is an unpretentious village version of Georgian ecclesiastical architecture. A slim, shingled steeple rises from a projecting brick tower. Damaged by fire in 1949, the church has since been completely renovated. Edenton's most distinguished building is the relatively small, two-story courthouse, which has been called "perhaps the finest Georgian courthouse in the South." Its discreetly projecting and pedimented bay with two narrow flanking elements, each with one window per floor, its handsome doorway, its prominently modillioned cornice and pediment, and its neat cupola topping the hip roof all add up to a well-organized and thoroughly pleasing structure. In front, a bowered village green slopes down to Edenton Bay and the Sound.

Chowan County Courthouse, Edenton, N.C. (1767)

Cupola House, Edenton, N.C. (about 1725)

Single Brothers' House, Old Salem Restoration (1769)

The Moravian followers of Jan Hus (about 1369–1415), one of the earliest of Protestant dissenters, having had their troubles in Bohemia for several hundred years, finally established a refuge in the New World in the eighteenth century. Moving first to Georgia in 1735, they left five years later when the struggle for possession of Florida between England and Spain threatened their pacifistic life in Savannah. As did others from Germany and Czechoslovakia, they then settled in Pennsylvania creating a flourishing community at Bethlehem. The Lords Proprietors of North Carolina, who admired the diligence of these newcomers and who wished to build up the center of their colony's holdings, offered to sell them a sizeable tract of land. Large numbers of Moravians then moved on to the rolling piedmont of North Carolina, taking with them a carefully selected group of expert craftsmen. With their dedication to hard work these "brethren" soon developed one of the most unusual communities in eighteenth-century America at what they called Salem. In recent years concerned citizens have undertaken painstaking restoration of that community to its earlier state. It has become one of the most revealing "ethnic" restorations and one of the finest town museums in the country. As mentioned in the introduction to this chapter, the Single Brothers' House, as restored, is an unmatched example of German half-timber-and-brick architecture in America.

Old Salem Restoration, Winston-Salem, N.C. (1766–1830; 1950–   )

Unlike so many American churches in the Georgian style, Pohick Church has no transept. In plan it is a simple brick rectangle and resembles a domestic structure in its outward appearance. Within, the building consists of a single elegant chamber with a "grid" of waist-high box pews divided by two long aisles. The pulpit, with a wine-glass-shaped base and, above, a cantilevered canopy for a sounding board, directly faces the main entrance. All the elements are painted the same putty color. George Washington, who was a member of the vestry, had a strong hand in the design of the church, and the master craftsman-architect William Buckland, whose work at Annapolis and elsewhere has been noted earlier, was probably responsible for carving the woodwork. Built at about the same time in St. Stephen, South Carolina, St. Stephen's Church offers a sharp contrast to Pohick. Its gable ends are curved in the manner of Jacobean styles of the seventeenth century. This, with its gambrel roof, which returns across both ends, its unusual brick Doric pilasters, and its roundheaded windows and doors, makes it a surprisingly sophisticated structure for the time and place—a place once made wealthy by its abundant crops of indigo.

St. Stephen's Church, St. Stephen, S.C. (1769)

Pohick Church, near Fort Belvoir, Va. (1769-74)

Somerset Place, Pettigrew State Park, Creswell, N.C. (about 1830)

The Burgwin-Wright-Cornwallis House was saved from destruction during the Revolution by being commandeered as the headquarters of Lord Cornwallis. Its double-decked piazza with Ionic columns, the well-turned balusters, and an elaborate Palladian door, the entry accented by the roof pediment, all add distinction to this North Carolina city house—as do the magnolias in front and the richly restored garden behind. It is one of the few colonial structures surviving in Wilmington. Somerset Place was built on the site of an old rice plantation as a winter home. (Heat and mosquitoes prompted the owners to go north in the summers.) Here again, double-decked porches so typical of Carolina coastal dwellings—as of West Indian architecture—provide shade by day and a place to enjoy refreshing breezes in the evenings. A projection at the rear, with its own double porches, gives the house a T-shaped plan. There are reputedly more than a hundred century-old buildings in Beaufort, North Carolina. The house built by Josiah Bell in the 1820's once again expresses the Carolina seashore vernacular with the familiar arrangement of porches.

Josiah Bell House, Beaufort, N.C. (1820's)

Burgwin-Wright-Cornwallis House, Wilmington, N.C. (1771)

Tryon Palace, New Bern, N.C. (as of 1770). John Hawks, architect

Shortly before the Revolution, Britain's royal governor, William Tryon, built an enormous palace to serve as his official residence at New Bern, North Carolina (a place so named by Swiss settlers in 1710). To design and supervise the construction of this great edifice, the governor brought one John Hawks from England, and with references to Gibbs' *A Book of Architecture*, Hawks produced what one respected architectural historian has with good reason termed "beyond question the finest house in North Carolina and perhaps in any of the Colonies." When George Washington visited New Bern in 1791 he wrote in his diary: "Dined with the Citizens . . . and went to a dancing assembly in the evening; both of which was at what they call the Palace, formerly the Government House and a good brick building but now hastening to ruins." A few years later, as a result of fire, the ruin was complete. In the 1950's the Tryon complex was completely rebuilt on the excavated foundations of the original buildings and the surrounding grounds restored and carefully replanted. The whole project was sumptuously carried out in the house itself, the furnishings, and the gardens—and, as in the case of Colonial Williamsburg, with a minimum of conjecture. Almost unbelievably, Hawks' original drawings were found in London, and there remains a precise inventory of the furnishings, also found in London, that was made for Tryon in 1771 when he left New Bern to become royal governor of New York. With the single exception of Williamsburg, this is the most significant colonial reconstruction in the United States.

Rehoboth Church, Union, W. Va. (1785)

Fort Harrod, Old Fort Harrod State Park, Harrodsburg, Ky. (as of 1776)

Rocky Mount Historic Shrine, near Johnson City, Tenn. (1772)

Beginning late in the 1700's the log cabin was practically ubiquitous in timber-rich borderland areas; it could be built with the aid of only an ax, and required no costly nails. The Rehoboth Church is considered the westernmost colonial church still standing. (It was restored in 1927). Fort Harrod, on the old Wilderness Road to the West, served the first permanent English-speaking settlement west of the Alleghenies. (It was reconstructed fifty years ago.) Rocky Mount Historic Shrine, built shortly before the Revolution, remains a good example of trans-Appalachian domestic log vernacular.

OVERLEAF: *Mount Vernon, Fairfax County, Va. (1735-87).* It is almost impossible to consider Mount Vernon in terms of its architectural merits (or deficiencies). Because of its important historical associations the estate has become a shrine and a symbol. The house was built in various stages. In 1754 Washington inherited a small house his father had raised. Four years later he enlarged it to receive his bride, Martha Custis, and between 1774 and 1787 he further enlarged it to its present appearance, including the first two-story, full-width portico in our domestic building. The house, its commanding situation, its outbuildings, and its extensive gardens were all woven together to provide one of the highlights of late-eighteenth-century American architecture.

Like Mount Vernon, Monticello is a famous national shrine, the home of the author of the Declaration of Independence, which tends to sway critical judgment of it as architecture. Also like Mount Vernon, it evolved in stages. Monticello was a laboratory for Thomas Jefferson's ever-developing studies in architectural design. It was put together, taken apart, and eventually fashioned—over a period of forty years—into the stunning, intricate, and occasionally puzzling building we see today on its superb hilltop site overlooking Charlottesville and the distant Blue Ridge Mountains of Virginia. While he was in France on government missions from 1785 to 1789, Jefferson provided a design for the Virginia State Capitol, inspired by the first-century Roman temple the Maison Carrée at Nîmes, a gem of classical architecture. With this structure and his other inventions, he made a complete and revolutionary break with the traditions of the Georgian style. He was the first architect anywhere in the world of his time to design a "modern" functional building, in the approximate form of an ancient temple, and as such was an innovator in the revivalist style that became so popular in later years.

OVERLEAF: *Rotunda, University of Virginia, Charlottesville, Va. (1817-26). Thomas Jefferson, architect.* Jefferson's providential architectural achievement was his design of the "academical village" for the University of Virginia, whose lawn and rotunda are here illustrated. This sensitively coordinated "museum of classical form" is one of the nation's greatest architectural creations. It is within view of Monticello's hilltop site.

Monticello, Charlottesville, Va. (1769-1809). Thomas Jefferson, architect

State Capitol, Richmond, Va. (1790). Thomas Jefferson, architect

Joseph Manigault House, Charleston, S.C. (about 1802). Gabriel Manigault, architect

The Charleston town house built about 1808 in the Federal style by Nathaniel Russell, a transplanted Rhode Islander, for what was then the very considerable sum of $80,000, features an extraordinary "flying" staircase of mahogany that coils upward to the third floor without touching a wall. It is a rare technical achievement and an esthetic delight. Farther down the same street, a few years earlier, Gabriel Manigault, Charleston's "best-known amateur architect," had designed another singularly attractive house for his brother Joseph, one of the city's wealthiest men. A most interesting feature of the exterior is a circular, pedimented gatehouse (porticoed on the inner side), the edge of which shows at left in the photograph here reproduced. A two-story piazza enlivens the façade of the main building. Gabriel Manigault, who had studied law in London, was a rice planter and merchant by profession. With this house he introduced the newly fashionable Adam style to South Carolina.

Nathaniel Russell House, Charleston, S.C. (about 1808)

Bethesda Presbyterian Church, Camden, S.C. (1822). Robert Mills, architect

Born in Charleston, South Carolina, in 1781, Robert Mills was one of the first native-born, adequately trained American architects. He was as well an accomplished engineer. His Bethesda Presbyterian Church, one of the earliest examples of the Greek Revival style in South Carolina, has two formal ends—one with a four-column Roman Doric portico, the other with an unusual three-column portico. Behind the latter, which frames the main entrance, are twin flights of stairs that meet and double back as they rise to the gallery over the two main doors of the church. The structure is topped by what Mills called "a neat" spire. The brick house that stands as a memorial to Mills at Columbia is one of the few of his dwellings to survive. A seven-arch projecting colonnade resting on a high basement of as many smaller brick arches graces the garden side of the building. Although the building was designed for Ainsley Hall and his wife, they never moved in.

Robert Mills Historic House, Columbia, S.C. (1825). Robert Mills, architect

Owens-Thomas House, Savannah, Ga. (1819). William Jay, architect

William Jay, a bright English architect, arrived at Savannah in 1817 at the age of twenty-two to supervise the final design and the construction of a spirited Regency house for Richard Richardson. (Preliminary drawings had been finished in England.) Many consider this to be the finest Regency house in America. It is now known by the names of its last two owners. Like so many Savannah houses, the Davenport House rests on a raised basement to move its main rooms above dampness and street dirt. A double stair with delicate wrought-iron railings curves up to the fanlighted front door. The shuttered windows create almost solid bands of alternating glass and wood across the façade. Isaiah Davenport, the builder, was born in Rhode Island and trained in Massachusetts.

OVERLEAF: *Orton Plantation, near Wilmington, N.C. (1725; 1840; 1910).* This is the only survivor of the several score plantations that once lined the Cape Fear River when timber and its by-products and then rice formed the basis of the area's economy. The structure grew over a period of almost two centuries. A small house built in 1725 was enlarged in 1840 at the height of the Greek Revival style. Two side wings and a chapel were added to the original structure early in the present century.

Davenport House, Savannah, Ga. (1820). Isaiah Davenport, master builder

Charleston has suffered five great fires, many hurricanes, and two severe earthquakes (in 1811 and 1886). Nevertheless, it can still boast of a rich assortment of historic houses, many of which continue to be lived in. Like many of the others, that built by Charles Edmonston—one of the few now open to the public—has evolved through the years, with floors and piazzas added to the original structure. Most of the early dwellings are in one or another of two categories, the "single house" or the "double house." In the case of the former, the gable faces the street with a street entrance giving onto a porch overlooking a side yard or carriage drive. The entrance of the double house, usually a symmetrical and almost square structure, fronts the street. In either case, the plans of such buildings typically include one or more piazzas or gallery porches (often later additions) on the front or side, as in all the examples here illustrated.

64 Meeting Street, Charleston, S.C. (early 19th century)

Edmonston-Alston House,
Charleston, S.C. (1829; 1839)

30 Meeting Street, Charleston, S.C.
(early 19th century)

54 Meeting Street, Charleston, S.C.
(early 19th century)

Charles B. Aycock House, Fremont, N.C. (1850)

Cades Cove Community, Cades Cove, Tenn. (early 19th century)

Covered Bridge, Philippi, W.Va. (1852).
Lemuel Chenoweth, engineer

Old Mill, Pigeon Forge, Tenn. (1830)

The structures illustrated on these pages, far from the sophisticated coastal cities, characterize building in the back country in the nineteenth century. A group of farm buildings at Fremont, North Carolina, includes the house in which Charles B. Aycock, later a distinguished governor of the state, was born in 1859. Early-nineteenth-century farmhouses at Cades Cove Community in Tennessee are nestled in a remote upland valley, with the Great Smokies as an incomparable backdrop. Some of these are still operated by descendants of the original settlers. At Philippi in West Virginia a picturesque and historic covered bridge that provided critical service in the Civil War has been reinforced with steel beams and concrete piers to handle today's heavy traffic. The Old Mill at Pigeon Forge, Tennessee, nicely supported on long beams resting on stone piers, still produces flour from various grains.

Actors' Theatre, Louisville, Ky. (1837). Gideon Shryock, architect

Old State House, Frankfort, Ky. (1829). Gideon Shryock, architect

Gideon Shryock's father sent him east from Kentucky to serve an apprenticeship with the well-known Philadelphia architect William Strickland. Returned to his native state, the young Shryock was soon master of the Greek Revival style in areas that were still remote from eastern seaboard culture, and his influence beyond the mountains was considerable. In 1821 he won a competition for the design of a new capitol building at Frankfort. (It was the third on the site, the earlier two state houses having burned.) He crowned this structure with a dome on pendentives with rich interior reliefs and encircled it with rosetted panels. Some years later he designed the Bank of Louisville, which was recently remodeled as the Actors' Theatre. The two towering Ionic columns set within enclosing side walls whose outer edges cant inward produce a deceptive impression of greater height and scale than the structure actually achieves. It is a mere thirty-eight feet wide and the same distance from base to cornice. A large cast-iron acroterium adds a note of opulence at the roof line.

Edward B. White, who, as both architect and engineer, designed many buildings in Charleston, produced the miniature Roman temple, elevated on its high basement and with a fine double stair, that for years served as a market hall. Since 1899 it has been used as a Confederate museum. The Tennessee State Capitol was the work of the Philadelphia architect William Strickland, who settled in Nashville in 1845 and who died there nine years later and five years before the last stone was set in this monumental structure. (He was buried in the north wall of the unfinished building, and his son Francis supervised the work that remained to be done.) A portico with eight Ionic columns terminates each gable end of the capitol, with porticoes of six columns projecting from the two sides of the building. From the center rises a square tower surmounted by a circular lantern designed after the Choragic Monument of Lysicrates built at Athens in the fourth century B.C. At Raleigh, in neighboring North Carolina, a state capitol was designed by Ithiel Town and Alexander Jackson Davis, a famous partnership, who formed the nation's first professional firm of architects. The structure has been called "the most distinguished of all our state capitols."

OVERLEAF: *Old City Hospital, Mobile, Ala. (1830). Thomas S. James, architect.* With its parade of fourteen Doric columns before its two-storied front, this is one of the most original examples of Greek Revival architecture in America. Until recently it served as the city's general hospital.

Market Hall, Charleston, S.C. (1841).
Edward B. White, architect

State Capitol, Nashville, Tenn. (1845-55). William Strickland, architect

State Capitol, Raleigh, N.C. (1833-40). Town & Davis, architects

Belle Meade, near Nashville, Tenn. (1854)

Log Cabin, Belle Meade (1793)

The stately white marble façade of Belle Meade, with its six square and slender Doric piers capped by a narrow pediment, is plausibly said to follow the design of the noted Philadelphia architect William Strickland, who was responsible for the state capitol at Nashville. So many additions have been made to the house that the purity of the original element has become compromised, although it remains discernible. Among other buildings on the plantation grounds, which once comprised fifty-three hundred acres, is a log cabin, built late in the eighteenth century—or rather rebuilt after Indians had burned an earlier structure. Its two parts, each the length of conveniently handled logs, are separated by the typical southern open way, or "dogtrot." General William Giles Harding, owner of Belle Meade, was born in this primitive building in 1808.

OVERLEAF: *Richards House (detail), Ideal Cement Corporation, Mobile, Ala. (1860).* Starting around the middle of the last century the use of cast iron as a building material —and indeed for almost everything else from furniture to street lamps—became a raging fashion. Some of the finest examples of architectural embellishment utilizing this material are presented by the portico, balustrade, and fence of the house built in Mobile by Charles G. Richards, a Maine-born steamship master. Such ornamental work had been introduced to the area toward the end of the eighteenth century by either the French or Spanish settlers there. Sixty years later, dwellings throughout the land flowered with such decorative tracery, much of it produced in the northeast, principally in Philadelphia. The lacelike balustrade of the Richards House, carefully restored by the Ideal Cement Corporation, includes representations of the four seasons.

In 1860, Dr. Haller Nutt commissioned Samuel Sloan, one of the most able of early American architects, to design a dwelling at Natchez. If the six-story octagonal structure (basement, three main floors, solarium, and observatory—all topped by an onion dome) had been completed, it would have been one of the nation's most unusual and interesting houses. Nutt devised an elaborate system of mirrors to reflect sunlight down the towering central hall even to the basement level. He also planned devices to use solar heat in winter and to ventilate the house in summer by drawing in cool air at the lower level and exhausting it at the top of the building. All thirty-two major rooms open onto both the central hall and exterior loggias so that each has two exits and assured cross ventilation. With the outbreak of war, all the workmen quit the job to return to the North and it was never finished. (Nutt died before the war was over.)

Longwood, Natchez, Miss. (1861). Samuel Sloan, architect

Fort Pulaski, near Savannah, Ga. (1829-47)

Some twenty-five million bricks were reportedly used in building Fort
Pulaski over a period of eighteen years. President James Monroe ordered
the construction of the fort after the War of 1812 had revealed the vulner-
ability of the eastern coast to attack. A distinguished French military engineer, General Simon Bernard, once aide-de-camp to Napoleon, helped with
the design. Under bombardment by the latest rifled cannon, in April, 1862,
the fort quickly capitulated to northern forces. It was now obsolete. Towering to a height of 193 feet, the famous Cape Hatteras lighthouse surveys
the notorious "graveyard of the Atlantic." A magnificent, sculptural sen-
tinel rising amidst its flat, impressively desolate setting, its spiraling bands
of black and white (it is built of stuccoed brick) render it a beacon by day as
its 250,000-candlepower light does by night.

Lighthouse, Cape Hatteras, N.C. (1870)

When it was built in 1849, the original 10th Street bridge was the longest suspension bridge in the world, with a span of more than one thousand feet across the Ohio River. The structure was destroyed in 1854 by wind oscillation. Two years later the illustrious engineer John Augustus Roebling replaced it with a new bridge, which offers an interesting preview of his famous Brooklyn Bridge built years later at New York. With its squat towers and seemingly delicate double cables stretched across their turrets, the Wheeling bridge epitomizes stone's compressive and steel's tensile strength. It was a daring engineering achievement for the time. A number of historic houses have been restored across the state at Harpers Ferry, a site made memorable by John Brown's abortive attempt to capture the arsenal to procure arms with which to free the slaves. The town's old Stage Coach Inn is currently used as a visitors' center.

10th Street Suspension Bridge, Wheeling, W.Va. (1856). John Augustus Roebling, engineer

Stage Coach Inn, Harpers Ferry, W.Va. (1826)

Carter Dry Goods Building, Louisville, Ky. (1878). C. J. Clarke, architect

In recent years Louisville has been renovating its long-neglected collection of venerable buildings along Old Main Street, a block or two south of the Ohio River. These structures represent a notable inheritance of the country's nineteenth-century commercial architecture. One of the highlights of this district is the old Carter Dry Goods Building, built in 1878, with its street-floor façade of cast iron and its upper three stories of light masonry. It was diligently restored in 1974–75. The Old City Hall at Richmond, Virginia, built in the late Victorian Gothic manner, has recently been cleaned. It remains, inside as well as out, a solid monument to the post-Civil War era.

Old City Hall, Richmond, Va. (1894). Elijah E. Myers, architect

The formal opening of "the world's finest hotel," the Ponce de León, built for Henry Morrison Flagler at St. Augustine, was an important event for Florida, which was now becoming a winter playground for half a continent. Perceptively, Flagler built a railroad down the coast to haul materials and to facilitate his guests' arrival at this remote spot. As architects he chose two young men, John Merven Carrère and Thomas Hastings, still in their twenties, whom he first sent to Spain to study the styles of that country. The job done, they vaulted to instant fame. The building, since become Flagler College, was one of the first poured concrete structures in the country. The Spanish Revival idiom of the hotel set an architectural mood in Florida that has lasted for almost a century. A few years later the same architects created the Roman splendor of Richmond's Jefferson Hotel.

Flagler College, St. Augustine, Fla. (1888). Carrère & Hastings, architects

Jefferson Hotel, Richmond, Va. (1895). Carrère & Hastings, architects

The fine old single-level railroad terminal at Chattanooga, Tennessee, built early in the century by Donn Barber, has been rescued from destruction and imaginatively transformed into an attractive up-to-date inn. Its domed waiting room is now used as the main dining room; Pullman cars have been converted into a fixed row of forty-eight family suites; a new two-story motor inn athwart the tracks supplements the Pullman accommodations. The central tracks have been removed to make way for a spacious garden complete with gazebo, whose landscaping is hemmed by original train sheds. The transformation was accomplished by Klaus Peter Nentwig. It would be hard to conceive of a more refreshing and useful rehabilitation of a terminal no longer needed for its original purpose. The Broad Street Station in Richmond, Virginia, along with the Union Station at Washington, ranks among the finest railroad terminals in the land. It is not only impressively well designed in the neoclassical style, but with its spaciousness and the clarity of its plan, it functions superbly.

Choo-Choo Hilton Inn, Chattanooga, Tenn. (1909; 1973).
Donn Barber, architect (1909); Klaus Peter Nentwig, architect (1973)

Broad Street Station, Richmond, Va. (1919). John Russell Pope, architect

Vizcaya, Miami, Fla. (1916). Paul Chalfin and F. Burrel Hoffman, Jr., architects

Swan House, Atlanta, Ga. (1928). Philip T. Shutze, architect

The years from just before the outbreak of World War I to the first dark days of the Great Depression marked a period of abounding eclecticism in American domestic and official architecture. Frank Lloyd Wright and a few others had planted the seeds of modernism, but the growth of their ideas was widely disregarded. No trace of such advances is visible in the three ambitious structures here illustrated. Vizcaya, on Biscayne Bay, in all its opulence has been described as a "70-room Mediterranean Xanadu." Built for the wealthy industrialist James Deering, this imposing structure with its borrowed grandeur directly embraces the open bay—a happy relation of house and waterside that was rare in Florida at the time it was built. In more restrained and different fashion, Swan House also suggests a congregation of styles looking to the past for inspiration. So indeed does the Morgan County Courthouse at Madison, Georgia, a preposterous, but civicly enthusiastic, pile that resembles several structures atop one another.

OVERLEAF: *Horse Farms, Lexington, Ky.* The horse and cattle farms along the northern arch of Lexington, with their painted fences extending across the undulating countryside, create deeply satisfying geometrical patterns of white and green. This regional expression of man and land in harmony, which characterizes the bluegrass area of Kentucky, may well represent the most sympathetically fashioned landscape in the United States.

Morgan County Courthouse, Madison, Ga. (1906)

Lake Anne Village, Reston, Va (1965-   ). Whittlesey, Conklin & Rossant, planners

Reston, Virginia, is a planned community comprised of seven villages, the first of which is Lake Anne. Developed by a concerned realtor, Robert E. Simon, Jr., Reston reflects Simon's social theories and his artistic tastes. It is one of our finest new town plans. The heart of Lake Anne Village is a lakeside plaza ringed by low buildings with shops, apartments, and open-air cafés, reminiscent of a European piazza. For housing, Reston's planners grouped clusters of dwellings together in a manner that utilized the surrounding open space for common recreation. According to the master plan, 70 per cent of the dwellings in Reston are to be town houses and garden apartments, 15 per cent are detached houses, and 15 per cent high-rise buildings. In order not to be solely a commuter community, Simon set aside one seventh of the land for industrial development, thus attracting government offices as well as private industry. One of the most meaningful aspects of the overall design is the ingenious use of bridges and underpasses that permit vehicles to traverse an entirely separate system of arteries than the pedestrian. The residents of Reston can walk to school, work, or play without ever crossing a street.

Paradise Steam Plant, Paradise, Ky. (1969). TVA, architects and engineers

The three groups of structures here illustrated stand as monumental sentinels of America's ever-advancing demands for energy and power. Near Athens, Alabama, the Brown's Ferry installation is the largest nuclear plant in the United States (possibly in the world). It is the first of ten that the Tennessee Valley Authority plans to construct. Among other complicated factors in these constructions, the 607-foot-tall stack that vents the gases generated when the reactors are fueled was built to withstand the violence of tornadoes and earthquakes. The hyperbolic cooling towers of the coal-fed steam plant at Paradise, Kentucky, another Tennessee Valley Authority installation, lend this complex an air of outdoor sculpture on an ultimate scale. It is said that the shovels used for stripping coal from neighboring beds are "the largest self-propelled land vehicles in history, and can scoop up, swing, and dump a third of a million pounds of earth at a time." The Bull Run Steam Plant at Knoxville is dominated by an 800-foot-tall chimney, anchored by its powerhouse, and tethered to the land by giant conveyors that feed it more than five tons of coal a minute.

Bull Run Steam Plant, near Knoxville, Tenn. (1966). TVA, architects and engineers

Brown's Ferry Nuclear Plant, near Athens, Ala. (1967-74). TVA, architects and engineers

The brilliantly designed Tampa International Airport may well be the best-functioning airport in the country. It is based on a plan of one main building for all ground-generated passenger needs and four widely separated satellite terminals for airplanes and air-related needs. The main terminal is connected to the airside units by elevated, automatic shuttle cars that can move about a hundred people in either direction in a forty-second ride. The ground floor of the central terminal is devoted to the arriving passengers and baggage claim; the second floor to departing passengers and ticketing; the main concourse comprises the restaurants, shops, and shuttle level; and the top three floors provide parking facilities for travelers and visitors.

RIGHT *and* OVERLEAF: *Dulles Airport, Chantilly, Va. (1962). Eero Saarinen & Associates, architects.* The Dulles Airport provides another solution to the passenger-to-plane logistics. A mobile lounge backed up to the terminal buses the passengers to the plane on the airstrip a mile away. The terminal is visually dominated by its fantastic suspended roof and sculptured control tower which rises over the flat Virginia countryside. Sixteen heavily reinforced concrete piers on each side incline outward to counteract the roof load. The 65-foot-high main façade, with its great canted windows, is a breathtaking architectural statement.

Tampa International Airport, Tampa, Fla. (1971).
Reynolds, Smith & Hills, architects

Piers, Dulles Airport

VOLUME II

A Pictorial History of

ARCHITECTURE IN AMERICA

by G. E. KIDDER SMITH

Fellow, American Institute of Architects

Chapter Introductions by

MARSHALL B. DAVIDSON

Editor in Charge

AMERICAN HERITAGE PUBLISHING CO., INC.

BONANZA BOOKS
———
NEW YORK

MIDWEST

POWESHIEK COUN
NATIO

ILLINOIS

INDIANA

IOWA

MICHIGAN

MINNESOTA

OHIO

WISCONSIN

What is often referred to as the heartland of America has been given various boundaries. For the purposes of this publication it embraces the seven midwestern states here listed. Most of that large area was incorporated into the United States as the Northwest Territory shortly after the conclusion of the Revolutionary War, when it was largely a wilderness yet to be subdued. Its typical architectural form was then the fortified frontier post and in certain areas the simple homestead of the French *habitant*, who had been the first white man to settle in those remote parts. For years this had been contested ground, fought over by an assortment of Indian tribes and by their French and British allies, before the American colonists successfully challenged the others for possession and authority.

Today it is a land of apparent paradox. It contains some of the nation's most spacious and productive farmlands and also some of its greatest industrial complexes and urban centers. Midwestern cities are far from either ocean, landlocked in the center of the continent, yet Michigan, bordering its three great lakes, has one of the longest coastlines of any state in the United States and its cities and those of neighboring states have easy access to the major waterways of the outside world. Principally through the enterprise of Chicago and its environs, the Midwest has contributed enormously to the architectural heritage of America.

Daniel Webster once observed that no law in history produced more beneficent and lasting results than the Northwest Ordinance of 1787, which secured the administration of that territory. Its enlightened provisions banned slavery, going beyond the Declaration of Independence and the Constitution in that respect; it assured religious freedom over a wide area; and it actively encouraged education in all the land north of the Ohio River. It denied once and for all the ancient contention that colonial territories were subordinate to the mother country in their political and social interests. The future states of that area were to enter the Union "on an equal footing with the original states, in all respects whatever." In short, it announced a new, organic concept of empire, a concept that dictated the future history of the United States.

However, any fulfillment of that farsighted plan had to await the pacification of those borderlands. Although the Revolutionary War campaigns of George Rogers Clark had established America's claim to the territory, it remained hostile Indian ground for a decade and more to come. Many of the frontier forts continued to be under control of the British, who were allied with various Indian tribes. In the summer of 1794 this issue was largely settled when Anthony Wayne sallied forth from Fort Defiance, not far from the western tip of Lake Erie, to do battle. He was dubbed "Mad Anthony" because of his tactical boldness and his personal courage, but he was anything but mad, for he took elaborate precautions to ensure the success of his operation. In the sanguinary Battle of Fallen Timbers he broke the natives' resistance, and with this turn of events the British were forced to evacuate those border forts they had continued to occupy.

Now that the new frontier was relatively quiet, the westward movement of Americans took on a new momentum. Even before the Indian menace had been removed, migrants from the East were surging into Ohio by the thousands searching for new

Ornament detail, Poweshiek County National Bank, Grinnell, Iowa (1914). Louis H. Sullivan, architect   423

homesites at the risk of their scalps. Revolutionary War veterans established a settlement, named Marietta in honor of Marie Antoinette, on the north bank of the Ohio River as early as 1788. Here the little office of the Ohio Land Company, originally raised within a stockade, still stands, and is considered the oldest building in Ohio. In 1790 Gallipolis was first settled by hopeful Frenchmen lured into the West by speculative land jobbers. (George Washington, Benjamin Franklin, and others among the Founding Fathers owned tracts of land in the western country which they held and sold for whatever profit they might make.) These first settlers were but a trickle presaging the flood of humanity to follow. The pace of migration became spectacular, especially after the War of 1812, during which bloody turmoil again broke out along the borderlands. Then, with the extension of the National Road from Baltimore to the Ohio River and the opening of the Erie Canal, the floodgates were wide open. "All America seems to be breaking up and moving westward," one British traveler reported as he watched this great swarm of westering people. From New England and from Virginia came laments that the exodus might soon depopulate the older regions and leave them wastelands. Within less than a decade after Fallen Timbers, Ohio was populous enough to qualify as a state of the Union; by 1830 the western state had more inhabitants than the old New England states of Massachusetts and Connecticut combined.

In this new land Yankees and Yorkers mingled with Virginians and Pennsylvanians and with first generations of Americans from European countries to breed a typical New World civilization of mixtures within mixtures of people. The earliest settlers inevitably tended to perpetuate their separate and familiar cultures. Immigrants from Connecticut, for example, traveling westward through New York for the most part, soon laid out tidy village greens graced with steepled meetinghouses amidst the rolling hills of northern Ohio, and gave such good old Connecticut names as Greenwich and Norwalk to their newly established villages. The Virginians and Pennsylvanians took to the National Road as it pushed westward until they reached the Ohio River at Wheeling, West Virginia. (Traffic was so heavy, wrote one historian of that road, that it looked more like a leading avenue of a great city than a road through rural districts.) From Wheeling they moved on to easily accessible sites across the river to transplant their own architectural heritage. In those early years, the architecture of Ohio became to a large degree a recapitulation of the building styles and methods that had prevailed up and down the Atlantic seaboard for the preceding century.

Year after year what had been a West became an East with bewildering speed. To the west of Ohio, Indiana became a state in 1816, Illinois in 1818, Michigan in 1837, Iowa in 1846, Wisconsin in 1848, and Minnesota in 1858. Unlike great migrations of the past, this westering movement of Americans was not a wandering of tribes or, with important exceptions, the settlement of compact colonies. Individuals, families, and small groups, on their own initiative, found their way through the wilderness to new homes and new adventures. "How beautiful," Thomas Carlyle rhapsodized in a letter to Emerson, "to think of lean tough Yankee settlers, tough as gutta-percha, with most occult unsubduable fire in their belly, steering over the Western Mountains to annihilate the jungle, and bring bacon and corn out of it for the Posterity of Adam.—There is no *Myth* of Athene or Herakles equal to this *fact*."

Those who so quickly peopled the heartland wilderness were not, of course, all Yankees by any means—or even natives of other eastern coast regions. Immediately following the first wave of pioneers came Germans, then Irishmen, in turn followed by people from the shores of the Mediterranean, by Russians, Poles, and Balkan and Baltic immigrants. A great influx of Scandinavians settled the northlands of Michigan, Minnesota, and Wisconsin that so closely resembled their homelands. Meanwhile, Swiss came to Indiana and Wisconsin, Dutch to Michigan, and so on down a long list of nationalities, each adding another patch to this large and varied quilt of American life.

It was a world of promise and, in addition to the host of newcomers who came to realize their individual dreams, there were a number of organized groups of all descriptions and of both native and foreign conception who moved into the West, each intent on building a perfect community according to its lights. In 1817 a "holy experiment," the Separatists Society of Zoar, Ohio, was established by Germans who had emigrated from Württemberg and who laid out their vast central garden in a radial plan of the New Jerusalem envisioned in the Apocalypse. The community ceased to exist as such in 1898, but a number of its buildings, including a meetinghouse on a hill overlooking the town, still stand as witness to the lofty convictions of these enterprising immigrants. In Iowa there remain seven villages of the Amana Society, another German religious group who were led to America in 1843 by Christian Metz and moved into the West in 1855. (Amana is the biblical term for "remain faithful.") Descendants of the first colonists still live along the quiet streets of these towns. Amana itself is reminiscent of a German village.

The Shakers founded several communities, one on the site of what is now the prosperous Cleveland suburb of Shaker Heights. Mormons also looked for utopia in the heartland. At Nauvoo, Illinois, they laid the foundations for an extravagant temple in what had by then become the largest city in the state, but the structure was never completed because the Church's founder, Joseph Smith, was assassinated and his people moved on to Utah under the leadership of Brigham Young in quest of a site beyond reach of persecution.

One of the bravest of such efforts to reclaim man from social evils was the communitarian colony established in 1825 at New Harmony, Indiana, by the Scottish reformer Robert Owen. Owen had the good luck and good sense to find and prefer a site that had already been cleared and built upon by an earlier group of pioneering idealists, the German Rappists, who sold out to return east. Thousands of colonists from almost every state in the Union and from most of the countries of northern Europe came to the settlement. These hopefuls included numerous men of marked ability and high purpose. A vast and complex structure composing a square enclosure one thousand feet wide was envisioned as the nucleus of the settlement, but it was never built. The community dissolved. Those modest dwellings the members did live in for a while are preserved as a national historical landmark.

More practical and enduring were the cities that sprang up with such astonishing rapidity from one edge of the heartland to the other. With access to flourishing farmlands and with trade outlets to East, West, and South by ample waterways, Cincinnati became the crossroads of an active traffic, and would soon be aptly known as the "Queen City of the West." With a large number of Germans among its inhabitants, Cleveland, founded in 1796, was an outpost one day, a great lakeside port the next. The American flag was not raised over the frontier outpost at Detroit until 1796. When the settlement burned to the ground in 1805, it was only a cluster of wooden buildings covering a few acres of ground and surrounded by a stockade. But it, too, was on the main route to the West, and once the great migration started, the little village, almost as old as Philadelphia (it had been founded by the French in 1701), suddenly awoke from its long sleep. In 1836 one visitor remarked on the thousands of settlers who were pouring in every year, many of them Irish, German, or Dutch, pausing there to make money before working their way farther west.

Urban developments were far from predictable. A century ago Galena, in Illinois, was bright with the promise of future growth. Today its population is half what it was in 1856, and Galena remains an almost perfect prototype of the mid-nineteenth-century midwestern town. On the other hand, the growth of Chicago defied credulity. For nearly a half century after the founding of the nation, this tiny settlement remained almost invisible in the midst of a vast, undeveloped prairie. The small town was incorporated in 1833. After being burned down a few times, thought one English observer in 1846, the village might amount to something. No city on earth was to amount to something more suddenly, burn down more thoroughly, and rise again from the flames more lustily. Chicago's surging growth had its real beginning in 1852 when for the first time the railroad linked the future metropolis with the eastern seaboard. Four years later a Scotch visitor to Chicago encountered railroad lines then in the course of speedy construction that would open up 6,738 miles of trackage leading in all directions out of the city. At the center of what Abraham Lincoln termed the "Egypt of the West," Chicago was by then the greatest primary grain market in the world and was fast becoming the railway hub of the nation.

Then, in October, 1871, the booming city, already boasting a population of almost a third of a million people, burned level in one of the major catastrophes of the century. But that proved an incentive rather than a deterrent. Within less than a decade the city was not only rebuilt, but greatly enlarged. With a population of over one million people, it was America's second city. Chicago was classified with Niagara Falls as one of the great wonders of the United States. In a few years it would initiate contributions to American architecture that were in some ways greater than those of any other contemporary city, as its skyscraping structures would so proudly testify.

Generally speaking, the same sequence of styles that characterized developments along the eastern seaboard attended building in the Midwest, with some time lag in the beginning and with variations dictated by available building materials. (An exception to this was in those areas in the Mississippi Valley where the French had settled and for a time to come continued to build in their traditional manner, but this was largely a localized expression.) One important technological advance was apparently introduced by a Chicago builder in 1839. As earlier mentioned, for hundreds of years men had framed their wooden dwellings and other buildings of heavy timbers, often more than a foot square, that were mortised, tenoned, and pegged together, and then raised into position by group labor. As one traveler pointed out, in the headlong rush to occupy the land of the prairies, where heavy timber, labor, and carpentry skills were unavailable, homebuilders were obliged occasionally "to do with make-shift" to get a home at all. The Chicago-born innovation of the 1830's known as balloon framing was a construction of light two-by-four studs nailed, rather than joined, in a tight framework, the studs rising continuously from foundation to rafters. Uninjured by mortise or tenon, with every strain coming in the direction of the fiber of some portion of the wood, the numerous, light sticks of the structure formed a fragile-looking skeleton that was actually exceptionally strong.

This radically new method of construction, inevitable as it seems in retrospect, had awaited two technological advances: the mass production and distribution of dimensioned lumber and the production of cheap machine-made nails. With these available, a whole new order of speed and economy in wood framing was made possible. Balloon-frame houses were more than makeshift; the method has been generally used throughout the country ever since it was first conceived. Without its advantages, Chicago and other mushroom cities of the Midwest could never have risen, or been rebuilt, as fast as they did and were.

Practical and economic as it was for domestic building, the balloon-frame structure was hardly adequate to cope with the architectural problems created by the surging economic and industrial growth of the Midwest, pivoting on Chicago, in the late nineteenth century. For the accommodation of this booming commercial enterprise, planning and building had to be projected on a bolder scale and with more imagination than had yet been attempted. Chicago, after the Great Fire, provided an electric environment, an urgent demand for offices, an abundance of capital, and a progressive spirit of prodigious vigor. Out of this combination of circumstances emerged what has been called the "Chicago School" of architecture, ever since famed for accomplishments unmatched during the next several decades anywhere else in the nation.

Among the assemblage of brilliant talents who contributed to this phenomenal outburst of creativity, three men stand out with special distinction: Henry Hobson Richardson, Louis Henri Sullivan, and Frank Lloyd Wright. Richardson can fairly be called a prime mover. His work in the eastern states, some of it earlier discussed, spread its roots into the Midwest and came to fresh flowering in the advanced constructions of Sullivan and Wright. Richardson was keenly aware of the needs and circumstances of his time. He once exclaimed that he most wanted to design a grain elevator and the interior of a great river steamboat, two prime symbols of progress at the time. He never realized either of those aspirations, but among his many other accomplishments before his early death he did see to completion several memorable railroad stations, symbols of another mightily important aspect of the new industrial age.

In 1885 Richardson went to Chicago to design a wholesale store for Marshall Field. This massive, seven-story structure, solidly built of sandstone and covering an entire city block, was the greatest of Richardson's designs for the world of commerce. It was a magnificently simple building. The only ornament, if it could be called that, consisted of the placement of stones of various sizes and the graduated sequence of the building's round-arched window embrasures. But these façades precisely expressed the internal organization of the store. "Four-square and brown, it stands . . . ," Louis Sullivan observed admiringly, "a monument to trade, to the organized commercial spirit, to the power and progress of the age, to the strength and resource of individuality and force of character; it stands as the index of a mind large enough, courageous enough to cope with these things, master them, absorb them, and give them forth again, impressed with the stamp of larger and forceful personality."

When Richardson died in 1886 at the age of forty-eight he was at the height of his career. He had been a fundamental force in developing and dominating architectural trends, in private dwellings as well as in public edifices, occasionally in wood as well as in stone; what he might have accomplished had he lived longer can only be imagined. Brief as it was, however, his invasion of the Chicago scene with what Sullivan termed his "direct, large, and simple" construction was to have an important influence on the future of the city's architecture. Richardson died at the dawn of the age of steel-frame construction—the age of the skyscraper—and with his straightforward functional designs he had foretold its advent.

No one better appreciated the organized planning of Richardson's constructions than Louis Sullivan, who would for a brief time enjoy eminence as a prophet of modern architecture, the unchallenged master of the skyscraper. Richardson had opened Sullivan's eyes to a vision that was revolutionary for his generation. He was determined to create an architecture that would necessarily evolve from and express the American environment, and for him the center of that environment was Chicago, although he had been Boston-bred, the son of an Irish dancing master and a Swiss pianist. "The function of a building must . . . organize its form . . . ," he wrote, "as, for instance, the oak tree expressed the function oak, the pine tree the function pine." The Crystal Palace of the Exposition of 1851 in London, the Brooklyn Bridge in New York, and the Eiffel Tower in Paris had already indicated how large a part engineering and iron and particularly steel would play in this approaching day of giant buildings.

Sullivan had attended the Massachusetts Institute of Technology in 1872, worked in Philadelphia as a draftsman, and in 1874 enrolled in the École des Beaux-Arts in Paris to receive the highest training in architecture then available. As he remembered it in his autobiography, when he visited Chicago after the fire and during the panic year of 1873, he found the city "magnificent and wild: a crude extravaganza, an intoxicating rawness, a sense of big things to be done. For 'big' was the word . . . and 'biggest in the world' was the braggart phrase on every tongue . . . [the men of Chicago] were the crudest, rawest, most savagely ambitious dreamers and would-be doers in the world . . . but these men had vision. What they saw was real." Sullivan entered the great period of his career in the early 1890's. He had joined a fruitful partnership at Chicago with the German-born Dankmar Adler, whose knowledge of engineering and acoustics had earned him wide respect in the city. Assisted by Adler, and stimulated by the young Frank Lloyd Wright, who had joined the firm in 1887 and become his chief apprentice, Sullivan's genius came to flower.

Focusing his attention on the skyscraper, he pondered the problem of "How shall we impart to this sterile pile, this harsh brutal agglomeration, this stark, staring exclamation of eternal strife, the graciousness of those higher forms of sensibility and culture that rest on the lower and fiercer passions?" His solution was to combine the traditional elements of classic composition—proportion, scale, rhythm, and ornament, to name a few—with the new skeletal structure of the tall, steel-frame commercial buildings. Sullivan did not invent the steel frame or the many-storied building, but he produced outstanding examples which in their plans and their expressive façades were not substantially improved upon for another fifty years to come. His work, by no means confined to Chicago, consisted of more than one hundred buildings in various states, and through these highly diversified structures, ranging from tombs to department stores, and through his philosophical essays, he was for a time an important energizing force in the theory and practice of advanced American architecture. He provided a basic approach for the tall office building.

Sullivan also realized that the skyscraper represented a potential social menace when it was built in "surroundings uncongenial to its nature." "When such buildings are crowded together on narrow streets or lanes," he pointed out, "they become mutually destructive." That warning has since been largely ignored in the building and rebuilding of our large cities, with the unhappy consequences that he foresaw would result when the multitudes working and living in these great piles swarm in and out to choke the limited spaces available at street level.

Sullivan's later life was a sad anticlimax. When an economic depression caused the firm of Adler and Sullivan to dissolve, the sensitive architect no longer had his partner to shield him from the harsh world of business outside his drafting room. His commissions drastically diminished, and he was also beset by a series of humiliating personal tragedies that included the failure of two marriages, the loss of his country retreat, the auctioning of his art and furniture, and the removal of his offices where he had long done his work. He ended his days in a dingy hotel room on Chicago's South Side, all but forgotten, despondent and, not without reason, cynical about the immediate future of American architecture.

The financial panic of 1893 that led to the dissolution two years later of Sullivan's partnership with Adler coincided with the opening of the World's Columbian Exposition at Chicago. This great fair was staged to celebrate (one year late) the four hundredth anniversary of Columbus' discovery of America. It also celebrated (a few years early) the rounding out of a century of progress. By extension of that record, with its impressive displays of technological achievements, it forecast a more promising tomorrow for Americans and for the rest of the world. The fair, it was announced, would "awaken forces which, in all time to come, [would] influence the welfare, the dignity and the freedom of mankind."

If the industrial and scientific displays at Chicago foretold a future of progressive advances, the buildings that housed them gave no indication of such an outlook. Almost all of them turned back to models from the classical past for their inspiration—largely to the styles and canons of ancient Rome. A host of distinguished architects, sculptors, and painters had been brought together to create this "inconceivable scenic display," as Henry Adams termed it. The Chicago architect Daniel Hudson Burnham was charged with the allover planning, but most of the others were easterners of unassailable reputations. Richard Morris Hunt, famed for the magnificent châteaux he designed for the very wealthy in Newport and New York, was among them, as was Stanford White, of the prestigious firm of McKim, Mead, & White, whose buildings in period styles were renowned throughout the East. The result was a monumental midwestern extravaganza, with glittering façades of plaster of Paris rising with fluttering flags on the shores of Lake Michigan. This, remarked Burnham, was "what the Romans would have wished to create in permanent form." He also predicted that all America would soon be constructed in the "noble, dignified classic style," and in this he came close to the truth. In the years that followed, that style did become almost a standard brand for state capitols and official buildings in general, banks, libraries, railroad stations, and other types of public edifices.

Others viewed the Exposition scene differently. To a number of critics the thin veneer of classical order imposed on most of the buildings, and which bore little or no relation to the demonstrations within, seemed like a sickly-sweet frosting laid on by the chill, dead hand of the past. Predictably, Sullivan was appalled. (His nonclassical Transportation Building at the fair, in the designing of which he was assisted by his protégé Frank Lloyd Wright, was the one structure that caught the special attention of foreign observers.) He thought that the influences of the fair on American architecture would be all but disastrous. The epidemic of neoclassicism that had germinated in the East, he wrote, had spread westward, contaminating all that it touched. "Thus did the virus of a culture, snobbish and alien to the land of the free and the home of the brave, subvert the cause of progress. Thus ever works the pallid academic mind, denying the real, exalting the fictitious and the false, incapable of adjusting itself to the flow of living things." Architecture would be a living art, he was convinced, only when the form of a building was dictated by the function it was to serve.

No one can reasonably contest Sullivan's original contributions to the art and science of building. However, without stretching the point too far, his ideas could be viewed as an extension of much earlier American theories and practices. In 1851, the Yankee sculptor Horatio Greenough wrote to Ralph Waldo Emerson explaining his theory of structure, which he saw justified in the sailing ships of the time—the time of the magnificent clipper ships and the cup-winning yacht *America*—and which he thought offered a "glorious foretaste" of what could be accomplished elsewhere in the near future. "Here is my theory of structure," he wrote. "A scientific arrangement of spaces and forms to functions and to site—An emphasis of features proportioned to their *gradated* importance in function—Color and ornament to be decided and arranged and varied by strictly organic laws—having a distinct reason for each decision—The entire and immediate banishment of all makeshift and make-believe." Greenough was an outspoken functionalist before that word had been coined. "By beauty," he once wrote, "I mean the promise of function. By character I mean the record of function." In such a spirit he would remove design from the thralldom of the past.

When those words were written, the industrial revolution had not yet had any profound impact on American life, at least compared to the changed conditions that would result from the explosive growth of technology in the decades to follow. Greenough could not have visualized the new possibilities that would open up to architects and engineers of the next generation or two, technical developments that were far advanced when Sullivan voiced his protest on the occasion of the Chicago fair—his complaint against the "fraudulent and surreptitious use of historical documents" such as he saw there and that caused him to despair. In later years, from the depth of his despondency, as he awaited commissions that too rarely came, he confessed, "American architecture is composed, in the hundred, of 90 parts aberration, eight parts indifference, one part poverty, and one part Little Lord Fauntleroy. You can have the prescription filled at any architectural department store, or select architectural millinery establishment." He had lost all hope that his work or his ideas would be remembered.

The year that the fair opened, the young, Wisconsin-born Frank Lloyd Wright quit his apprenticeship under Sullivan to start a practice of his own. He was only twenty-four years old at the time, but he took with him a precious legacy from his six years of close association with his *lieber Meister*, as he reverently referred to Sullivan. Like Sullivan, Wright resolutely turned away from everything the classical buildings at the Chicago fair stood for. Those reactionary forces, however, put a harsh limit on the market for his brilliant but unorthodox proposals. Referring to those circumstances through which he would adamantly have to cut his highly individual way as his career progressed, Wright later remarked that "they killed Sullivan and they nearly killed me!" Like Sullivan, Wright was to know misadventures and tragedies, periods of failure, and frustration. But, whereas Sullivan's career was in effect over by 1910, Wright persisted, survived, and when he died in 1959 at the age of ninety he was widely recognized, even by some of his many critics and enemies, as the greatest American architect of the twentieth century.

Actually, Wright won quicker and greater critical acclaim abroad than in his own country. As early as 1910 and 1911 two reports of his architecture that were published in Germany spread his fame across Europe. An architect from Holland who came to the United States early in the century to see Wright's buildings at first hand and to talk with the man himself, went away "with the conviction of having seen a genuinely modern work, and with respect for the master able to create things which had no equal in Europe." That was a degree of recognition that few if any of his American colleagues at the time were ready to give Wright; and the American public at large was very far from understanding his aims.

As Wright repeatedly explained, his buildings looked the way they did on the outside chiefly because of what he did with them on the inside. He decried the box-within-box arrangement of rooms in earlier dwellings as a "cellular sequestration that implied ancestors familiar with penal institutions." Democracy, he claimed, "needed something basically better than a box to live and work in. So I started to destroy the box as a building." In his autobiography he wrote that he saw a house "primarily as livable interior space under ample shelter. . . . So I declared the whole lower floor as one room, cutting off the kitchen as a laboratory. . . . Scores of unnecessary doors disappeared and no end of partition. . . . The house became more free as space and more livable too. Interior spaciousness began to dawn." Like the medieval cathedral builders, Wright used light and space as the equivalent of natural building materials, in his public and commercial structures as well as in the private dwellings he designed.

Wright once remarked that the "real American spirit, capable of judging an issue for itself upon its merits, lies in the West and the Middle West . . . where breadth of view, independent thought and a tendency to take common sense into the realm of art, as in life, are more characteristic. It is done in an atmosphere of this nature that the Gothic spirit of building can be revived." However, for the better part of a generation, what Wright was propounding and his buildings themselves were all but ignored in America. About 1911 an issue of *The Western Architect* remarked that "none have gone so far into the realm of the picturesque, or failed so signally in the production of livable houses, as Frank Lloyd Wright." (Wright later confessed that he was "black and blue in some spot" almost all his life from too intimate contact with the furniture he had designed early in his career.) Nevertheless, he persevered and by constantly renewing his vision lived on to confound many of his critics, to win most of them over, and to irritate others with his everlasting innovations.

From the early years of the century to the dark days of the Great Depression, most traces of modernism as represented by Wright's work and that of some of his advanced contemporaries were eclipsed by conservative trends in America, trends that looked to "period" styles of accepted worth and attraction for solution to problems of design and style. Up until the beginning of that regression, Europe could offer no comparable achievements in progressive architecture to those that featured the height of the Chicago movement. However, during the years between the two World Wars, while America remained relatively isolated in its outlook, the avant-garde European architects developed the strictly modern, so-called "international style" that swept all before it overseas. It was in the early 1930's that Americans, architects and public alike, were first shocked by the realization of what had been transpiring on the Continent while, so to speak, their backs were turned. In no small part those developments stemmed from ideas that Wright had been expounding and that had found their way abroad, there to receive a more generous welcome than they had at home.

It was after World War II that the new architectural language was widely imported into the United States and rapidly found acceptance here. By the end of the war, as well, many of Europe's most forward-looking builders, including Ludwig Mies van der Rohe, Marcel Breuer, Walter Gropius, and others, were living in this country and giving fresh impetus to developments here. Once again the provocative but neglected or half-forgotten issues so much earlier raised by Louis Sullivan and Frank Lloyd Wright were brought out into open controversy. Wright himself was rediscovered by a new generation, and his subsequent years proved to be his most prolific ones. A new "Chicago School" was established, a movement sharply spurred by the influence of Mies van der Rohe, who took that city as the base for his operations, and by the continuing presence of Wright. "Chicago has reasserted its great building tradition," writes one critic of our day, "in a body of work that may be traced directly back to the days when the city launched the modern movement in architecture and structural techniques." What has regerminated there has spread over the entire Midwest and far beyond.

OVERLEAF: *Fort Michilimackinac, Mackinaw City, Mich. (as of 1715).* In its duel with England for an empire in North America, France thrust its way through the heart of the continent from the rocky eminence of Quebec in the North down the length of the Mississippi to distant New Orleans in the South. At a vital point in their line of communication, near the site where the waters of Lakes Michigan and Superior unite with Lake Huron, early in the eighteenth century the French built the palisaded outpost known as Fort Michilimackinac. This roughly square enclosure, about 320 by 360 feet, was a primitive wood construction that has recently been as meticulously re-created as the technology of modern archaeology can contrive. Of basic architectural interest are the *poteaux*, or vertical posts, which were driven into the ground—a speedy method of building typical of the French frontier. However, unless the posts were of cedar, which resists the dampness underground, they tended to rot and disintegrate, as happened with the original structure at Michilimackinac. All the reconstructed buildings here, both within and without the enclosure, rest on their original foundations.

Church of the Holy Family, Cahokia, Ill. (1799)

Cahokia Courthouse, Cahokia, Ill. (1737)

The structures on these pages are survivors from the eighteenth century when the French controlled the Great Lakes-Mississippi Valley from Canada to New Orleans. In 1737 Captain Jean Baptiste Saucier built a dwelling in Cahokia, Illinois (opposite St. Louis), in the traditional early French *poteaux-en-terre* method—hand-hewn timbers set vertically in the earth and caulked with a mixture of lime and rubble. In 1793 the house was purchased for use as a courthouse, making it the oldest surviving public building west of the Alleghenies, and the first court sessions and the first elections in Illinois were held there. The building was moved several times and is now reconstructed on its original foundation. The Church of the Holy Family, built in Cahokia in 1799, is believed to be the oldest church in Illinois. Also constructed in the *poteaux* style, it is one of the very few eighteenth-century French churches surviving in the United States or Canada. In 1776 Wisconsin's oldest extant house was erected by the fur trader Joseph Roi, one of the first permanent white settlers at Green Bay. Judge Joseph Porlier later held probate court at the house, which served as British military headquarters during the War of 1812. In 1850 the property was purchased by Nils Otto Tank, who hoped to establish a Moravian colony for Norwegian immigrants. He enlarged the clapboard cottage by adding wings to either side. The center section with its original wattle-and-daub walls—willow branches interwoven on an upright frame, packed with mud, and generally faced with rough boards—is an index of the building means of frontier America.

Roi-Porlier-Tank House, Green Bay, Wis. (1776; 1850)

Gristmill, Spring Mill Village, Spring Mill State Park, Mitchell, Ind. (1817)

Two midwestern villages established in the early years of the nineteenth century have been restored to give a good insight into living conditions in the frontier states that were once the old Northwest Territory. Spring Mill Village, Indiana, is dominated by the three-story stone gristmill with its waterwheel, twenty-four feet in diameter, and its elevated flume. The mill machinery has been restored to working condition to grind out corn for those who visit the mill museum of early Indiana history. Also in the village, which became a ghost town in the 1870's when it was bypassed by the railroad, are shops, a tavern, a distillery, and a mill office, all restored or reconstructed to their earlier appearance. Many of the residences, even when built of wood, are enclosed by low stone walls around house and garden to keep out animals. In 1817 in Zoar, Ohio, members of a German pietist sect established a village that became an exemplary communal enterprise. Most of the early individual houses are log-based and the restored tinsmith shop is a good example of half-timber construction as it was traditionally practiced in the Black Forest. By 1852 the self-contained village, made up of hard-working peasant stock, had a brickyard, iron foundry, and woolen mill among its industries, as well as a great central garden to sustain its primarily agricultural economy. By 1898 the community ceased to exist, but the physical nucleus remains.

Zoar Village Restoration, Zoar, Ohio (1817-98)

Sibley House, St. Paul, Minn. (1835)

Situated at the confluence of the Minnesota and Mississippi rivers, Mendota (now St. Paul)—the oldest permanent settlement in Minnesota—was a trading village for the American Fur Company in the 1820's and 1830's. Henry Hastings Sibley, who became Minnesota's first governor, built a relatively sophisticated stone dwelling at the outpost to serve as home and office in 1835 when he was a factor for the fur company. The Joseph Smith Mansion was the second Illinois residence of the Mormon leader when Nauvoo flourished as headquarters for the Church of Jesus Christ of Latter-day Saints from 1839 to 1846. The white wooden Congregational church was built in Tallmadge, near Akron, Ohio, by no mere accident, for that section of Ohio was part of the famous Western Reserve, land that Connecticut set aside for emigrants from that state after relinquishing the rest of her western claims to the federal government.

Joseph Smith Mansion, Nauvoo, Ill. (1844)

First Congregational Church, Tallmadge, Ohio (1825). Lemuel Porter, architect

Cotton House, Green Bay, Wis. (1840)

Taft House Museum, Cincinnati, Ohio (about 1820)

In 1820 Martin Baum, one of Cincinnati's prominent early citizens, who introduced viticulture to the region, built an elegant residence of white-painted wood in the Greek Revival style, with a two-story central block, a handsome portico, and an unusual play of oval window lights. It was subsequently the home of Charles Phelps Taft, whose half-brother, William Howard Taft, accepted the presidential nomination from the porch. With its inset porch, two-story Doric columns, and flanking wings, the handsome house built by Captain John Winslow Cotton at Green Bay, Wisconsin, is in the Greek Revival style. In Dayton, Ohio, the august courthouse, also Greek Revival in style, with

its tawny limestone walls and unfluted Ionic columns, is now serving as a museum of local history. It has a temple front, pilastered sides, and a coffered Roman dome over the old courtroom.

OVERLEAF: *Amana Village, Iowa (1855).* A German religious sect resettled from western New York to Iowa and founded a group of seven villages, the most successful of the utopian communities that flourished in America in the mid-nineteenth century. The industrious, God-fearing Amana settlers shared communitive living in plain houses and farm buildings that reflected their dedication to strict principles.

Old Courthouse, Dayton, Ohio (1850). Howard Daniels, architect

State Capitol, Columbus, Ohio (1839-61). Henry Walter and Alexander Jackson Davis, principal architects

The weather-beaten sandstone temple at Springfield, which served as Illinois' fifth state house from 1840 to 1869, and thereafter as the Sangamon County Courthouse, is linked to the political careers of Abraham Lincoln, Stephen A. Douglas, and Ulysses S. Grant. Lincoln sat in the state legislature here (1840-41) and in 1858 accepted the Republican nomination for the United States Senate and made his famous "house divided" speech in the structure. Its Greek Revival design, with two Doric porticoes and with a lantern surmounted by a dome, was undoubtedly the work of the eastern architects Town & Davis, and John Rague may 'have acted as superintendent. The two-story limestone classical revival building in Columbus, Ohio, is one of our state capitols of great distinction. The design—a solid rectangle with recessed porches on all four sides, a triangular pediment above the entry, and a cylindrical drum above—required the services of seven architects over a period of twenty-two years.

Old State Capitol, Springfield, Ill. (1840). Town & Davis, architects; John F. Rague, associate

Hillforest, Aurora, Ind. (1856)

Honolulu House, Marshall, Mich. (1860)

The houses on these pages reflect the remarkable eclecticism that was so pervasive in architecture as well as in the decorative arts during the middle years of the nineteenth century. In 1856 a leading Ohio Valley skipper and industrialist, Thomas Gaff, built his mansion on a green-carpeted hill in Aurora, Indiana. Although semi-Italianate in style, it is sometimes called the "steamboat mansion" because its verandahs and wrought-iron balconies offer views of the Ohio River and its cylindrical cupola resembles a riverboat pilothouse. The lavish limestone Tuscan villa designed for James Burbank in St. Paul, Minnesota, has bracketed eaves running around the roof edges and an elaborate belvedere. A later owner, Mary Livingston Griggs, added a wing in the 1920's and then imported ten complete period rooms of European antiques which are now on display in this Victorian mansion. In Marshall, Michigan, stands an exotic house that Abner Pratt built as a replica of his residence in Honolulu, when he was United States consul to the Sandwich (Hawaiian) Islands. It is dominated by a high gallery which rises into a central tower and is set off by triple-scrolled brackets on the porch and around the eaves.

Burbank-Livingston-Griggs House, St. Paul, Minn. (1865; 1920's). Otis E. Wheelock, architect

The Culbertson mansion at New Albany, Indiana, overlooking the Ohio River and Louisville, Kentucky, across the way, is an inspired Victorian dwelling that has been restored to pristine condition. With its unusual balustrade topping a dark, shingled mansard roof, its variety of arched windows and doors, and its light yellow exterior walls, the house presents a façade that is both an attractive and colorful statement of its age. That age is even more extravagantly expressed in Terrace Hill, built a year later in Des Moines. This is one of the most representative examples of high Victorian architecture in the country, even though it was built when Des Moines had a population of but seventy-five hundred persons. The architect was the same William Boyington who designed Chicago's beloved Old Water Tower, a credential that gives the structure special interest. It was originally commissioned by Benjamin Franklin Allen, Iowa's first millionaire, and for a long time it was occupied by the successive presidents of the Equitable Life Assurance Society of Iowa.

Culbertson House, New Albany, Ind. (1868)

452

Terrace Hill, Des Moines, Iowa (1869). William W. Boyington, architect

The Old Water Tower in Chicago remains the city's only public building to have survived the Great Fire of 1871. Because of its interest as a historic relic and its endearing Gothic Revival fancifulness it has been called a structure "as sacred as a religious symbol." It was built to contain a standpipe 138 feet high and three feet in diameter, providing a hydrostatic head to equalize the pulsation of the pump and thereby achieve a continuous flow of water drawn from a spot several miles offshore in Lake Michigan. The tower has not been needed for years but it has long been regarded with affection by local citizens. Another sturdy suspension bridge designed and engineered by John Augustus Roebling crosses the Ohio River at Cincinnati. More than one thousand feet in length, it was the longest such span in the world at the time—as each of Roebling's bridges were as he built them in succession with increasing scale, until his final achievement with the Brooklyn Bridge at New York. The Cincinnati example combines suspension cables with Howe trusses for strengthening. By the time he designed the Brooklyn Bridge Roebling had refined his suspension techniques and dispensed with such trusses.

Bridge, Cincinnati, Ohio (1856-67).
John Augustus Roebling, engineer

Old Water Tower, Chicago, Ill. (1869).
William W. Boyington, architect

Iowa's fourth state capitol, here illustrated, is a many-domed building. The scale of the central vault, rising to a height of 275 feet and covered with gold leaf, is emphasized by similar but smaller domes at each of the structure's four corners. In an open competition New Hampshire-born John C. Cochrane along with French-born Alfred H. Piquenard won first place and were awarded the commission to undertake construction of their unusual variation on classical themes. About the same time, in Bellville, Ohio, some inspired soul designed what may well be the most engaging village bandstand that remains in the United States. It is a gem of Victorian fancifulness, and a nostalgic reminder of a time when musical entertainment came from the community itself, not to the community over the air waves from sources far distant from the village green or local park.

Bandstand, Bellville, Ohio (1879)

State Capitol, Des Moines, Iowa (1871-84). Cochrane & Piquenard, architects

Isaac M. Wise Temple, Cincinnati, Ohio (1866). James K. Wilson, architect

The Isaac M. Wise Temple, a synagogue that ornaments Plum Street in Cincinnati with its two minarets and other elements of Saracenic design, stands directly opposite the Roman Catholic Cathedral of St. Peter in Chains, "one of the handsomest and most monumental of Greek Revival churches in the United States," a corner of which can be seen in the above illustration, in a fascinating confrontation. The interior of the temple presents an extraordinary mixture of architectural motifs derived from Middle Eastern and Gothic sources, combined with disciplined judgment. It is one of America's outstanding religious monuments, inside and out.

Two of the most ebullient office structures of the 1870's and 1880's, the Mitchell Building and the Mackie Building, stand cheek by jowl in downtown Milwaukee. Their unabashed architectural hedonism was achieved with knowing talent and without timidity by a designer with invincible trust in the taste of his day, and an indulgent budget. In McLeansboro, Illinois, the People's National Bank goes even farther, incorporating in one structure half the architectural motifs known to architects in the latter part of the last century (plus metal awnings of the twentieth century). Its banded columns, roundheaded windows, outward-splaying chimneys, mansard roof, topped by a square dome, which is in turn surmounted by filigreed ironwork, are just a few of the elements that have been brought together in a colorful combination of red brick and white stone.

People's National Bank, McLeansboro, Ill. (1881)

Mitchell Building (1876) and Mackie Building (1879-81), Milwaukee, Wis. Edward Townsend Mix, architect   461

Vanderburgh County Courthouse, Evansville, Ind. (1891). Henry Wolters, architect

The courthouses of Indiana, especially those of the 1880's and 1890's, comprise one of the most astonishing arrays of municipal buildings in the United States. No other state in the nation can equal their determined ostentation. During the course of the nineteenth century, it has been said, all ninety-two Indiana counties built at least two and several as many as five courthouses in a span of less than ninety years. Some smaller towns splurged on such structures in the hope of being named the county seat. In all cases they bear witness to extravagant demonstrations of civic pride.

Lake County Courthouse, Crown Point, Ind. (1879). John C. Cochrane, architect

Tippecanoe County Courthouse, Lafayette, Ind. (1884). James F. Alexander and Elias Max, principal architects

The published guide to the courthouse at Fort Wayne alleges with apparent reason that the building is "the largest, most beautiful, costly, safe, and the most splendid structure designed for County uses, of any in Indiana, or indeed, the entire West." It is, as the guide further attests, "a combination of the Renaissance, Roman and Grecian, in architecture." The exterior of the structure, built of the famous Indiana limestone, is hardly less imposing than the Vanderburgh Courthouse, just noted; but the interior is unrivaled in its splendor. The dome and its pendentives and arched supports blaze with a whirling kaleidoscope of colored glass and bright murals of allegorical interest or depictions of various aspects of regional history.

Allen County Courthouse, Fort Wayne, Ind. (1900). Brentwood S. Tolan, architect

Early in the nineteenth century, skylighted arcades (as opposed to covered sidewalks) began to grace Paris, London, Milan, and Naples as smart meeting and shopping locales—so successfully, it might be added, that many of them are still preserved and actively used for their original purposes. The arcade at Cleveland, built almost ninety years ago, is America's unparalleled example of this highly agreeable and convenient urban form. Not only does it provide a protected pedestrian link between two downtown thoroughfares, it transacts the change in level between them, and it does both things within a light, superbly and daringly engineered enclosure of cast and wrought iron. The engineering problems were such that only a bridge-building firm—the Detroit Bridge Company—would undertake it. A success from its opening day, the Cleveland arcade is still a highly significant urban achievement. It is 290 feet long, 60 feet wide, and 110 feet high. One engaging aspect of its design is that no floor level is treated precisely like the one above or below. As the arcade rises it steps backward in the second level, admitting a maximum of daylight from the skylight-capped roof. The Butler Building (now known as Butler Square), an impressively scaled structure reminiscent of both Italian Renaissance designs and those of H. H. Richardson, was erected in 1906 as a warehouse. It had been vacant for a decade when, in 1975, the firm of Miller, Hanson, Westerbeck, Bell, carefully preserving the essence of its exterior, transformed it into an up-to-date office building and thus preserved an architectural ornament of the Minneapolis scene.

OVERLEAF: *Carson, Pirie, Scott & Company Store (detail), Chicago, Ill. (1904). Louis H. Sullivan, architect.* To give relief to the basic plainness of his Schlesinger and Mayer Department Store (now the Carson, Pirie, Scott & Company store) and to entice customers into it, Louis Sullivan traced out and his associate George G. Elmslie detailed an incredible filigree of cast-iron ornament which comes to full bloom over the corner entrance. It is doubtful that we will ever again see such inventiveness in design and such skilled craftsmanship in American architecture.

Butler Square, Minneapolis, Minn. (1906; 1975). Harry W. Jones, architect (1906); Miller, Hanson, Westerbeck, Bell, architects (1975)

Arcade, Cleveland, Ohio (1890). George H. Smith, architect; John M. Eisenmann, engineer

National Cash Register Company, Dayton, Ohio (1888-1906). Frank M. Andrews, architect

Carl Schurz High School, Chicago, Ill. (1909). Dwight H. Perkins, architect

In the years just before and after the turn of the century certain buildings in the public and industrial sectors showed some of the innovations that became commonplace in twentieth-century architecture, while others continued to look to the past for inspiration. The late-nineteenth- and early-twentieth-century buildings in Dayton, Ohio, designed for the National Cash Register Company were pioneers in industrial design. The architect, Frank Andrews, encouraged by an enlightened management, created a comfortable working environment, with a maximum amount of cross ventilation and glass, for the assembly of high-precision machinery. The double-hung windows fill four fifths of most of the walls, which are constructed of reinforced concrete. The Carl Schurz High School in Chicago exhibits a dignified play of angles and planes that has worn well since it was constructed in 1909. High-pitched roofs with deep overhangs suddenly stop the rising verticals of the brick walls. In 1917 with the limestone Marion County Public Library, Paul Philippe Cret produced a superb building in the Greek Revival manner.

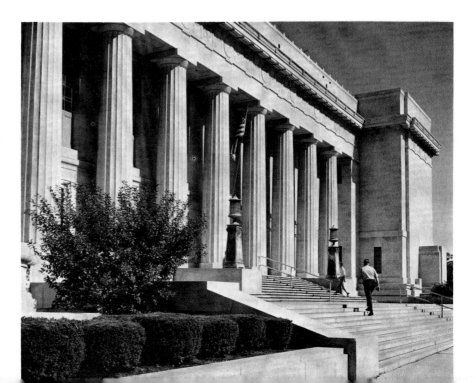

Marion County Public Library, Indianapolis,
Ind. (1917). Paul P. Cret, architect

Following the Columbian Exposition at Chicago in 1893, neoclassicism became a prevailing style in architecture, particularly in public buildings over the next several decades. Just after the turn of the century two impressive edifices arose in St. Paul, Minnesota, that were in the best classical tradition. A young Minnesota-educated architect, Cass Gilbert—who later gained national prominence for the Woolworth Building in New York City and the Supreme Court Building in Washington, D.C.—won the national competition to design a new Minnesota State Capitol. The white marble building in the Renaissance style boasts a dome that is a scaled-down copy of Michelangelo's dome atop St. Peter's Cathedral in the Vatican. Inside, the grand stairways and upper halls recall the splendor of imperial Rome. In 1906 Emanuel L. Masqueray, a Frenchman from the École des Beaux-Arts in Paris, designed the Cathedral of St. Paul in a triumphantly Beaux-Arts manner. A monumental arch frames a central rose window over the main entry. The Greek cross plan is crowned by a great dome 175 feet high and 96 feet in diameter.

Cathedral of St. Paul, St. Paul, Minn. (1915).
Emanuel L. Masqueray, architect

State Capitol, St. Paul, Minn. (1902).
Cass Gilbert, architect

S. C. Johnson Offices (1939) and Research and Development Tower (1950), Racine, Wis. Frank Lloyd Wright, architect

Some thirty-seven years after its completion, the administration building of the Johnson Wax Company in Racine, Wisconsin, can still claim to have one of the great interior spaces in U.S. corporate architecture. For the central office area Frank Lloyd Wright used fifty-four slender dendriform columns—suggestive of those in King Minos' palace in Crete—to uphold this two-story (128-by-228-foot) room. The concrete columns increase in diameter as they rise and spread into eighteen-foot-wide lily-pad tops. From between these flowerlike circles comes natural light through glass tube skylights. The adjacent fourteen-story Research and Development Tower, with bands of red brick alternating with glass tubing to provide light, is a welcome vertical accent to the low units about it.

OVERLEAF: *Ceiling (detail), S. C. Johnson Offices*

Chapel, Concordia Senior College, Fort Wayne, Ind. (1958). Eero Saarinen & Associates, architects

Abbey Church, St. John's University, Collegeville, Minn. (1961).
Marcel Breuer, architect; Hamilton Smith, associate

The triangular chapel and its slender bell tower, resting on a terraced podium at the head of a large lake, is the visual and spiritual center of the Lutheran Concordia College. The church's sharp roof is covered with dark gray tiles as are the roofs of all the secular buildings on the campus, recalling a northern European village. The focus of the St. John's Abbey Church is the stupendous bell banner, some hundred feet wide and slightly higher, resting on four sculpted supports that straddle the entry to the church. The trapezoidal banner is pierced by a horizontal rectangle for bells and above it a vertical opening for a cross. Sun from the southern quadrants picks up facets of bells and cross and bounces from the bell banner to the honeycombed concrete and glass façade of the church rising behind.

When Frank Lloyd Wright designed the Greek Orthodox church at Wauwatosa, Wisconsin, he turned to the mother Byzantine church, Hagia Sophia in Istanbul, for reference. The dome of the Wauwatosa church is 104 feet in diameter, just three feet smaller than the one topping Hagia Sophia, even though it is much shallower. Wright employed a lunette motif on the eaves' edge and repeated it in larger size in the band of windows, and designed an even larger lunette at the entry. This interlocked circular and semicircular geometry is echoed in the interior. Marcel Breuer and Herbert Beckhard created a Roman Catholic church at Muskegon, Michigan, of almost brutal strength. The warped concrete walls rise virtually windowless, while roof skylights provide effective interior illumination.

*Annunciation Greek Orthodox Church, Wauwatosa, Wis. (1959).
Frank Lloyd Wright, architect*

St. Francis de Sales Church, Muskegon, Mich. (1966). Marcel Breuer and Herbert Beckhard, architects

Cummins Engine Company Technical Center, Columbus, Ind. (1967). Harry Weese & Associates, architects

The south central Indiana town of Columbus, population 28,000, has the most extraordinary building program of any city of any size in the country. Through the enlightened generosity of the Cummins Engine Foundation, the company being the largest manufacturer of diesel engines in the world, and the chairman of its board, Columbus-born J. Irwin Miller, some of the nation's most noted architects have been commissioned to design local buildings. The architects are chosen by the citizens from a panel recommended by outside experts and the foundation pays the architects' fees. The result has been an outstanding parade of fine structures, only a few of which can be illustrated here and on the next two pages. The First Baptist Church and Chapel dramatically cap the brow of their hill; their steeply pitched roofs and semicircular ends set up a geometric interplay. The North Christian Church by Eero Saarinen is in the form of an oblate hexagon whose steel roof ribs continue into a tall spire. A square, six-story administration building and a research and testing unit of prefabricated concrete panels house the Cummins Technical Center.

North Christian Church, Columbus, Ind. (1964). Eero Saarinen & Associates, architects

First Baptist Church and Chapel, Columbus, Ind. (1965). Harry Weese & Associates, architects

The county library, shown below, forms one of the harmonious components of an urban plaza set off by a magnificent walk-through "Large Arch" by Henry Moore. The plaza is paved in red brick which steps up to make a low podium for the library and then rises vertically to form the walls. The planar white metal exterior of the Fodrea School, which functions as an elementary school and community facility, wraps around an open inner court planted with grass and trees. Inside the junior high school just southeast of town, an inner court illuminated by daylight from overhead provides a lively meeting place for students.

OVERLEAF: *Roofless Church, New Harmony, Ind. (1960). Philip Johnson, architect.* One of the most profound religious constructions in the country today stands behind a twelve-foot brick wall set off by living trees and open to the sky. The fifty-foot-high, softly undulating sanctuary, covered with cedar shingles over a wooden arch frame, hovers over a bronze Virgin in the center, sculpted by Jacques Lipchitz, who also created a gilded ceremonial gate at the east end of this unusual building.

Cleo Rogers Memorial County Library, Columbus, Ind. (1968). I. M. Pei & Partners, architects; Henry Moore, sculptor

Southside Junior High School, Columbus, Ind. (1969). Eliot Noyes, architect

Fodrea Community School, Columbus, Ind. (1973). Caudill, Rowlett, Scott, architects

A meticulous analysis of urban educational needs for commuting students and the proper architectural expression of those needs was made before any building was undertaken at the Circle Campus of the University of Illinois in Chicago. It was decided to group facilities by function rather than by discipline: that is, one cluster of rooms for lectures (no matter what the subject), all laboratories together (whatever the science), and a separate office building for professors (as opposed to departmental buildings). The highlight of the campus is the roof-top agora above the cluster of lecture halls, which comprise one enormous rectangle. This ample piazza, or court concourse, shown below, lies at the confluence of elevated granite walks. Four inward-oriented "exedras" stand near its corners. In the center, twin flights of curved steps march down to the lecture room level in the form of a split amphitheater. This elevated core is one of the great spaces in college architectural planning. The campus is so named for the adjacent Congress Circle Interchange. Cars are allowed only on peripheral parking lots.

Circle Campus, University of Illinois, Chicago, Ill. (1972). Skidmore, Owings & Merrill, chief architects and planners

Assembly Hall, University of Illinois, Urbana, Ill. (1963). Harrison & Abramovitz, architects; Ammann & Whitney, engineers

The assembly hall at Urbana rests lightly on the horizon like some gigantic space ship. In the simplest terms, the structure consists of two domes, the one serving as a roof resting on the upturned base, creating an interior completely free of columns. It represents magnificent coordination between architect and engineer. St. John's Preparatory School consists of terraces of classrooms that step down a hillside, with space allowed for full windows at each level looking over the next lower level to a pine-edged lake beyond. The McGregor Memorial Conference Center is dominated by its full-height central hall and lounge, which bisects the mass of the building, and is topped by a translucent ceiling that, with the glass end walls, suffuses the interior with radiant natural light. This architectural gem is set in an immaculate garden that enhances its luster.

St. John's Preparatory School, Collegeville, Minn. (1962). Hanson & Michelson, architects

McGregor Memorial Conference Center, Wayne State University, Detroit, Mich. (1958). Minoru Yamasaki, architect

College Life Insurance Company of America, near Indianapolis, Ind. (1972). Kevin Roche, John Dinkeloo & Associates, architects

The hard-edge, geometric, sculptural approach to architecture has probably reached a climax in the three startling structures (there will eventually be six) of the College Life Insurance Company of America on the plains of Indiana northwest of Indianapolis. Vertical, but splayed, walls of solid concrete form two sides of each structure; sloping, right-angled walls of bluish mirror glass form the other two. The interiors are all interconnected by bridging, and bands of windows overlook the countryside, which includes the group's own pool and landscaped surroundings.

The Blossom Music Center is situated on an ample site covering 526 acres. Under a great pavilion, partially open on two sides and completely so across the front, are some 4,500 seats, an orchestra pit for 110 musicians, and a stage accommodating 200 performers. The structure is based on a large inclined parabolic arch supported by ten inclined exposed steel columns, which together form a structural spine that is stable in all directions. This auditorium looks outward and upward to a bowl-shaped hillside where ten to twelve thousand additional listeners can sit on the grass under the stars of a summer night. The E. J. Thomas Performing Arts Hall, the first phase of an ambitious cultural complex, lies just across the bridge from downtown Akron. A multiterraced, thoughtfully landscaped area leads to this bold, provocatively angled concrete structure. The capacious lobbies have twenty-seven stainless steel cylinders which serve as counterweights for the adjustable ceiling of this highly flexible auditorium.

Blossom Music Center, near Akron, Ohio (1968). Schafer, Flynn & Van Dijk, architects; R. M. Gensert Associates, structural engineers

E. J. Thomas Performing Arts Hall, University of Akron, Akron, Ohio (1973).
Caudill, Rowlett, Scott; and Dalton, Van Dijk, Johnson, architects

Orchestra Hall in Minneapolis is one of the most remarkable interiors of its kind. Its excellent acoustics are controlled by a startling arrangement of relief surfacing of plaster cubic shapes that begin at the rear wall behind the orchestra and proceed across the ceiling to the rear of the auditorium in a precise pattern. At first sight these sound-reflecting geometric forms seem to encroach on the visual setting of the hall, but they are soon accepted as an intrinsic part of the over-all design. Also in Minneapolis, the exterior of the Tyrone Guthrie Theater, with its inviting large areas of glass, encloses an intimate interior. Although it accommodates 1,437 persons, no one of them sits more than fifty-four feet from the stage. The spectators in the orchestra seats virtually surround the players on the theater's projecting stage, a variation on the ancient Greek theme in which steeply banked seats fan out approximately 200 degrees about a central stage, reminiscent of the fourth-century-B.C. theater at Epidaurus designed by Polyclitus the Younger.

Tyrone Guthrie Theater, Minneapolis, Minn. (1963). Ralph R. Rapson, architect

Orchestra Hall, Minneapolis, Minn. (1974). Hardy Holzman Pfeiffer and Hammel Green & Abrahamson, architects; Dr. Cyril M. Harris, acoustical consultant

The Hennepin County Government Center is housed in two parallel office blocks—according to the function of courts and municipal offices. These nearly identical units are sheathed in reddish South Dakota granite and are separated by a sixty-foot-wide atrium which is glazed at the ends, X-braced for stability, and roofed with glass to make a covered garden concourse. The resulting inner space, which rises through most of the height of the building, is breathtaking. The nearby Crystal Court (see following page) is another brilliantly airy example of the new architectural trends changing the face of downtown Minneapolis. Directly across the street from Hennepin Center the turreted and beautifully preserved City-County Building (1905) is a fine reminder of the best of the past.

Hennepin County Government Center, Minneapolis, Minn. (1975).
John Carl Warnecke & Associates, architects

Interior Atrium (detail), Hennepin County Government Center

Ceiling (detail), Crystal Court

The IDS complex is comprised of a fifty-seven-floor skyscraper and its enclosed mall, the Crystal Court. Vertical setbacks at the corners, seven uniform notches, soften the profile of the tower, which is wrapped in a greenish-blue glass. The lower section contains the multilevel Crystal Court, a spirited mid-city crossroads of shops and cafés embellished by plantings and banners; a glazed roof floods the interior with sunlight.

OVERLEAF: *Federal Reserve Bank, Minneapolis, Minn. (1973). Gunnar Birkerts & Associates, architects.* The façade of the bank is attached to cables which are slung from the tops of two great piers ten stories high, creating a column-free basement floor so that armored cars could have free access to the gold bullion stored below. On the carefully landscaped terrace are several fine pieces of contemporary sculpture.

Interior (detail), Crystal Court

IDS Building and Crystal Court, Minneapolis, Minn. (1972). Philip Johnson and John Burgee, architects

The sixty-story twin towers of Marina City, strategically situated at the edge of the Chicago River within a few hundred yards of Lake Michigan, form a microcosm of a city where one can live and work, find recreation and exercise, shop and dine, and park a car or boat without leaving the premises. The circular towers are constructed on a central core of reinforced concrete about which the apartments and their semicircular balconies fan out. The seventy-story Lake Point Tower at the Navy Pier promontory of Lake Michigan is a masterpiece of design. The concrete frame—the highest concrete building in the world when built—is sheathed in bronze-tinted glass set in a framework of bronze-colored aluminum. The architects, once students of Mies van der Rohe and members of his office staff, were influenced by the trefoil shape of the tower on a drawing the master had created in 1921 in Berlin.

Marina City, Chicago, Ill. (1962). Bertrand Goldberg Associates, architects

Lake Point Tower, Chicago, Ill. (1968). G. D. Schipporeit and John C. Heinrich, architects

Civic Center, Chicago, Ill. (1966). C. F. Murphy Associates, architects; Skidmore, Owings & Merrill; and Loebl, Schlossman and Bennett & Dart, associates; Pablo Picasso, sculptor

The Chicago Civic Center is comprised of a thirty-one story skyscraper containing a new courthouse, one venerable old (1906) courthouse, and a polished plaza (345 by 220 feet). The design of the tower, clad in Cor-Ten steel and complemented by bronze-colored plate glass, was dictated by the need of an unusually large bay size (free floor area) to accommodate the numerous courtrooms and was accomplished by the use of large columns to frame these bays and support the building. The central feature of the granite plaza, alive with the interplay of fountain jets and rustling trees, is the fifty-foot-high Picasso sculpture "Woman," made of the same Cor-Ten steel as the building. It was given by the artist to the citizens of Chicago.

Like the pioneering Marina City, the hundred-story John Hancock Center is a microcity, with shops, restaurants, parking areas, skating rink and pool, offices, television and radio stations, and apartments from the forty-sixth to ninety-second floors. Skidmore, Owings & Merrill created the steel-framed, tapered form of "Big John"—all four walls incline inward from the large base—in response to the heavy wind load from the lake. The prominent exterior diagonals, each pair extending across eighteen floors, provide bracing against the wind and form the strongly visual exoskeleton. The 110-story Sears Tower, also designed by Skidmore, Owings & Merrill, is the tallest building in the world. The technically ingenious structure consists of nine independent units strapped together—the units on the corners terminate at different levels, producing the notched profile of the exterior. The steel frame is clad in black aluminum and sixteen thousand bronze-tinted windows.

John Hancock Center, Chicago, Ill. (1970).
Skidmore, Owings & Merrill, architects

Sears Tower, Chicago, Ill. (1974). Skidmore, Owings & Merrill, architects

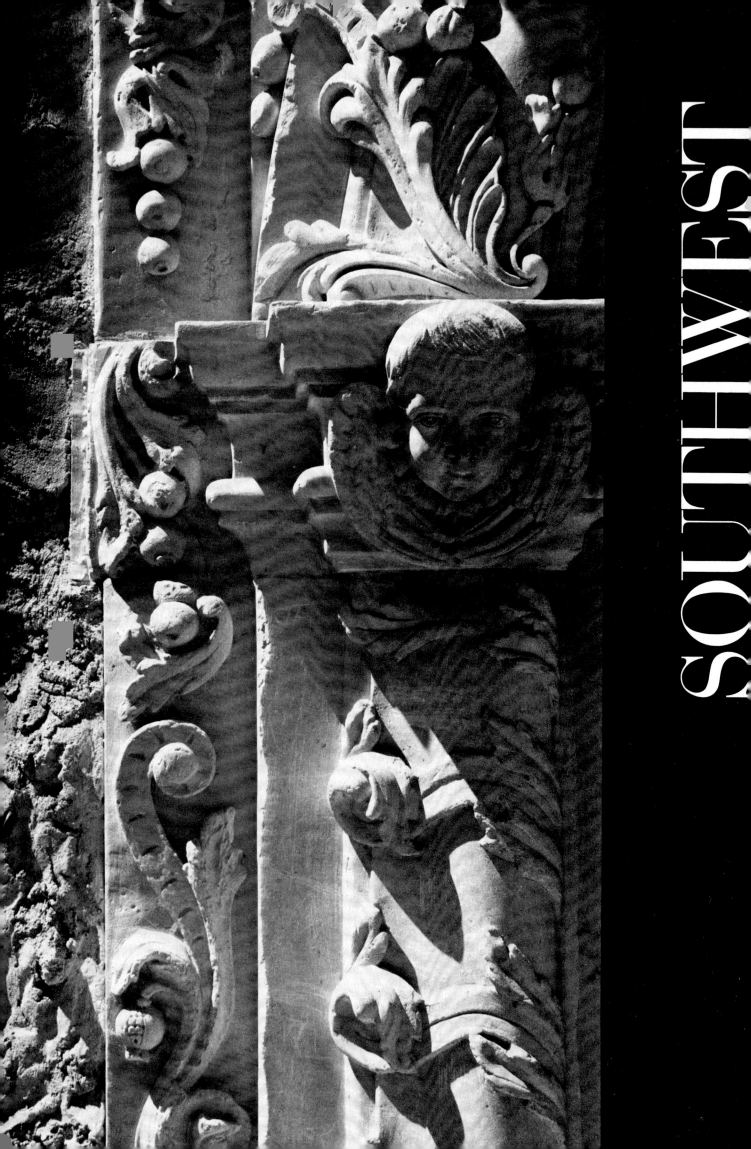

SOUTHWEST

ARIZONA
ARKANSAS
LOUISIANA
NEW MEXICO
OKLAHOMA
TEXAS

The six southerly states that range from the western bank of the Mississippi River to the borders of California and Nevada contain some of the oldest habitations in the United States, as well as some of the nation's oldest public buildings and oldest cities. Long before the white man appeared in the Americas, the natives in what is now New Mexico, Colorado, and Arizona, ancestors of the present-day Pueblo Indians, had developed a unique type of architecture culminating, almost a millennium ago, in large apartment-house complexes, some with hundreds of rooms and capable of accommodating as many as a thousand persons. In New Mexico's Chaco Canyon alone are the ruins of twelve such multistoried masonry developments, one of them the largest ever uncovered on the continent.

At about the time of the Norman conquest of England, the Chaco area was a lively community of about seven thousand inhabitants. Although these natives knew nothing of writing, the wheel, or elementary metallurgy, they had the advantages of a network of surfaced roads and an elaborate system of irrigation. They had domesticated corn and beans, and their farming methods provided the surplus that sustained their civilization. Here there are no special apartments or buildings for an elite. Almost all rooms are of the same size, as in modern low-cost housing, indicating an egalitarian society that flourished some seven centuries before the Declaration of Independence was signed in Philadelphia, far across the continent.

It was not until the sixteenth century that the first Europeans found their way into this American Southwest, Spanish conquistadores bent on epochal discoveries that would make their fortunes and redound to the glory of Spain and of Christianity. Actually, the expedition of the first of them, Álvar Núñez Cabeza de Vaca, came of an accident that resulted in one of the most remarkable adventures in the annals of exploration. Although the details remain vague, it is evident that this intrepid pioneer along with several companions was shipwrecked off the coast of Texas in 1528 and was enslaved for some years by the local Indians. With his companions he escaped and after much wandering through the Southwest came safely to Mexico City eight years after his shipwreck. (According to one account they arrived stark naked, their clothing having shredded away.)

Almost certainly these were the first white men to see the buffalo, those "wild hunch back cows" that were the very substance of life for the natives of the West and whose incredible numbers blackened the illimitable prairies far beyond reach of the eye. Less probable were stories about the Pueblo Indians, which gave rise to the legend of the Seven Cities of Cibola, famed for immense wealth; a legend that grew more fabulous with retelling and inspired a vast treasure hunt. Within less than a decade Francisco Vasquez de Coronado had wandered as far north as Kansas and as far west as the Grand Canyon, the land where Montezuma's proven wealth was said to be equaled in yet undiscovered hoardings. Coronado's search revealed only humble native pueblos. But years later Spaniards were still hoping and looking for riches north of the Rio Grande. Meanwhile, they were spreading a thin web of empire over that great area. All this wandering and searching took place many years before the English laid serious claim to any

San Ildefonso Pueblo, N.M. (about 1300)

Palace of the Governors, Santa Fe, N.M. (1612)

With the severe drought of 1276–99 in the Southwest, many of the Pueblo Indians abandoned their cliff dwellings and began to move to other adobe communities. These so-called pueblos are large, terraced community houses, with walls of adobe and roofs supported by projecting vigas, or heavy beams. They are entered through the upper story by ladders. At San Ildefonso Pueblo, on the east bank of the Rio Grande, one- and two-story buildings accented by dome-shaped, outside ovens frame the main plaza. In 1609 Santa Fe was founded as the capital of the Spanish Southwest, and the next year work began on the Palace of the Governors on Santa Fe Plaza. The low, viga-punctured, adobe structure, with its shaded passageway across the front and a patio behind, is a graceful blend of Indian and Spanish architectural styles.

Set against the harsh landscape of an upland mesa, a new cultural center-restaurant-motel complex accommodates those seeking to explore the vast Hopi Reservation.

OVERLEAF: *Taos Pueblo, Taos, N.M. (rebuilt about 1700)*. Nestled against New Mexico's high Taos Mountains, the communal dwellings of Taos Pueblo—the tallest in the Southwest—are little changed from those described by Spanish explorers as early as 1540. The several units of the still-occupied pueblo echo the hills beyond with cube piled upon cube in abstract geometric forms. The solid adobe walls—doors and windows were added only in the nineteenth century—contrast with the wooden outrigging of several storage shelters, and with ladders arranged to reach the upper terraces.

Hopi Cultural Center, Oraibi, Ariz. (1971). Gonzales Associates, architects

San Francisco de Asis, Ranchos de Taos, N.M. (about 1772)

By the early seventeenth century, churches and missions had been installed in most of the Pueblo Indian villages, adding to the Indians' resentment of Spanish rule. In 1680 they revolted in an armed protest that forced the Spanish to retreat to the El Paso area of Texas; they did not reconquer New Mexico until 1692. The ancient mission of San Geronimo, first built about 1598 near the entrance to Taos Pueblo, was rebuilt after 1694 and continued to operate until 1847 when it was reduced to ruins by American troops. About four miles southwest of Taos the venerable church of San Francisco de Asis still stands at Ranchos de Taos. The exterior, with its two belfries and Gothic-style pointed arch door, is wrapped around by a low adobe wall. The buttresses which cluster about the base of the apse and lend lateral support to the adobe walls are the remarkable and much photographed feature of San Francisco. Differing from the sophisticated flying buttresses of the medieval cathedrals of Europe, these bulky supports were at times reinforced because of weathering. Apart from their structural function, they appeal as abstract architectural sculpture.

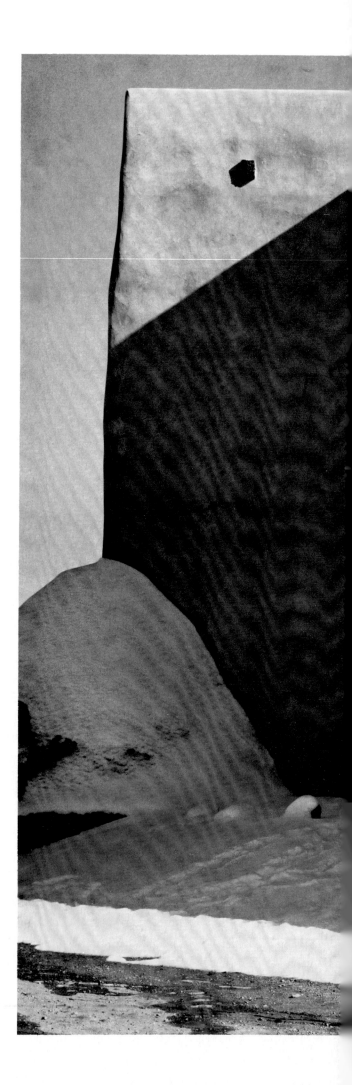

549

San Estévan del Rey, Ácoma, N.M. (about 1640)

Occupying the heights of a sandstone mesa some 357 feet above the plain, Ácoma Pueblo, established about 1300, claims to be the oldest continuously occupied settlement in the nation. From their aerie, the Indians of Ácoma successfully resisted the Spanish conquistadores for nearly a century, until 1629, when the Franciscans founded the San Estévan del Rey Mission at Ácoma. Materials of the mission's original church, so painstakingly hand-carried to the mesa top, are undoubtedly incorporated in the one built about 1640, which is still in use today. San Estévan epitomizes the thick-walled, narrow, flat-roofed churches with few windows built under Spanish religious influence in New Mexico with Indian labor. The interior illustrates the simple post-and-lintel construction—the supporting vigas of the roof placed atop the stone and adobe walls and braced by corbels often fancifully painted. The chapel at Laguna, New Mexico, is notable for its energetic wall decorations—boldly primitive wainscoting painted to represent the elements. In comparison to these primitive New Mexican examples is the startlingly ambitious church of San Xavier del Bac in Arizona—the high point of Spanish baroque architecture and sculpture in America. The vaulted and domed interior is dominated by its elaborately carved brick and polychromed stucco *retablos* behind the altar, flanked by richly treated transepts.

San José de Laguna, Laguna, N.M. (1706)

San Xavier del Bac, near Tucson, Ariz. (1783-97)

San José y San Miguel de Aguayo, San Antonio, Tex. (1768-78)

During the eighteenth century San José y San Miguel de Aguayo was one of the most important missions on the northern frontier of New Spain. Founded in 1720 by Captain Juan Valdez, lieutenant general of the province of Texas, San José was a thriving community by mid-century with some two thousand Indian converts caring for three thousand head of livestock and producing three thousand bushels of corn annually. The mission formed a large, walled compound composed of living quarters for the Indians and soldiers, a granary, and the church itself. After 1824, when the missions were secularized by the Mexicans, San José gradually fell into disuse and started to collapse, but it has now been restored. The façade of the church, started in 1768, is one of the glories of the Spanish contribution to architecture in this country. The main entrance sparkles with its Spanish baroque richness of ornament set off against the simple stuccoed walls of its semi-Moorish façade. Originally most of the building was covered with stucco decorated in brightly colored geometric patterns, a small sample of which remains near a lower corner of the tower. The highly accomplished carvings of the church's façade and of the rose window on the south wall were the work of Pedro Huizar of Aguascalientes, Mexico.

El Santuario de Chimayo, Chimayo, N.M. (1816)

In 1699 Jesuit Father Eusebio Francisco Kino converted the Pima Indians of Tumacácori village and introduced ranching to the area. After the Pima rebellion of 1751 the settlement was moved to its present site, where a small mission was erected. When the Franciscans took over the Sonora mission chain in 1768, San José de Tumacácori became the most important mission in the region. The present baroque adobe church—with its semicircular gable end, arched doorway, pilasters, attached baptistry with belfry on top—was built between 1796 and the end of Spanish rule in the region. The devout Indian converts abandoned it in 1848 and today the ruins of the church remain as a sturdy symbol of the mission period. A little-altered example of a Spanish village church stands at Chimayo village in New Mexico. El Santuario is currently a pilgrims' shrine.

San José de Tumacácori, near Nogales, Ariz. (1796-1806)

Spanish Governor's Palace, San Antonio, Tex. (1749)

The so-called "palace" at San Antonio was completed in 1749 as housing for commandants of the presidio of Béxar, and in 1772 it became the headquarters of the Spanish government in Texas. It was here that Moses Austin came in 1820 to secure the privilege of settling Anglo-Americans in Texas. The last governor left the next year, when Mexico proclaimed its independence from Spain. The Cabildo in New Orleans, with its massive arches and wrought-iron balconies, was built in 1795 of stuccoed brick as the seat of the administrative and legislative council for Spanish Louisiana. After the French returned to rule Louisiana for twenty short days in 1803, the sovereignty of Louisiana was ceremoniously transferred to the United States in this structure.

Cabildo, New Orleans, La. (1795)

Built during the early days of French colonization, Parlange is a fine example of the early Louisiana type of farmhouse in what is known as the "raised cottage style." Its ground floor is built of stuccoed brick as protection from water and dampness, with circular columns also of brick to help support the galleries that surround most of the house. The upper part was constructed of cypress and moss packed together with clay, topped by a steep-pitched roof in the French tradition. It has been lived in by eight successive generations of descendants of the early owners. The Acadian House was built in similar fashion by an early French commandant at Poste des Atakapas, later to be known as St. Martinville. This part of the state was settled by French Acadians who came there when they were forced from Nova Scotia in the middle of the eighteenth century because they would not swear allegiance to the British who had conquered their homeland. Their French-speaking descendants, the Cajuns, remain a group apart to this day.

Parlange, near New Roads, La. (about 1750)

Acadian House, St. Martinville, La. (1765)

Madame John's Legacy, New Orleans, La.

In the late 1720's a French sea captain, Jean Pascal, from Provence, built a country-style raised cottage in New Orleans' Vieux Carré. The house did not survive the great fire of 1788, but it was immediately rebuilt using the original plan and some materials salvaged from the burnt-out structure. Thus, the dwelling that stands today is almost precisely like the earlier one, although the verandah originally went around three sides, including that facing the essential patio. The house represents a rare and excellent souvenir of the intriguing but little-known French period of the city's architecture. (The dormer windows may be later additions.) In his romantic tales of old New Orleans, *Old Creole Days*, published in 1879, the author George Washington Cable dubbed the house "Madame John's Legacy," a name that has stuck to it over the years since. Madame John's Legacy stands just around the corner from Jackson Square, the heart of old New Orleans and long known as the Place d'Armes or, in Spanish, the Plaza de Armas, the most historic spot in Louisiana. (It was renamed Jackson Square in 1851 for Andrew Jackson, the hero of the battle of New Orleans during the War of 1812.) On the north side of the square stands the St. Louis Cathedral, built in 1794, adjacent to the Cabildo. It is the third church to have been raised on the site and christened with the name of the patron saint of Bourbon France.

Cabildo (1795) and St. Louis Cathedral (1794), New Orleans, La.

Fort Smith was established in 1817 to keep peace between the Osage Indians and the Cherokees. Starting in 1839, the original log structures were replaced by a new, more substantial fort built of stone. Ten years later it was observed that the "public buildings for Military purposes at this place are the finest, largest, and best buildings on the Western frontier." The Pentagon Barracks consist of four identical, angled structures built of brick painted pink with white Doric columns supporting galleries on both sides. They constitute a handsome example of military architecture. A fort had been built near this site by the French in 1719. Eight years later the British threw up a redoubt to ward off approaching Spaniards. In 1966 the American barracks, built between 1819 and 1829, were restored and remodeled on the interior to serve as very desirable apartments.

Old Fort Museum, Fort Smith, Ark. (1839)

Pentagon Barracks, Baton Rouge, La. (1829; 1966)

Shadows-on-the-Teche, New Iberia, La. (1834)

Rosedown Plantation, St. Francisville, La. (1835; 1844)

The surviving white-columned mansions of ante-bellum Louisiana are standing symbols of the affluent and suave society they so handsomely served. Shadows-on-the-Teche, facing the street rather than the bayou behind it, was commissioned by the planter David Weeks as a town house at New Iberia. The owner unfortunately died just after he moved in. During the Civil War, General Nathaniel P. Banks made his headquarters here. With its justly celebrated gardens, Rosedown Plantation covers ten acres of land. Six Doric columns support the gallery along the façade, and an identical set above supports the gabled roof. Side wings were added in 1844.

RIGHT *and* OVERLEAF: *Oak Alley, Vacherie, La. (1839).* One of the greatest of the plantation houses, Oak Alley is covered by an enormous hip roof supported by twenty-eight two-story Tuscan columns. Its double galleries are so wide that windows can be kept open virtually all the time, the interior remaining protected from a merciless sun or pelting rain; in clement weather each verandah serves as an open-living room. Thus did the southern adaptations of the Greek Revival style logically and effectively respond to the needs of a specific environment. The plantation derives its name from the twenty-eight almost unbelievably magnificent oak trees that, spaced exactly eighty feet apart, stretch in an *allée* down to the Mississippi.

Porch (detail), Oak Alley

San Francisco, Reserve, La. (1850)

Obviously influenced by the design of Mississippi river-boats that once steamed past its front door (the river was then without a levee), San Francisco is a maverick among Louisiana plantation houses. Its style has been variously described as "surrogate Greek Revival gone Victorian" and as an "improbable assemblage of Gothic, Classic and miscellaneous Victorian architectural elements . . . Louisiana's best known fantasy in architecture." The top floor is set back, largely camouflaged by a dominating cornice which surmounts the second-floor gallery. Within, the cornice and the cypress ceiling of the drawing room are exquisitely painted by Dominique Canova (nephew of the famous Antonio Canova), an Italian apparently influenced by wall paintings at Pompeii dating from the first century B.C.

Le Prète House, New Orleans, La. (1835)

The Le Prète House, noted for the beauty of the cast-iron ornament that embroiders its many balconies, is a landmark of the Vieux Carré. It was built by Dr. Joseph Coulon Gardette, a Philadelphia dentist who came to New Orleans during Spanish rule and created a flourishing practice here. In 1839 it was purchased by Jean Baptiste Le Prète, a prominent local merchant. James Gallier, Jr., was brought to this country at the age of five and, following in the footsteps of his father, recently mentioned, became a leading architect of Louisiana. In 1860 he completed his own residence on Royal Street in New Orleans, next to an earlier, commercial building. Each of these structures has the distinctive New Orleans balcony on the street façade, here upheld with the slenderest of cast-iron columns burgeoning into a fantasy of cast-iron grillwork at the balcony level and eave. When continued in adjacent buildings, the verandahs create a passage providing shade in the sunshine and an umbrella during a rain.

Gallier House, New Orleans, La. (1857-60). James Gallier, Jr., architect

St. Louis Cemetery #1, New Orleans, La.

Small Houses, Vieux Carré, New Orleans, La.

At first glance the St. Louis Cemetery appears to be a domestic annex to the Vieux Carré. Packed together along the *allées* of the burial ground, the vaults of its infinitely varied tombs are raised several feet above the ground and the underlying water table. These picturesque "homes of the dead" often resemble the houses of the living. Some of them are the work of such highly qualified architects as James Gallier, Benjamin Latrobe, and others. Parts of the Vieux Carré retain its early character, one which was fashioned long ago by local cultures and was shaped in part by the local climate and molded of local materials.

The Old State House at Little Rock was designed by Gideon Shryock, who had recently completed the Kentucky capitol at Frankfort, as earlier described. It ranks among the freshest examples of Greek Revival style in the country and is rightfully the pride of Arkansas. (The triple-tiered fountain in front was brought down from the Philadelphia Centennial Exposition.) In remarkable contrast, the Old State Capitol at Baton Rouge, built in 1850 and restored in 1882, presents a stiffly symmetrical block with octagonal turrets and a machicolated cornice outlining the roof line. The original design was by James Dakin, who for several years had been a member of the New York firm of Town and Davis, largely famous for their Greek Revival structures.

OVERLEAF: *Interior, Old State Capitol, Baton Rouge.* As part of the rebuilding of the old structure in 1882, a magnificent dome was added to the capitol, which had been gutted by fire twenty years earlier during the Civil War.

Old State Capitol, Baton Rouge, La. (1850; 1882). James H. Dakin, architect

Old State House, Little Rock, Ark. (1842). Gideon Shryock, architect

So long as they moved through timbered wilderness, pioneering Americans continued to find log cabins their most practical type of shelter, at least until which time something better could be built. It was not until they reached the sea of grass of the Great Plains that they ran out of timber and turned to sod for their building material. In the Ozark Mountains of northwest Arkansas a collection of mid-nineteenth-century log structures has been gathered at Prairie Grove, the site of a Civil War battle in 1862. The oldest units in the village are the restored F. F. Latta House and its barn, both of extremely simple notched-log construction. Another log cabin village of the same vintage has been assembled in Fort Worth and gives an insight into living conditions on the Texas frontier. Connecting the rooms of the Isaac Parker cabin is a typical "dog trot," a breezeway providing an open-air work space covered over by the roof.

Latta House, Vineyard Village, Prairie Grove, Ark. (1834)

Parker House, Log Cabin Village, Fort Worth, Tex. (1848)

Winedale Inn, near Round Top, Tex. (1834; 1850's)

Fort Davis, founded in 1854 to protect travelers on the San Antonio-El Paso road, played a major role in the defense system of western Texas. Federal troops garrisoned here patrolled the area, escorted stagecoaches and wagon trains, and pursued raiding Comanches and Apaches. In 1861, during the Civil War, Fort Davis was occupied by Confederate troops, who evacuated the post in the next year. It was subsequently destroyed by Apaches and in 1867 was rebuilt by federal forces, who protected the region from outlaws and hostile Indians for the next two decades. The fort was finally abandoned in 1891, and today the National Park Service has restored many of the fifty adobe and red-stone buildings of the western military outpost. The first part of the eight-room Winedale Inn, of native Texas cedar with its log outbuildings of cedar and oak, was built in 1834 by early settlers in the rolling countryside between the Brazos and Colorado rivers. It was subsequently added to and served as a stagecoach inn during the 1850's.

Fort Davis National Historic Site, Fort Davis, Tex. (1854; 1867)

U.S. Courthouse and Federal Building, Galveston, Tex. (1861). Ammi B. Young, probable architect

The former custom house at Galveston established a surprisingly sophisticated classic revival beachhead at this western site, a building which more than a century of hurricanes and man-made batterings has not diminished. The north and south façades are distinguished by inset columned porches on both floors, the whole suggestive of Inigo Jones' early-seventeenth-century Queen's House in Greenwich, England. At Tombstone, the courthouse where frontier justice was sometimes meted out is a surprisingly capable brick structure whose stone quoins, columned entry, and venturesome cupola recall influences from much farther east. At the time it was erected, the "Town Too Tough To Die" was earning an unparalleled reputation for lawlessness and violence.

Courthouse Museum, Tombstone, Ariz. (1882)

Bishop's Palace (Gresham House), Galveston, Tex. (1893). Nicholas J. Clayton, architect

Hill County Courthouse, Hillsboro, Tex. (1890). W. C. Dodson, architect

Texas can boast of some of the most unrestrainedly exuberant buildings of the late nineteenth century. In 1885 Walter Gresham commissioned his architect-neighbor, Nicholas Clayton, to build him the most elaborate house in the state, a task that was undertaken with unflinching confidence at the cost of a quarter of a million dollars. The exterior unfolds a catalog of virtually every conceivable architectural motif. With its combination of turrets and gables, roof lines of changing character, wrought-iron railings and brackets, and chimneys of assorted designs, the profile of the house reveals a thoroughly restless imagination. Since 1923 the house has served as the residence of the bishop of the Galveston-Houston Roman Catholic diocese. Somewhat less fanciful, the Ellis County Courthouse is still conglomerate in appearance, with its towers, turrets, and terra-cotta embellishments. The Hill County Courthouse is a foursquare, three-story structure of tawny limestone, topped by a dazzlingly white, triple-tiered metal tower above its Mansard roof.

Ellis County Courthouse, Waxahachie, Tex.
(1897). J. Reilly Gordon, architect

591

Santa Fe Railroad Station, Shawnee, Okla. (1901)

From 1877 to 1889 the Santa Fe Railroad developed from a prairie grain and cattle carrier extending a little more than 780 miles to a great transcontinental system reaching from Chicago to the Pacific and the Gulf of Mexico. In 1901 a new station was built at Shawnee, Oklahoma, with stepped gables and a staunchly turreted tower—a somewhat vagrant western outpost of H. H. Richardson's far-reaching influence. When it was completed in 1929, the Boston Avenue Methodist Church in Tulsa attracted international attention as a notable example of modern ecclesiastical architecture. The walls of the four-story-high main building, constructed of massive limestone, terminate in cubistic forms in the shape of praying hands. An illuminated central tower, rising 290 feet above the doorways, suggests the same symbolic imagery. The doorways themselves have pointed arches and are embellished with terra-cotta and bas-relief figures of memorable pioneers. Bruce Goff was the principal designer.

Boston Avenue Methodist Church, Tulsa, Okla. (1929). Rush & Endicott, architects

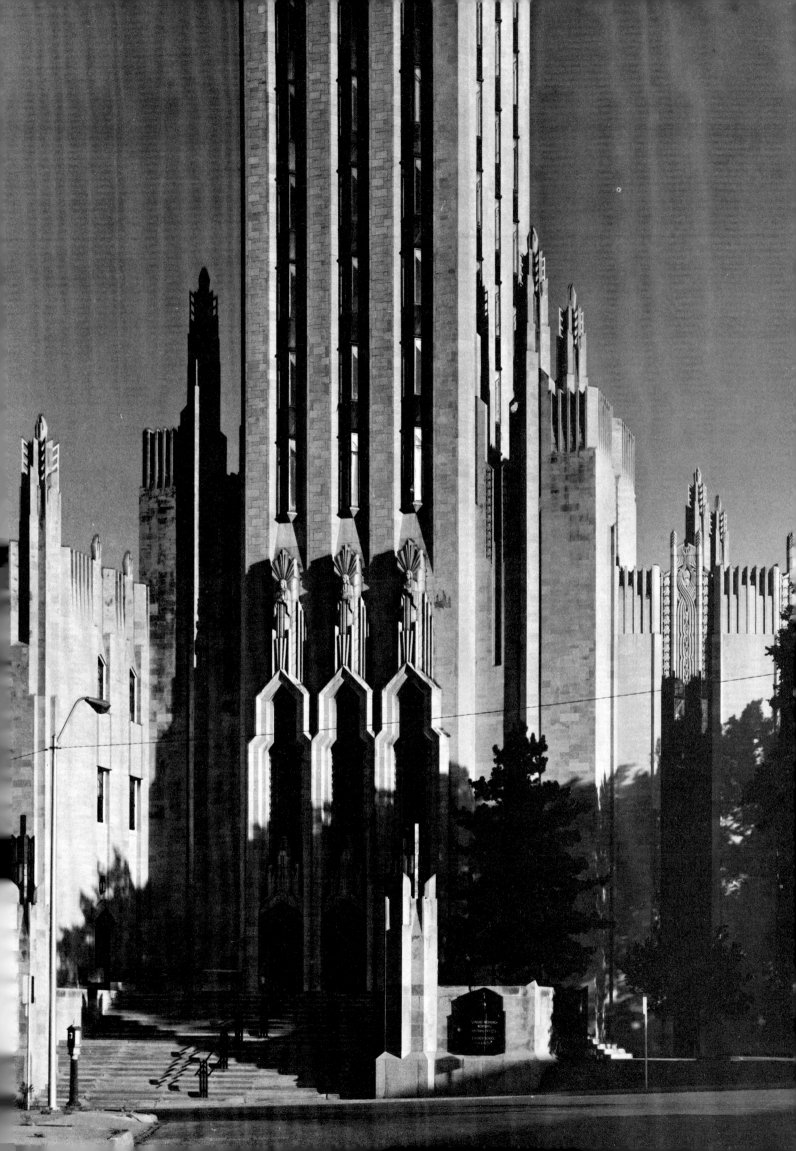

Meandering through the heart of the oldest city of Texas, San Antonio, with its wealth of historic landmarks—the missions of San José y San Miguel de Aguayo and Purísima Concepción, the Spanish Governor's Palace, and the Alamo—is a delightful river walk. The Paseo del Rio, lying some twenty to twenty-five feet below street level, winds for about three miles in a horseshoe shape through the downtown area. Pedestrians may stroll along footpaths or avail themselves of paddle boats or sightseeing barges on the waters. The Paseo, lined with diverting shops, cafés, and restaurants, and with its flowing water and attractive landscaping, offers a welcome respite from the noises, traffic, and concrete of the city above. An elegant tower originally designed for the San Antonio Hemis-Fair of 1968 is now a prominent part of the city's skyline. The 750-foot tower is anchored by fifty-five piers sunk more than sixty feet down to form a foundation base. External elevators move up and down the twelve-sided poured-concrete shaft of the tower; stairwells are within the hollow core. The steel-frame Top House contains a revolving restaurant, a stationary one, and an observation deck.

Tower of the Americas, San Antonio, Tex. (1968). Ford, Powell & Carson, architects

Paseo del Rio, San Antonio, Tex. (restoration begun 1939)

Cosanti Foundation Workshop, Paradise Valley, Ariz. (1962-70). Paolo Soleri, architect

Paolo Soleri, a gifted Italian-born architect, has spent years in the Arizona desert drafting what he calls "guidelines toward a new option" for modern man, the city dweller. Soleri has designed ideal possible cities that he calls "arcologies," a combination of architecture and ecology in new basic patterns of life for vast populations. In Soleri's visionary cities people are concentrated in elaborate, multileveled structures within small areas. These cities have definite boundaries, beyond which lay an unspoiled countryside within easy reach of the urban dweller. The hand-built desert workshop (left) in Paradise Valley, not far from Scottsdale, Arizona, serves as a gathering place for Soleri's disciples. Here, with spontaneous improvisation, the master and his dedicated student-apprentices have fashioned their "earth colony"—a workshop, living quarters, and small museum—mostly of concrete cast in desert silt. The structures, some below ground and cavelike, abound in circles, arcs, and apses and are enlivened by Soleri's famous ceramic wind bells, the sale of which helps support the foundation. At Arcosanti (below), about seventy miles north of his present headquarters, Soleri and his disciples are constructing the first application of his principles for the new utopia.

Arcosanti, near Dugas, Ariz. (1972-   ). Paolo Soleri, architect

Hopewell Baptist Church, Edmond, Okla. (1953). Bruce Goff, architect

The space requirements for three very different types of enterprises have been successfully met by three very creative architects. Buckminster Fuller's largest geodesic dome yet built, with an unobstructed interior diameter of over 375 feet, services tank cars near Baton Rouge, Louisiana. The all-welded-steel dome is made up of bright yellow hexagonal units supported by an exoskeleton of blue-pipe framing. Philip Johnson designed a beautifully landscaped, below ground-level library for Hendrix College in Arkansas. The roof deck on top of the library and the sunken plaza in front of it provide a gathering place for students; library functions are accommodated below. For a church in Oklahoma, Bruce Goff employed architectural symbolism to tie the religious activities of the parishioners to their working life. The supporting trusses of the twelve-sided church are of pipes ordinarily used in the rigging of oil wells.

Bailey Library, Hendrix College, Conway, Ark. (1967). Philip Johnson, architect

Union Tank Car Repair Facility, Baton Rouge, La. (1958). Synergetics, Inc., dome engineers; Battey & Childs, architects

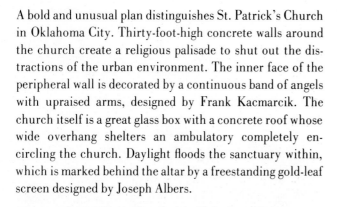

A bold and unusual plan distinguishes St. Patrick's Church in Oklahoma City. Thirty-foot-high concrete walls around the church create a religious palisade to shut out the distractions of the urban environment. The inner face of the peripheral wall is decorated by a continuous band of angels with upraised arms, designed by Frank Kacmarcik. The church itself is a great glass box with a concrete roof whose wide overhang shelters an ambulatory completely encircling the church. Daylight floods the sanctuary within, which is marked behind the altar by a freestanding gold-leaf screen designed by Joseph Albers.

BELOW *and* OVERLEAF: *Chapel of the Holy Cross, Sedona, Ariz. (1956). Anshen & Allen, architects.* An evocative memorial chapel is set against the towering red sandstone cliffs of central Arizona. The reinforced concrete walls rise from two rock outcroppings, and a ninety-foot-high cross projects from one of the glass ends. The dramatic cliffside chapel is approached by a sinuous footpath leading up from a parking area which is located below.

Chapel of the Holy Cross

The thirty-three-story Tenneco Building in Houston, Texas, ranks among a handful of great postwar skyscrapers in America. The outer walls are inset five feet from the peripheral structure to provide for sun and weather control by means of clever louvers and for window-washing platforms. This also provides the building with a subtly pierced profile. The ground floor is inset on four sides, creating a sheltered, fifty-foot-high galleria. Also in Houston, the Jesse H. Jones Hall for the Performing Arts is wrapped in Italian travertine. The theater-concert hall is surrounded by a peristyle of slender piers upholding a great sheltering roof. The peristyle is brilliantly illuminated at night and the marble facing is carried right into the lobby, inviting the theatergoer into the foyer. The auditorium itself, accommodating an audience of 3,001 persons, is a chamber whose electronically controlled acoustical devices and imaginative "theater mechanics" contribute to the structure's reputation as "the most sophisticated building of its kind anywhere in the world."

Jesse H. Jones Hall for the Performing Arts, Houston, Tex. (1966). Caudill, Rowlett, Scott, architects

Tenneco Building, Houston, Tex. (1963). Skidmore, Owings & Merrill, architects

Philip Johnson has described his memorial to John F. Kennedy as a "pair of magnets about to clamp together." The design forms an enclosure of two U-shapes, understated to the point of starkness and curiously unsettling in its emotional impact: The Dallas memorial is situated a few hundred yards from the spot where the late President was gunned down and suggests in contemporary architectural terms the inexorable turns of fate. Construction is of simple precast concrete slabs lightly elevated above the ground on short supports. In Houston a nondenominational chapel and meditation center commemorates two great twentieth-century American artists—Mark Rothko and Barnett Newman. A memorial to Dr. Martin Luther King, Jr., by Newman, a twenty-six-foot-high self-rusting steel "Broken Obelisk," points its shattered finger skyward and is reflected in a pool in the courtyard. In the chapel-gallery are fourteen enormous, almost solid-color canvases by Rothko, who died before the chapel was opened.

John F. Kennedy Memorial, Dallas, Tex. (1970). Philip Johnson, architect

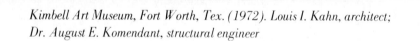

Kimbell Art Museum, Fort Worth, Tex. (1972). Louis I. Kahn, architect;
Dr. August E. Komendant, structural engineer

"Structure is the giver of light," wrote the late architect Louis I. Kahn, designer of the Kimbell Art Museum, and here light and life are fused throughout the structure. It has one of the country's greatest museum interiors. Although the Texas sun furnishes by far the greater part of the illumination, no direct rays strike the art on the walls; the lighting is all indirect. This is achieved by running continuous skylights down the center of fourteen of the sixteen cycloidal vaults that form the building's distinctive roof. Finely pierced metal screens, suspended directly beneath the skylights, reflect and disperse the light over the soffits of the vaults and thence onto the works of art. The vaults, the two forward of which form entry porches, are supported only at their ends. They measure 104 feet long and twenty-three feet wide and are separated by concrete channels containing air-conditioning outlets and electrical conduits.

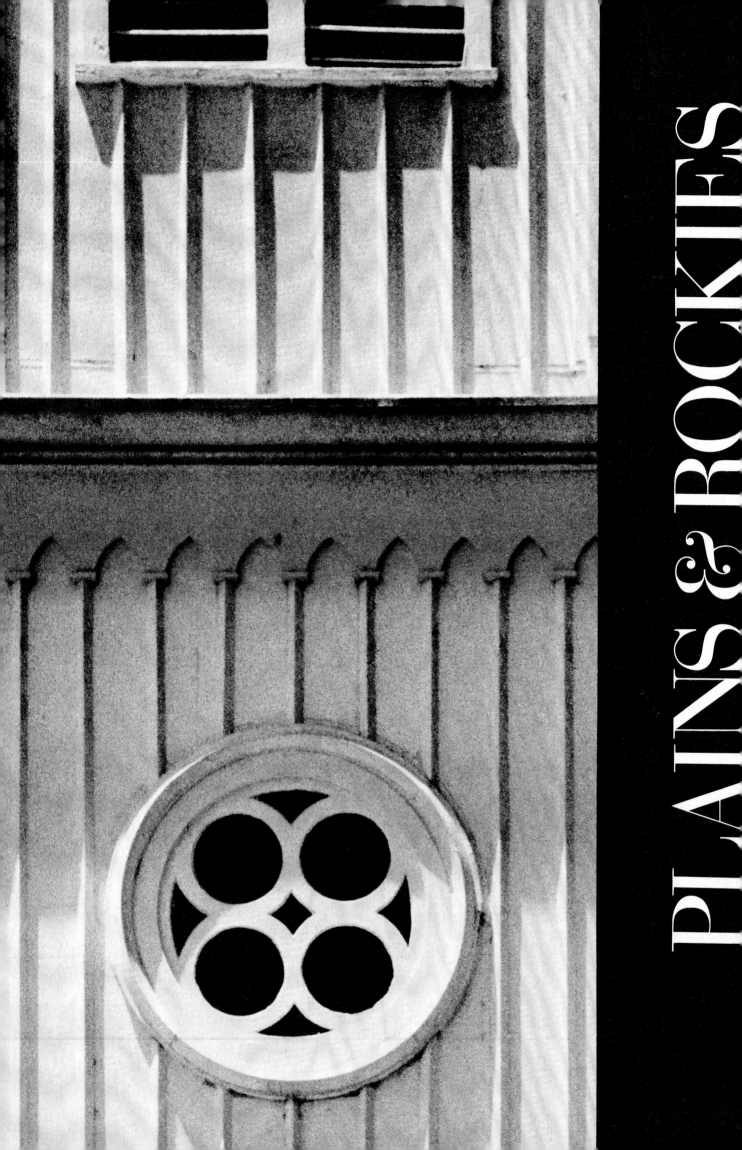

PLAINS & ROCKIES

COLORADO

IDAHO

KANSAS

MISSOURI

MONTANA

NEBRASKA

NORTH DAKOTA

SOUTH DAKOTA

UTAH

WYOMING

In the eighteenth century Benjamin Franklin, a major prophet and apostle of American expansion, grossly miscalculated that it would take ages to fill the North American continent. For once this very sage old man did not know what he was talking about. His younger contemporary Thomas Jefferson was hardly more prescient when, surveying the West of his day, he saw there "room enough for our descendants to the hundredth and thousandth generation." There was no sensible way of making sounder judgments, since at the time no one was sure what did lie to the west. From the East it looked at first like an interminable, dense, and dreary forest that the most determined and expert axmen might never be able to clear to let the sunlight in. Someone judged that squirrels might have hopped from tree to tree for a thousand miles without touching the ground and scarcely seeing the daylight. To travel weeks on end through that thick gloom among trees a hundred feet high was oppressive beyond the imagination of those who had not experienced it.

Beyond that, as reports by Lewis and Clark and other explorers revealed early in the nineteenth century, were the prairies and the plains, "a world of unexplored deserts and thickets," as the French traveler Constantin Volney wrote at the time of the Louisiana Purchase. And beyond that barren prospect rose the Rocky Mountains, standing "like a Chinese Wall," as one Congressman put it in 1828. For some years yet to come the territory between the Mississippi and the Missouri rivers and the Rockies continued to be labeled on maps as the "Great American Desert," a dry and treeless immensity fit for nomads but not for settlers. That "desert" today includes large parts of states discussed in this and the preceding chapter—land as productive in agriculture and in mineral wealth as any comparable area in the world. In some justification of Franklin's and Jefferson's predictions much of this territory does remain as open, relatively unoccupied land. However, as early as 1890 the Superintendent of the Census reported that to all intents the old frontier was closed. Geronimo had only recently been captured, a few straggling remnants of the once immense herds of buffalo remained on the plains, and several territories still awaited statehood. But the good free land to the west was largely staked out. The "interminable" forests were so far on their way to destruction that in 1891 President Theodore Roosevelt signed a Forest Reserve Act in an effort to save what remained. Lands "forever" set aside for the Indians by government regulation had been invaded from all directions; lands that were "impassable" had been crossed and recrossed by fortune hunters of one sort or another; land that was "uninhabited" had been opened for settlement.

As elsewhere on the continent, the big, open, western country had long been familiar to Indians before the earliest intrusions of the white men. There were Indians of many tribes, speaking various languages and following different ways of life. Along the eastern edge of this expanse were villages of farmer-hunter natives. Farther west were nomadic tribesmen who lived by hunting alone. An early legend told of a mysterious nation of white-skinned, Welsh-speaking Indians somewhere in the upper Missouri River Valley, who would become identified as the Mandans. The first white man to visit these people, in 1738 near what is today Bismarck, North Dakota, found them handsome, genial, hospitable, some of whom were indeed light-skinned but none of whom spoke Welsh. He was amazed by one Mandan village where he found hundreds of acres of tilled fields and a virtually impregnable palisaded fort. Within this compound he counted 130 "cabins," ranged along streets so uniform that he and his companions would lose their way trying to get about. What he called cabins were well-lit, spacious lodges, ranging from forty to ninety feet in diameter at the base, with a domed earthen roof supported by heavy cottonwood pillars and with sturdy crossbeams. These natives were carrying on a profitable trade in European goods and raising bumper crops, whose surplus they sold to other tribes. Then, just short of a century after their first contact with the white man, they suddenly vanished from the scene. A smallpox epidemic virtually wiped them out overnight.

Other distinctive Indian cultures have disappeared even more completely. On a bitterly cold and snowy day in 1888 two cowboys searching for stray cattle in the wild canyons of southwestern Colorado rode to the top of a mesa for a look about the countryside. Through a clearing in the junipers and piñon brush they suddenly saw what appeared to be the substantial remains of a whole city nestled in the opposite wall of the canyon. Finding their way to the site they there discovered several skeletons, clay pots, a stone ax, and other objects that gave indications of a hasty departure and that had lain there untouched by the weather and undisturbed by human intrusion for six centuries past. What fate had befallen the departed inhabitants was not apparent.

Others had earlier known of the existence of this site. In 1776 it was named Mesa Verde by a priestly Spanish explorer who, however, did not pause to investigate what he had seen in passing. The Utes in the region were awed by those "cities of the dead," and kept their distance. A United States government surveying party had also noted some such ruins, but without pursuing the matter. It was not until the two cowboys went there that the significance of the site was suspected.

These remains are, obviously, representative of the same prehistoric native culture as the neighboring cliff-dweller ruins in New Mexico discussed in the preceding chapter. What these people called themselves can never be known for they left no written records. The Navajos referred to these earlier people as "Anasazi," the "Ancient Ones," and, lacking a better designation, so they are called today by scholars who are trying to probe the mysteries of this complex and long-vanished civilization—a civilization whose influence apparently spread across the entire Southwest and into Texas and Nevada, and whose cliffside constructions remain to our wonderment.

Long before adventurers from the eastern United States had wandered so far in any numbers, French explorers, traders, and trappers had combed much of the land beyond the Mississippi and Missouri rivers. On their epic journey in the late seventeenth century the young priest Jacques Marquette and his companion Louis Jolliet reported seeing "prairies extending farther than the eye can see," covered by a sea of grass spangled with myriad flowers—a land, as one of the group wrote, "that somewhat resembles an earthly Paradise in beauty." "A settler would not there spend ten years cutting down and burning trees," wrote Jolliet; "on the very day of his arrival, he could put his plough into the ground." La Salle had written that this land of "vast meadows" was the best in the world—so the farther West seemed, at least, to the wondering eyes of these pioneers who journeyed down from Canada in the North.

However, after cutting and hewing his way through a thousand miles of forested land, the American farmer viewed the treeless expanse that lay beyond with some suspicion. It was true that such land needed no girdling and grubbing, but there was a scarcity of good water and little enough timber for fuel and building material. A land that grew no trees might not be rich enough to support crops of grain, vegetables, or fruit.

There were no nuts to feed the pigs. To break the thick and tough prairie soil was in itself a formidable challenge for the first plows to try it. The sticky, heavily root-matted earth did not yield easily to customary tools and methods. How to build houses and farms without available timber was another problem to be faced, along with the presence of inhospitable aborigines.

As the agricultural frontier paused temporarily before such obstacles, plainsmen and mountain men swarmed over this western expanse. They were men who came to know the wilderness beyond the wide Missouri more keenly and sensitively than the Indians and wild beasts which they had to outwit if they were to survive and make a living. When their heyday was over, the land had yielded both its precious furs, so prized in distant markets, from Leipzig to Canton, and most of its geographical secrets, and lay ready for the invasion of immigrants who would follow.

The town of St. Louis was born as a fur-trading post in the winter of 1763-64 when Pierre Laclède Liguest and a company of followers operating from that site obtained a monopoly of the trade with the Indians who hunted and trapped the plains and the Rockies before the white men had reached out first to plunder and then to settle those areas. Long after the Louisiana Purchase, the streets of that village swarmed with the frontiersmen who ventured to deal and compete with the natives in the more distant borderlands. St. Louis was soon celebrated as the gateway to the West, a city of proud buildings, which conspicuously included a cathedral along with extensive limestone warehouses along the river's edge and an abundant display of public and private structures typical of a flourishing community.

Few of those buildings survived a disastrous fire which swept through most of the waterfront area in 1849. One that did was the courthouse, which had been designed in the Greek Revival style a decade earlier. It was here that Thomas Hart Benton advocated a transcontinental railroad and that Dred Scott sued for his freedom. Another survivor, Old Rock House, for a while served as a warehouse for the great company with which John Jacob Astor hoped to win complete control over the western fur trade.

Following the conclusion of the War of 1812 the War Department had set up a series of garrisons to guard the extreme limits of the farmer's advance into the West. For some years to come these forts remained the most impressive buildings on the wide horizon. As early as 1819 Fort Snelling had been put up at the head of navigation on the Mississippi to dominate the northwestern wilderness. "It is built of stone," wrote Captain Marryat in 1839, "and may be considered as impregnable to any attempt which the Indians might make, provided that it has a sufficient garrison. Behind it is a splendid prairie, running back for many miles. . . ." Close by that remote outpost of civilization, St. Paul and Minneapolis grew up in another generation, but by then the farmers had advanced far beyond. (The fort's round tower, part of the original structure, is believed to be the oldest building in Minnesota.)

Such redoubts were not only fortifications; they became natural gathering places for fur traders, red and white, and for emigrants passing by. They served as social centers for a wide neighborhood, and not all were built by the government. Three miles above the mouth of the Yellowstone River, in what is now North Dakota, Fort Union was built by Astor's company in 1829 as a permanent trading post and as a depot for others farther out in the wilderness (hence its name). Palisaded with poplar logs and stone bastions, with towered blockhouses twenty-four feet square, it was the company's greatest fort and attracted a variety of curious visitors, from postgraduates of Europe's salons and studios eager for adventure and study to the roughest of hunters and Indians in from the surrounding prairie to swap their season's catch for tobacco, alcohol, firearms, or whatever seemed most appealing or necessary at the moment. Periodic balls were held at which the Indian wives of the factors appeared bedecked in the latest fashions that had reached the outpost via St. Louis from New York and Europe.

For thirty years, Fort Laramie, in what is now Wyoming, eight hundred miles northwest of St. Louis, remained a strategic point in the center of the Sioux country. The original quadrangle was built as a private fur-trading post in 1834, taken over by Astor's company, rebuilt in adobe, and sold to the government as a military post in 1849; new structures were then added. Lumber for the officers' clubhouse was hauled eight hundred miles by wagon from Fort Leavenworth in Kansas. One visitor was entertained in a room which he described as resembling the barroom of an eastern hotel. However, cannon were always at the ready to discourage marauders from the surrounding plains. Emigrants on their way to the farther West were expected to register here, as Francis Parkman did on his celebrated journey along the Oregon Trail to the Pacific coast. During the first six months of 1850, in the feverish rush to the gold fields, 37,570 men, 825 women, 1,126 children, 9,101 wagons, 31,502 oxen, 22,878 horses, 7,650 mules, and 5,754 cows were checked in at the post, and that apparently did not account for all the travelers and their equipment and beasts.

Once he had passed the limits of the eastern forests the settler was faced with unwonted building problems. He could hardly afford to freight in timber (it had cost between $60,000 and $85,000 to haul the lumber used for the officers' club at Fort Laramie), and in large areas stone was not available in any quantity and there were few masons to work it in any case. Under such circumstances his most sensible option was to use the earth itself for his building material. Western Kansas, for example, sprouted with sod houses—"soddies," as they have been called—built of heavy slabs of topsoil bound together by roots of growing buffalo grass. These elementary structures effectively served generations of Kansans.

In Utah and elsewhere adobe clay was shaped into sun-hardened bricks which were widely used in constructions of various sorts. Although not as durable as modern fired bricks, those made of adobe were easy and cheap to produce, they provided good insulation, and adequately protected with a coat of stucco or plaster, they were long-lasting enough for most practical purposes, as so many surviving and still-functioning early structures made of them in various parts of the West give evidence.

In 1834 Congress had forbidden any white person without a special license to set foot in Indian country beyond Missouri, an edict that as already indicated had become virtually a dead letter as soon as it was issued. By the 1840's the trails to Oregon and Santa Fe were deeply rutted by the passage of emigrants and traders; by 1849 the great rush was on to the California gold mines. In the summer of 1847 with Brigham Young in the lead, the first body of Mormons pushed westward to choose the site of a new state beyond reach of persecution by those who disagreed with their special religious beliefs —and, indeed, beyond reach of the restrictive laws of the United States. With directions from Jim Bridger, that almost legendary mountain man, Young found his way to the Great Salt Lake Valley, which he determined was the Promised Land of his people. Some of his followers thought that it was rather a blistering and interminable wasteland of sagebrush. However, within a month of their arrival the well-regimented brethren had, in the words of one of them, "broke, watered, planted and sowed upwards of 100 acres with various kinds of seeds, nearly stockaded with adobes one public square (ten acres)," and built cabins to live in. Two years later, visitors found there a city of eight thousand inhabitants, laid out on a magnificent scale, needing only trees to make it a "Diamond of the Desert." The first Mormon Tabernacle was raised in the city in 1851. Within two years after that, work was undertaken on Salt Lake's great Mormon Temple, to be built of granite hauled over twenty miles to the site by ox teams. That monumental structure, designed by the noted pioneer architect Truman O. Angell, took forty years to complete. In the meantime, a huge tabernacle boasting the world's largest domed roof was finished in 1868. (Ironically, Brigham Young's hope to escape any government but his own was almost immediately thwarted when the United States took over the entire area that is now Utah as part of the territory it claimed at the conclusion of the Mexican War.)

Throughout much of the West the coming of the railroad had a profound effect on architectural developments. Portable houses could be shipped in and quickly thrown up as a new settlement sprouted. If the community flourished, sometimes entire blocks of such provisional structures were set afire and destroyed to be replaced by more substantial buildings. And in the wake of the railroad came eastern fashions in domestic and public architecture, more or less undigested or sophisticated, according to varying circumstances. Virtually all the styles of the later nineteenth and early twentieth centuries that have been discussed in the opening chapters of this book took their turns. In the eighties and nineties it was not uncommon for county commissioners to buy plans for courthouses, mostly showing the influence of Richardson's Romanesque designs, from salesmen whose illustrated folders represented samplings.

At terminal points, wherever the railroad lines started or ended, they gave rise to colorful and prosperous communities. After a few short years of railroad activity, Omaha, Nebraska, which had been chosen as the starting point for the transcontinental Union Pacific, sprang from a small frontier settlement to what one early visitor described as "the liveliest city in the United States." Cheyenne, the site chosen by the Union Pacific as a division point in 1867, was soon made the capital of the Wyoming Territory and in good time developed into the largest city in the state. Elsewhere, as the tracks were pushed forward, provisional terminals that had supplied the "front" of operations and that briefly provided all the raucous, brawling excitement rude men of action could contrive, gave up their streets and rickety false-fronted buildings to wolves and coyotes that wandered in from the surrounding wilderness.

During the 1860's–80's, successive reports of rich mine discoveries in Utah, Montana, Wyoming, Idaho, and Nevada kept the whole mountain area of the West in an almost constant ferment. In these parts the wandering prospector replaced the frontiersman and the farmer as the first tester of the unsettled land. Unlike the gradual, continuous advance of the frontier east of the Mississippi and into the plains, the early rush into the mountains was explosive and erratic. Men and women of every sort and from all points of the compass joined the quest for sudden wealth and gave the upland wilderness a cosmopolitan cast. In one mining gulch a reporter from Connecticut met an old Boston merchant successfully running a quartz mill and a Presbyterian deacon from Kansas retailing whiskey and selling pies on Sundays. At another site the inveterate traveler Bayard Taylor met a Norwegian merchant he had last seen in the arctic wastes of Lapland. A German miner from San Francisco devised a new system for getting at the precious ore, and intrigued experts from many countries came to examine this engineering achievement.

Some of the communities born of these gatherings of adventurers grew into enduring, thriving cities. Denver, for example, soon became the capital of a large region, and Last Chance Gulch matured into Helena, Montana. It was with the great, nearby silver strikes of the late 1870's and 1880's that Denver boomed into its permanent prominence. Earlier discoveries of gold had brought treasure hunters to the area, and for some years the fortune of the little city fluctuated with the alternating hopes and disappointments of those mining adventurers. Early in the game, in 1859, Horace Greeley, on his way to the diggings, paused at Denver to lecture on temperance and reported

Spruce Tree House is one of three majestic cliff dwellings constructed by Anasazi Indians at Mesa Verde in the thirteenth century. (The other two are Cliff Palace and Square Tower House.) By then, possibly because of raids by covetous nomads, the Indians had retreated from their well-constructed stone pueblo apartment houses on the mesa top to the greater security of the cliff dwellings built in yawning caves just beneath the mesa rim. Each of these villages was comprised of a vast assembly of rooms, towers, kivas, courtyards, and terraced paths. The architectural features of Spruce Tree House are generally similar to other Anasazi cliff dwellings in the area: small rectangular doorways constructed well above ground level; thin slabs of sandstone for doors; roofs set on stout logs; masonry walls generally plastered inside; and small windows for light and air. These tiny chambers served exclusively as sleeping quarters and for storage. The kiva, the subterranean ceremonial chamber and men's gathering place, may be visited at Spruce Tree via a ladder through a small hole in its roof on the courtyard.

Entrance to Kiva, Spruce Tree House

Spruce Tree House, Mesa Verde National Park, near Cortez, Colo. (1200–1300)

Explorers Lewis and Clark spent the first winter (1804–05) of their epic-making journey to the Pacific on the Upper Missouri River near the earth-mound villages of the Mandan tribe. These handsome, hospitable Plains Indians and their distinctive domed dwellings were captured for posterity by George Catlin on a canvas, "The Bull Society Dance," in 1832. Five years later the Mandans suddenly vanished, obliterated by a smallpox epidemic. At Fort Abraham Lincoln State Park in North Dakota, five Mandan earth mounds have been reconstructed on the excavated sites of the originals. The inner framework consists of four stout tree trunks set in a square and braced at the top by horizontal crossbeams. Willow branches were laid on top of the angled roof rafters and then were packed with earth to create the domical effect. The central section was excavated to form a row of built-in seats around the fire. An engraving by the Swiss artist Charles Bodmer reveals the interior of a Mandan lodge as a commodious, well-lit, and seemingly comfortable place.

Slant Indian Village, Fort Abraham Lincoln State Park, near Mandan, N.D. (as of 1750)

*Interior detail,
Mandan Earth Lodge,
Slant Indian Village*

Bolduc House, Ste. Genevieve, Mo. (about 1785)

Ste. Genevieve, the first permanent settlement within the present boundaries of Missouri, was founded in 1732 on the west bank of the Mississippi River by French fur traders and was originally part of the vast French territory of Louisiana. Even after the United States acquired the territory through the Louisiana Purchase in 1803, French influence and culture lingered on through the entire Mississippi Valley from New Orleans to Wisconsin. The Louis Bolduc House, built by a wealthy merchant, is a fine example of the French colonial style, with its oak timbers set upright into a stone foundation—the space between the uprights filled with clay and straw—and its steeply pitched hip roof forming a gallery around the house. The Amoureaux House, an older dwelling, dates from about 1770.

Amoureaux House, Ste. Genevieve, Mo. (about 1770)

Sod House, Pioneer Village, Minden, Nebr. (as of 1860's)

The Homestead Act of 1862 entitled an American citizen to lay claim to 160 acres of unappropriated government land, which became his after he lived on it and cultivated it for five years. At Beatrice, Nebraska, the Homestead National Monument commemorates the legislation, and the story-and-a-half Palmer-Epard log cabin illustrates the simplicity of the lives of the homesteaders. The Pioneer Village in Minden, Nebraska, has reconstructed a typical sod house of the treeless plains. The crude rafters of the soddy's roof were usually covered with earth and planted with grass to reduce erosion. Jacob Hamblin, a Mormon pioneer and Indian missionary in Utah, erected a two-story house of red sandstone roofed with hand-split cedar shingles to shelter his several wives and two dozen children.

Jacob Hamblin House, Santa Clara, Utah (1862)

Palmer-Epard Cabin, Homestead National Monument, near Beatrice, Nebr. (1867)

Coeur d'Alene Mission of the Sacred Heart, Cataldo, Idaho (1853)

In the mid-nineteenth century, Christian missionaries to the Indians of the trans-Mississippi West played an important role in the settlement of that region just as they had in the previous century in the Southwest. In 1838 the Shawnee Methodist Mission, founded in 1830 by the Reverend Thomas Johnson, was moved to its present site in Kansas on the Santa Fe and Oregon trails, near their points of origin. The mission at one time covered more than two thousand acres and had sixteen buildings in which Indian youths were taught English, crafts, and agricultural skills. During the Civil War the mission was used as a barracks; the Kansas State Historical Society has restored the site. In 1848 Jesuit Father Anthony Ravalli drew the plans for the Coeur d'Alene Mission of the Sacred Heart—the oldest building still standing in Idaho—which he and the Indians erected over the next several years. The huge beams and columns were hewn and dressed only by a broadax and were mortised and pegged together without nails. The façade shows some architectural flair with its Greek Revival and baroque elements, and the interior has a carved and painted ceiling and an altar of some note. It has recently been completely restored.

North Building, Shawnee Methodist Mission, Kansas City, Kans. (1845)

As the pioneers pushed westward across the plains, military outposts were established to protect the trails and to keep open the lines of communication. Just after the outbreak of the Black Hawk War in 1867, the Mormons under the leadership of Brigham Young built Old Cove Fort to protect travelers on the Salt Lake–Pioche stage line as well as to guard the newly installed telegraph line. Constructed of local black volcanic rock and rubble, the square fort has six rooms on both the north and south sides with prominent chimneys rising from each room. In the summer of 1874 the Custer expedition to the Black Hills reported the likelihood of a gold strike, and the first group of prospectors, led by John Gordon, arrived the following winter and erected a primitive stockade, shown below in its reconstructed state. During the 1860's and 1870's Fort Larned was the principal guardian of the Kansas segment of the Santa Fe Trail. The buildings around the four-hundred-foot-square parade ground were rebuilt in local yellow sandstone in the years following the Civil War.

Old Cove Fort, near Beaver, Utah (1867)

Gordon Stockade, Custer State Park, Custer, S.D. (as of 1875)

Fort Larned, Larned, Kans. (1860's)

OVERLEAF: *Front Street Reconstruction, Dodge City, Kans. (as of 1870's).* Founded with the coming of the Santa Fe Railroad in 1872, Dodge City soon became a major shipping center for cattle, a rendezvous for cowboys and Indians, gamblers and outlaws, and famous lawmen. The two-block reconstruction of store fronts, guided by old photographs, recalls those wide-open days.

Hôtel de Paris, Georgetown, Colo. (1875)

From 1859, when gold was first discovered in Central City, Colorado, a series of boom towns was spawned to support the mining operations extracting gold, silver, lead, copper, and zinc from rich veins in the Rocky Mountains. Here Louis du Puy constructed one of the most celebrated hostelries west of the Mississippi and ran the Hôtel de Paris as though it actually was in Paris. Georgetown also affords glimpses of amusing Victorian domestic vernacular, such as the detail of the doorway and fenestration illustrated at right. The semi ghost-town of Victor boasts a Masonic Hall with three richly treated pediments.

OVERLEAF: *Elkhorn, Mont. (1870's)*. In its boom days, Elkhorn produced about $14 million in gold and silver and provided no less than fourteen saloons for the thirsty miners.

Masonic Hall, Victor, Colo. (1890's)

Domestic Vernacular, Georgetown, Colo. (late 1800's)

Katz Building (Boley Clothing Company), Kansas City, Mo. (1908). Louis S. Curtiss, architect

Brown Palace Hotel, Denver, Colo. (1892). Frank E. Edbrooke & Company, architects

The two buildings illustrated here represent landmarks in the country's architectural development. The little-known pioneer Boley Clothing Company, now the Katz Building, in Kansas City was one of the first expressions of continuous cast-iron–mullioned strip-windows alternating with uninterrupted metal spandrels to form a curtain-wall façade. The venerable Brown Palace Hotel in Denver creates a delightful inner space in its nine-story lobby topped by an enormous stained-glass skylight. Balconies embellished with bronze panels open out on this great interior courtyard. The Guggenheim Museum in New York and the Hyatt Regency Hotel in Atlanta are direct descendants of Denver's spatial masterpiece.

Annunciation Priory, Bismarck, N.D. (1963). Marcel Breuer, architect; Hamilton P. Smith, associate

The Annunciation Priory of the Sisters of St. Benedict and its nearby affiliate, Mary College, occupy rolling sites on opposite sides of a hill overlooking the Missouri River. The powerful buildings constitute one of the country's best architectural groups concerned with the Roman Catholic religion and education. The priory is marked by a three-dimensional, 100-foot-high bell banner, recalling a similar one by Marcel Breuer at Collegeville, Minnesota (see page 492), that lends a vertical accent to the landscape and to the long, low building mass of the four main units. The circular Priory of St. Mary and St. Louis at Creve Coeur, Missouri, is a skillful exposition of concrete design. The lower tier of twenty-one-foot-high arches is surmounted by a second tier twelve feet high and topped by a thirty-two-foot arched steeple belfry.

Priory of St. Mary and St. Louis, Creve Coeur, Mo. (1962). Hellmuth, Obata & Kassabaum, architects

A wondrous web of simple plastic panels and intricate aluminum struts, based on R. Buckminster Fuller's geodesic principles, forms an ideal canopy for the Missouri Botanical Garden in St. Louis. The geodesic dome sheltering a prodigal array of plants is 175 feet in diameter and seventy feet high and forms a low vault that rests on five concrete piers. The exoskeletal framing of the Climatron is composed of hexagonal components of aluminum tubes in two planes connected by aluminum rods. A weather skin of some four thousand triangles of acrylic plastic is hung about a foot below this frame—the Plexiglas is unbreakable and permits photosynthesis. Inside under one partitionless roof, two major meteorological zones ranging from hot tropics to cool uplands are maintained by an ingenious air-conditioning system. A peripheral walk encircles the flourishing gardens on several levels and there is even a waterfall within.

Climatron, St. Louis, Mo. (1961). Murphy & Mackey, architects; Synergetics, Inc., dome engineers

The striking geometric form of the McDonnell Planetarium has made it a landmark since it appeared in St. Louis in the early 1960's. The planetarium dome nestles within the curves of the outer shell and an internal ramp around the half-dome leads to an observation deck on top. In Colorado, against the backdrop of the Rocky Mountains, the buildings of the Air Force Academy stand sharply etched on a partly natural, partly man-made acropolis.

RIGHT *and* OVERLEAF : *Chapel, Air Force Academy, and Exterior (detail), Colorado Springs, Colo. (1956-62). Skidmore, Owings & Merrill, architects.* The heavenward-thrusting spires of the chapel provide the architectural as well as the spiritual focus of the academy. Its dramatic profile has been likened to the folded plane wings on the flight deck of an aircraft carrier. Actually, it is comprised of a technically ingenious geometric steel-tube framing with aluminum panels separated by narrow bands of stained glass.

McDonnell Planetarium, St. Louis, Mo. (1963). Hellmuth, Obata & Kassabaum, architects

National Center for Atmospheric Research, near Boulder, Colo. (1967). I. M. Pei & Partners, architects

Situated on the edge of a mesa south of Boulder, Colorado, a complex of buildings—illustrated on these two and the following two pages—stands dramatically silhouetted against the backdrop of the Rockies and with the flat plains stretching before it.

OVERLEAF: *National Center for Atmospheric Research*. A winding road leads up to the summit and through a sculptured gate to the brownish-pink-colored concrete units—two tall structures connected by a lower base—of the Atmospheric Research Center. The two office and laboratory blocks, rising five stories above ground, flare out at the top like mysterious, hooded sentry posts. Narrow bands of dark windows run up the center of the broad sides of each tower and open up in wide canopied glass horizontals in the top-floor meeting spaces.

The United States Corps of Engineers has designed over fifty dams—two of which are illustrated here—thus making it the developer of the largest number of hydroelectric power plants in the country. One of its grandest architectural-engineering achievements is Libby Dam stretching over twenty-nine hundred feet across the rocky cleft gouged by the Kootenai River in northwestern Montana. The 448-mile Kootenai River rises in British Columbia, flows south into Montana, turns northwest through Idaho, and empties into Kootenay Lake in British Columbia. The building of the regal dam prompted a formal diplomatic treaty between the two nations to ensure proper attention to environmental concerns. Garrison Dam extends over eleven thousand feet—one of the world's longest earth-filled dams—across the Missouri River near Riverdale, North Dakota. Like the TVA undertaking, this dam has transformed an entire region, controlling and utilizing the river for irrigation, power, and recreation—the dam created 178-mile-long Lake Sakakawea.

Garrison Dam, Riverdale, N.D. (1959). U. S. Corps of Engineers, engineers; Charles T. Main, Inc., power plant designers

Libby Dam, Libby Mont. (1975). U. S. Corps of Engineers, engineers; Paul Thiry, architect

Base of Gateway Arch (detail)

Soaring 630 feet skyward on the levee of the Mississippi, Eero Saarinen's great stainless steel arch proudly proclaims St. Louis' historic gateway role in the settlement of the West. The nation's tallest man-made monument is situated in a national memorial park commemorating the vast expansion of the United States following Thomas Jefferson's Louisiana Purchase of 1803. Saarinen's catenary arch was raised nearby the famous Eads Bridge, which in 1874, in fact, opened up the trans-Mississippi West to the railroad. The arch is not only a great symbol of history, it is also a unique expression of the ongoing renaissance of downtown St. Louis. In cross section the arch is an equilateral triangle, fifty-four feet wide at the base tapering to seventeen feet at the tip. A capsule transporter in each leg carries visitors to an observation platform at the top, and a Museum of Westward Expansion occupies the underground visitor's center. The arch is a supreme achievement of twentieth-century American architecture, engineering, and sculpture.

Gateway Arch, Jefferson National Expansion Memorial, St. Louis, Mo. (1965).
Eero Saarinen & Associates, architects

FAR WEST & PACIFIC

ALASKA
CALIFORNIA
HAWAII
NEVADA
OREGON
WASHINGTON

West of the tall mountains that once seemed—and were in fact—such formidable barriers to migrants from the East lies the Pacific Coast, the restless edge of American dominion on the continent. During the last several generations, this long, relatively narrow region of the country, long since become easily accessible to easterners, has in many ways become the epitome of changing America. Here, the centuries-old westward movement has since World War II approached a climactic stage. In the course of recent years California has become the most populous state of the Union. Los Angeles has become the third largest city in the nation. As have some other fast-growing, western communities, Portland, Oregon, has even attempted to discourage the influx of new settlers, whose numbers threaten to burden its existing population with unwanted civic and economic problems (much as California tried to exclude the Oakies and the Arkies more than a generation ago during the Great Depression).

The West Coast is a region of many extremes, and of contrasts. In Mount Whitney (14,494 feet) it has the highest peak in the country, except for Alaska; nearby, Death Valley drops to 282 feet below sea level, the lowest point in the United States. There are rain-drenched forests in the north and scorching deserts to the south. In some parts these contrasts are so immediate that it is possible to swim in the ocean within view of snow-capped highlands, or swim in a desert pool overlooked by not-far-distant ski slopes. In spite of such sharp differences, however, there remains a fundamental uniformity that has helped to develop a special quality of life throughout most of the region, a quality of life that is importantly conditioned by the climate. Some years ago in the early autumn it was observed that at a given hour the temperature at Seattle, Portland, San Francisco, Los Angeles, and San Diego—and at Anchorage, Alaska—was at an even 72 degrees. Although that was an unusual phenomenon, it could hardly have happened in any other part of the world over such a wide range of latitude.

The millions of Americans who have settled in the Far West from every other part of the United States have been in good part attracted by this generally benign climate that makes possible a year-round way of life in the open. A large proportion of the populace is composed of fairly recent settlers. Within a very few generations they have produced a society that is in a real sense a synthesis of American society at large, adapted to a distinctive regional environment. Here, too, it is a land of extremes. "In a prosperous country," wrote the adopted California writer Wallace Stegner in 1959, "we are more prosperous than most; in an urban country, more urban than most; in a gadget-happy country, more addicted to gadgets; in a mobile country, more mobile; in a tasteless country, more tasteless; in a creative country, more energetically creative; in an optimistic society, more optimistic; in an anxious society, more anxious. Contribute regionally to the national culture? We *are* the national culture, at its most energetic end."

Long before eastern Americans had any awareness of the West Coast, men of other nations were scouting the possibilities of settlement in and domain over that remote area. In September, 1542, the Spanish explorer Juan Rodríguez Cabrillo landed at San

Diego Bay, the first European to step on California soil. (The name California was derived from that of Calafía, a legendary black Amazon who ruled over a far western island rich in gold.) Cabrillo sailed north, possibly as far as what is now the Oregon border, but returned to California without having found gold anywhere. There he died and was buried, the first European to be buried in California soil. The intrepid Englishman Sir Francis Drake apparently visited the San Francisco Bay area in 1579, after having cruised possibly as far north as the present state of Washington (and finding there only the "most vile, thicke and stinking fogges"), but he paused at that site only to await favorable weather for crossing the Pacific, without entering San Francisco Bay itself.

But it was not until two centuries later that interest in the American Pacific was seriously aroused. Then, during the last decade of the eighteenth century, a number of maritime powers—Britain, France, Holland, and even the infant United States—became aware of the colonial and commercial possibilities in those far western reaches; and Russian fur traders who had gained a solid hold in the Aleutians and Alaska through the discoveries of Vitus Bering, a Danish-born Russian Navy commander, were pushing southward to confront these others. The restored remains of their stockaded settlement at Fort Ross in northern California, built in 1812 and held by the Russians until 1841, may still be seen. Short of cash, Spain met these threats to her extended claims by wielding her most effective instrument of defense, her Sword of the Spirit. Under the inspired direction of Junípero Serra, a lame and aging Franciscan friar who traveled on mule-back, a chain of twenty-one red-tiled adobe missions was stretched up the coastal valleys at intervals of a day's march, with four modest presidios—fortified posts—for their protection. The first California mission was established at San Diego in 1769, the first presidio was founded at Monterey a year later. That same year a party under Gaspar de Portolá exploring the territory farther north by land spotted the majestic harbor that lay within the Golden Gate. In 1775, as other men far across the continent were stirring in rebellion against British rule, Manuel de Ayala took the first ship through the Golden Gate to survey the great untenanted bay within. (Cabrillo, Drake, and others had missed the port completely in their excursions up and down the coast.) The San Francisco presidio was dedicated in the summer of 1776, the unhappy season that saw Washington retreating before the British army.

The effort to settle California strained the resources of the Spanish outposts there. The primitive native Indians offered little resistance to the Spanish advances northward. One eighteenth-century French explorer described the straw huts of these indigenes as "the most miserable one could find anywhere." Father Junípero Serra and his companions baptised thousands of them and taught them the mysteries of farming and of adobe construction, but in the end, aside from the mission compounds, the colonizing efforts of the Spanish in California left very little trace. Nevertheless, ever anxious to affirm Spain's claims to the whole far western region, an expedition was sent to the Northwest in 1789. In 1778, on his tragic last voyage, Captain Cook had explored that area in quest of the Northwest Passage, and succeeded in charting the western coast as far north as the Bering Strait. Among his crew were William Bligh, later master of the *Bounty*, George Vancouver, who was subsequently to make a more detailed survey of the northwestern coast, and the young Connecticut Yankee John Ledyard, a corporal of the Marines who had joined the expedition just before the Declaration of Independence was signed. Ledyard was "painfully afflicted" with nostalgia at the sight of the American coast, he later wrote, although it was "more than 2,000 miles from the nearest part of New England." However, he noted that the Indians of that region, who had never before seen a white man, nevertheless carried European-made knives and bracelets. "No part of America," he concluded, "is without some sort of commercial intercourse, immediate or remote." Ledyard planned to return to the Pacific Northwest one day and make his fortune dealing in the abundance of furs to be had there from the natives in exchange for all but valueless trinkets.

When an expedition from Mexico arrived in those waters they were faced with English trading ships which had already established bases there and which repulsed the Spanish advances. Also present was the brig *Columbia* out of Boston with Captain Robert Gray in command. After garnering a cargo of precious furs for an ordinary chisel apiece, Gray returned to Boston via Hawaii and China, the first American sea captain to sail around the globe. Gray was welcomed at his home port by a "great concourse of citizens assembled on the various wharfs." To their amazement they saw Gray march off to call on Governor Hancock in the company of a Sandwich Islander clad in a feather cloak of golden suns set in flaming scarlet, with a gorgeous feather helmet to cap his elegance. Two years later Gray was back in the Pacific. He found ships of six other nations cruising those newly important waters. After swapping for more pelts at Nootka Sound, at the site of present-day Vancouver, Gray turned southward down the coast, hailing Captain George Vancouver who was on the way up with a commission to reclaim any territory in the Northwest seized earlier by the Spanish. On May 11, 1792, two days after Vancouver had, in passing, advised him that nothing of importance was to be observed to the south, Gray sailed into a "spacious harbor" and up a "fine river" which he named the Columbia, after his ship. He had discovered the great River of the West that had for centuries troubled the dreams of the world's most hopeful adventurers. To all intents the ancient riddle of the Northwest Passage was finally solved by the little brig from Boston. It was by then no anticlimax that its waters did not reach back into the eastern ocean. Gray had planted the flag of empire on the other side of the continent and opened a world-wide dominion for American trade. With the publication of Cook's account of his voyages, in 1784, which was peddled by no less a character than Parson Weems and was, as well, reprinted in the Pennsylvania *Packet*, Ledyard's dreams came back to life in the visions of other Americans. By the turn of the century, as Yankee traders found their way to the Northwest, in the wake of the *Columbia* the fur trade of that region had become an exclusively Boston business.

Just a dozen years later, Captain Meriwether Lewis and William Clark reached the Columbia River after a heroic overland trek and, in November, 1805, came to the coast where they "saw the waves like small mountains" rolling out of the Pacific. A few years after that John Jacob Astor, following John Ledyard's earlier design, launched his plan to drain the northwest country of its furs from both ends. The divide was to be from a post on the Columbia River, sea otters going west into the China Trade, beaver and other furs going to the American and European markets. Slipping in before Russia or England could lay claims to the spot, Astor's agents completed a stockaded fort—Fort Astoria—between the mouth of the Columbia River and Young's Bay. However, two years later the English took over that modest redoubt practically at the point of a frigate's guns, and changed the name to Fort George. At the time, that was too removed a matter for most Americans to worry over. As one representative derisively asked Congress as late as 1828, "What can lead any adventurer to seek the inhospitable regions of Oregon unless, indeed, he wishes to be a savage. . . ." As for Oregon entering the Union as a state, in 1843 congressional spokesmen ridiculed such a notion, pointing out that it would take ten months for representatives from such a remote point to travel to the District of Columbia and back again, which would leave them practically no time at either end of their business. Oregon became a state in 1859.

Nevertheless, the groundwork for the great migration had been laid, a migration which in the 1840's became almost epidemic as thousands of westering Americans crossed nearly two thousand miles of raw country to reach the wooded and well-watered lands of the northwest coast. To Horace Greeley this phenomenal wandering of peoples wore "an aspect of insanity." But by 1846, it was reported, the American Village in Oregon, flourishing under the good management of the Hudson's Bay Company, boasted "two churches, and 100 houses, store houses, etc. all of which has been built in five years." The Oregon Trail had become a national highway. Twenty years later Portland was a budding metropolis of a large region, with "water, gas, and Nicholson pavements; and had more of a solid air and tone, than any city we had seen since leaving the Missouri," as one visitor reported. "Several daily papers, two weekly religious ones, and a fine Mercantile Library, all spoke well for her intelligence and culture, while her Public Schoolbuildings and her Court-House would have been creditable anywhere. . . . Nearer to the Sandwich Islands and China, by several hundred miles, than California, she had already opened up a brisk trade with both, and boasted that she could sell sugars, teas, silks, rice, etc., cheaper than San Francisco." In 1873, Portland opened its New Market Theater, where celebrated artists drew audiences that came as far as two hundred miles to attend performances.

South of Oregon, for years California had hung like a ripe plum at the far end of Spain's vulnerable American empire. Little was changed by Mexico's revolt from Spain in 1821. United States squadrons, eager to improve this nation's opportunities, kept watch on the war vessels habitually maintained in the eastern Pacific by Russia, France, and England. Fired by one incentive or another, by the early 1840's Americans were already filtering into the territory through the mountain passes or by sea, some to settle, some to return home with tales of a fertile land of genial climate, of picturesquely decaying missions, and of tranquil ranches where *mañana* was always the day of action—a land of sunshine, lazy Indians, and gracious Latins. What a land it *could* be, mused Richard Henry Dana in *Two Years Before the Mast*, if it were governed and worked by people with Yankee enterprise. At Monterey and Santa Barbara he discovered that already most of the chief *alcaldes* were Yankees by birth, men who had "left their consciences at Cape Horn" and renounced their Protestantism to enjoy political liberty and trading opportunities in the land of sun-soaked, decaying Catholic missions. Dana had visited Yerba Buena, the future San Francisco, when that peninsula site had nothing to show but a few adobe huts besides its presidio and nearby mission. But, like others before him, he foresaw the ultimate importance of the place with its magnificent harbor rimmed with impressive hills. In a few years the enterprising people Dana looked for were arriving in earnest. By the winter of 1847-48 the little settlement had grown into a modest trading community with about eight hundred people, two small hotels, a few shops, and a sprinkling of private residences.

The most active focus of American interest in California was the semifeudal fort that had been built by John Augustus Sutter, directly in the line of overland travel from the East at a site that would become the present-day Sacramento. When California "revolted" against Mexico, General Vallejo and his brother were imprisoned in that compound, and in July, 1846, the American flag was raised over it. In 1841, the Russians, who had been hunting fur seals and sea otters out of Fort Ross for the past twenty-nine years, had sold their outpost to Sutter for $30,000 in gold and produce. (Their chapel, stockade, and blockhouse have been restored, and the Commander's House, an almost unaltered example of Russian log housing, all may be seen there today.) It was near there a year and a half later that "some kind of mettle was found in the tail race that looks like goald," as a contemporary record announced. Further reports embellished that statement with all but incredible claims, and an unprecedented gold rush was on its way. President Polk solemnly acknowledged that a strike had been made that would make Cortez seem like a smalltime operator.

Men who had never before dreamed of leaving home found themselves swept into one of the great pioneering adventures of the age—or of any other age, for that matter. This great treasure hunt took on something of the fervor of a crusade. Groups went to church to receive blessings before starting out, and sometimes the preacher left his pulpit to join them on their way. Farmers, clerks, doctors, lawyers, mechanics, left their callings and joined men of leisure to head westward to pan and dig for the precious metal. One forty-niner reported that San Francisco attracted "one of the most heterogeneous masses that ever existed since the building of the tower of Babel." Hopeful prospectors came from France, Germany, England, Japan, China, Australia, Peru, Chile, Mexico, as well as from other parts of the United States—men of all nations, creeds, and colors, dressed in every variety of costume, and babbling a medley of tongues. There were "Yankees of every possible variety, native Californians in *sarapes* and sombreros, Chilians, Sonorians, Kanakas from Hawaii, Chinese with long tails, Malays armed with everlasting creeses, and others in whose embrowned and bearded visages it was impossible to recognize any special nationality." Among them, according to one witness, were more well-informed and clever men than might be found in any other community of its size. In 1851 there were 136 lawyers in the city, more than half of them from eastern cities and some from the Midwest; and there were, it was reported, a sprinkling of women, most of whom were "neither maids, wives, nor widows."

For some time to come architectural niceties could wait until at least minimal accommodations could be contrived for the growing and floating populations, be they sheds, tents, or whatever. Houses of one sort or another were going up at the rate of fifteen to thirty a day, without satisfying the demand. Some were imported from Canton to be raised by Chinese carpenters. Others were imported prefabricated from the East and from England. Ships deserted by sailors who had quit their posts to try their luck in the gold fields were pulled up on the beach to serve as lodgings and warehouses. The flimsily built city was burned nearly to the ground half a dozen times during the first few years of its growth, but it shot up again after each disaster to harbor a growing population drawn from every corner of the earth, as happened so dramatically after the devastating fire and earthquake of 1906. By the end of the Civil War it had a population of more than one hundred thousand persons and a history like Alladin's palace. It was accurately reported to be "far more cosmopolitan than any other city except New York." Architecturally, the vigor and the confidence in the city's unlimited possibilities is probably best represented by the colonnaded Palace Hotel, opened in 1875, with its great glass-roofed center courtyard where San Franciscans still dine in splendor. (The hotel, now known as The Sheraton Palace, was destroyed in the fire and earthquake of 1906, but was quickly rebuilt along the original lines.)

Parenthetically, the Boston ships that plied the western waters were as well known in Hawaii. China Traders and whalemen, in fact, made those Pacific islands practically a suburb of Boston and, according to one visiting mariner, almost a facsimile of the New England city in some spots. For years the most conspicuous building in Honolulu, and a landmark for seamen, was the large church built of coral blocks by American missionaries in the image of a New England frame meetinghouse. Looking back on his own adventures in the South Seas, Herman Melville earnestly thought for a while that his countrymen had more to learn from the natives of those parts, cannibals though some of them were, than the natives could learn from the missionaries.

The first white men to visit the islands of Hawaii (then known as the Sandwich Islands) did not come there to conquer the land and subjugate its people. However, the advent of Europeans and, later, Americans inevitably resulted in vital changes in the

Meanwhile, north of California, Oregon and Washington had also been spurred to new growth when a transcontinental railroad reached that area in 1883. In 1870 more persons were living in San Francisco than in Oregon and Washington combined. Then, between 1880 and 1890, the population of Seattle increased more than twelve times over; Tacoma's, more than thirty-six fold in that same decade. Although Portland also grew, it lost its pre-eminence to its northern neighbors.

Still farther north, in 1867 Secretary of State William H. Seward purchased the huge Alaska territory from the Russians for $7,200,000, a bargain which was commonly referred to at the time as "Seward's Folly." (The price paid was less than two cents an acre.) The Russians, who had claimed this land for more than a century past, were at this point—following the Crimean War—eager to strip off their outlying possessions in order to gather strength for a struggle with Great Britain for the control of Asia. They had, moreover, already reaped a colossal harvest of furs from these northern climes. The impress they left on Alaska was picturesque but generally insignificant. All that is left today of their imperial adventure in Alaska are a few unpretentious structures still standing among the colorful totem poles and other artifacts of native origin. Under American administration the pattern of life in Alaska changed little for years to come.

Then in 1897 the S. S. *Excelsior* and the S. S. *Portland* came down from Alaska with a great fortune in gold drawn from the streams and mountains of that farthest North American territory. Seattle became the nation's chief link with Alaska, as several hundred thousand treasure hunters came to the city. By 1910 the population of the state of Washington was twice that of Oregon. Alaska went through its period of rough and lawless mining camps—a period made romantic by the writings of Jack London and Rex Beach. It did not get a territorial representative in Congress until 1906, and even then did not enjoy self-government for another six years. Alaska's greatest boom would come with the approach of World War II, when the area's strategic importance became a matter of national concern and its unfathomable natural resources a matter of growing interest. In 1959 it became the largest state in the Union, some two and a third times as large as Texas.

Throughout its history the Far West has faced the problem of water: too much in a few areas, not enough in by far the greater part of the region. To control and distribute the flow where it was destructive or imbalanced, to introduce it where the supply was otherwise meager or nonexistent, to harness it for power needed throughout the most rapidly growing region of the United States, required heroic measures. Without water supplies contrived by ingenious means and often from far distances, much of southern California would have remained virtually a desert. Hoover Dam, described in the previous chapter, has enabled southern California—along with other regions—to tap the great reserves piled up in Lake Mead by the Colorado River. Shasta Dam, north of Sacramento and at the head of the Central Valley Reclamation Project, stores enough water to serve two million acres of land, the agricultural heartland of California. Another great enterprise, the California Water Project, dwarfs every other water-transfer system in history. Farther north, the Grand Coulee Dam in eastern Washington, the world's most massive concrete dam, is one element of a project that, in all its ramifications, will serve still another empire of land in the Columbia River Basin with its increasing population. On one of the state buildings in Sacramento is inscribed a line from a popular nineteenth-century poem: "Bring me men to match my mountains." Such were the men who envisioned, planned, engineered, and realized these vast constructional schemes—modern pioneers who have opened up new frontiers for their restless fellow countrymen.

The problems and possibilities that contemporary architecture confronts in the states facing the Pacific Ocean are basically the same as they are elsewhere in the country. Here as elsewhere the planner has been freed from the necessity of limiting his project only to locally available materials. The natural materials of the entire world and new synthetic ones are accessible to architects everywhere in developed areas. Technological advances have made human habitation possible in almost any environmental circumstances (including outer space). Communication at the speed of light and transportation faster than sound have made the exchange of ideas, in architecture and engineering as well as in all other matters, virtually instantaneous. However, the tendency of such factors to reduce architectural designs to a universal idiom, as encouraged by the theories and practices of the so-called international school, has been countered by other tendencies that reassert a traditional regionalism in architecture. Frank Lloyd Wright, a modernist if there ever was one, did this by disassociating regionalism from its old dependence on archaic, historic formulas and orienting it towards the living present. Other architects who have worked in the Far West—John Yeon and Pietro Belluschi in the Pacific Northwest and William Wilson Wurster, Harwell Harris, and Gardner Dailey in California, for example—have won international respect for their essentially regional approach to architectural problems. In very recent years a threatened lack of the energy and resources needed to overcome demands of local circumstances by costly expedients has led to more imaginative and innovative accommodations to local climates and local expectations. For various sound and practical, as well as esthetic, reasons, regionalism remains a continuing aspect of American architectural progress.

OVERLEAF: *La Purísima Concepción Mission, Lompoc, Calif. (as of 1818)*. Occupying an unspoiled little valley, La Purísima Concepción Mission was first established in 1787 some four miles southwest of its present location. In 1812 it was destroyed by an earthquake. A decision was made the next year to move to the site the mission now occupies on the famous Camino Real. It was the eleventh of the twenty-one Franciscan missions stretching from San Diego to Sonoma, 650 miles to the north. In 1824, three years after Mexican independence from Spain, the local Indians revolted. In 1834 the mission was secularized, and after that the entire establishment began its decline. There were further earthquakes, and vandalism added to the destruction. However, from 1934 to 1939 the mission was carefully rebuilt, and this splendid reconstruction provides a convincing indication of the full cycle of mission life, its functions of housing and converting Indians and of teaching them skills, of the shops and quarters required by such routine activity, of the facilities for accommodating travelers, and, of course, of the chapel used for religious purposes. This was one of the most ambitious reconstructions in the Far West.

San Diego de Alcalá, near San Diego, Calif. (1813)

On July 16, 1769, Father Junípero Serra founded the mission San Diego de Alcalá, the first and "mother mission" of the chain of missions that were subsequently established at intervals up the western coast. Moved in 1774 from its original site on Presidio Hill in what is now Old Town San Diego, the mission seen today is the fourth of its name and the third on this site. The present church, completed in 1813, with its complex of patio, garden, mission school and quarters, is evocative of the mission era in California. San Carlos de Borromeo at Carmel was the second mission in the chain and the final resting place of Father Serra and his successor, Father Fermín Francisco de Lasuén. Completely restored, with its lovely gardened court-yard, the stoutly constructed stone church has an unusual vaulted roof, two towers of unequal size, and a fine baroque star-shaped window over the prominent central doorway.

San Carlos de Borromeo, Carmel, Calif. (1797)

Russian Blockhouse, Sitka, Alaska (as of about 1805)

The octagonal Russian blockhouse illustrated above commemorates Sitka, Alaska's, early days as a fortified fur-trading post. Old Sitka, founded in 1799 by the manager of the Russian-American Trading Company, Alexander Baranof, was burned in 1802 in a surprise attack by the Tlingit Indians. Baranof subsequently resettled about six miles to the south, and within a short time Sitka became the flourishing capital of Russian America. Eventually the Tlingits returned to Sitka, which remained a thriving fur-trading center for over sixty years. On nearby Castle Hill, which was the site of Baranof's castle, in October of 1867 the Russian flag was lowered and the American flag was raised over Alaska for the first time. The native Alaskan Indians left their cultural imprint on the land in the form of their magnificent totem poles. These painted wood carvings celebrated family history, mythological beliefs, deaths, and tribal events. The Old Witch Totem Pole at left, carved by the Haidas, was moved to Juneau from Prince of Wales Island in southern Alaska.

Old Witch Totem Pole, Juneau, Alaska (about 1860)

737

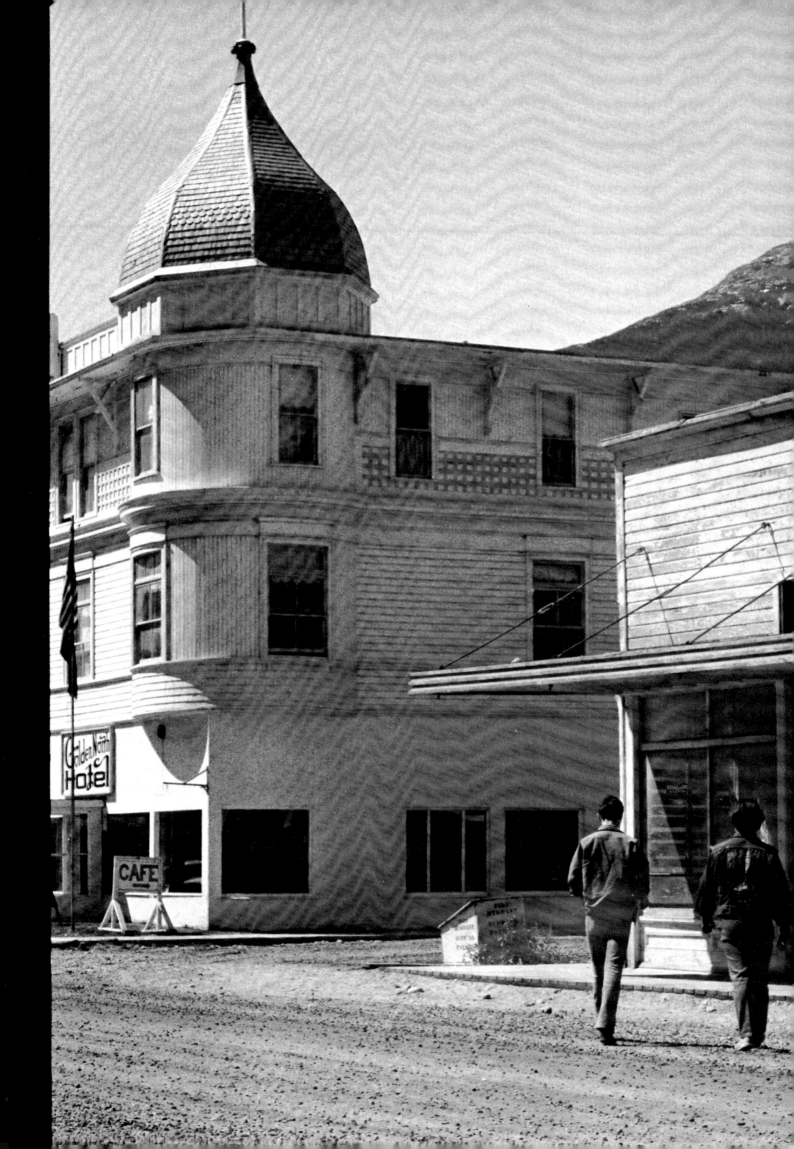

In their quest for suitable forms and designs for their public buildings, American communities have looked in all directions. With all its classical dignity the Capitol at Washington, D.C., set a precedent for the new nation that could hardly be ignored as regional and local state houses and courthouses were raised across the land. Traces of such classicism, mingling pleasantly enough with Victorian features, can be seen in the state capitol at Carson City, Nevada, built just over a century ago by an architect from California. The roundheaded paired windows, the prominent quoins, and the capably handled hexagonal cupola contribute strong accents to the design of the structure. At Spokane, Washington, on the other hand, the county courthouse owes a recognizable debt to the French châteaux of the Loire Valley. It was built at a time when Richard Morris Hunt was lining Fifth Avenue with fashionable buildings in the châteaux manner. The Pioneer Post Office and Courthouse at Portland, Oregon, is the oldest standing federal structure in the Northwest, a mellow and pleasant reminder of the classical dignity of the faraway National Capitol, built almost a century earlier.

Pioneer Post Office and Courthouse, Portland, Oreg. (1873).
Alfred B. Mullett, architect

State Capitol, Carson City, Nev. (1870).
Joseph Gosling, architect

County Courthouse, Spokane, Wash. (1895). W. A. Ritchie, architect

New Market Block, Portland, Oreg. (1872). Piper & Burton, architects

Like almost every other city of consequence in the nation, Salem and Portland in Oregon went through a cast-iron phase in the nineteenth century. As everywhere else, the metal fronts of these buildings generally followed formal historical designs, such as had originally been realized in carved stone. Salem's Ladd & Bush branch of the U.S. National Bank was patterned directly after the Ladd & Tilton Bank built in Portland in 1859. The almost identical cast-iron façades of the two buildings were turned out by the Willamette Iron Foundry and are examples of the finest cast-iron work in the country. When the Salem Bank was expanded in 1969 by the architectural firm of Skidmore, Owings & Merrill, carefully preserved sections of the old Portland bank, which had been replaced by a new structure in 1955, were incorporated into the addition. The first floor of Portland's old three-story New Market Block, now used as a garage, presents a startlingly rich mixture of white-painted cast-iron columns and fancifully carved wood cornice.

Ladd & Bush Bank, Salem, Oreg. (1869). John Nestor, architect

Pioneer Square Historic District Redevelopment, Seattle, Wash. (1890's; 1970's)

Spritely in spite of its years, having survived fire, earthquake, semineglect, and even scorn, in a once deteriorating section of downtown Los Angeles, the five-story Bradbury Building remains a treasure of its architectural kind. Lavish use of French-fashioned wrought iron, especially in the open elevator cages, distinguishes its skylit central court. Like an increasing number of other cities, Seattle is awakening to the architectural heritage from its early years. The Pioneer Square area was once the heart of the old city. Among the historic district's attractive features is the glass and cast-iron pavilion, which originally stood over underground municipal restrooms and was restored in 1972 to its present use as a bus-stop shelter.

Bradbury Building, Los Angeles, Calif. (1893). George H. Wyman, architect

David B. Gamble House, Pasadena, Calif. (1908). Greene & Greene, architects

Hollyhock (Barnsdall) House, Los Angeles, Calif. (1920). Frank Lloyd Wright, architect

In 1907 Henry Mather Greene and his brother Charles Sumner Greene were commissioned by Mr. and Mrs. David Berry Gamble to design a house for them in Pasadena, California. The Gamble House "will be somewhat Japanese in feeling," reported a local newspaper when plans were announced. The resulting structure remains today the most complete and best preserved of the Greene brothers' "California bungalows." The structural woodwork, inside and out, expresses elements of the composition and design—the rounded and corbeled beams that support the overhanging eaves and porches constitute a decorative pattern that casts shadows across the hand-split cedar shingles of the walls. Hand-finished teak, mahogany, quartered oak, cedar, and other attractive woods were used for the paneling and trim of the interior. Fixtures and furnishings were also designed by the architects as part of the totally integrated scheme. About ten years later Frank Lloyd Wright designed the famous Hollyhock House for Aline Barnsdall, the first of seven of his works in the Los Angeles area. The house suggests a Mayan influence in its plain concrete walls set off by a band of rich decoration, an abstract motif of the hollyhock in the cast concrete on both exterior and interior.

Mann's (Grauman's) Chinese Theater, Los Angeles, Calif. (1927). Meyer & Holler, architects

Architect Bernard R. Maybeck, even with his Beaux-Arts classical training, was at heart a romantic eclectic. For the Palace of Fine Arts at the Panama-Pacific International Exposition of 1915 in San Francisco, Maybeck sketched a building of vanquished grandeur in the manner of a Piranesi engraving. Comprised of an arc-shaped gallery, an elliptical colonnade, and a circular rotunda, the Palace was constructed of a mixture of plaster of Paris and hemp fiber over a wood frame meant to be demolished after the fair. But as the years passed, the colonnade and rotunda grew dearer to the hearts of San Franciscans, and in 1959 philanthropist Walter S. Johnson donated two million dollars which the state of California matched for its rebuilding in permanent materials. In Santa Barbara the handsome county courthouse epitomizes that area's continuing romance with the Spanish colonial style. And an exotic movie palace has survived from Hollywood's heyday in the twenties. In the forecourt of what was long known as Grauman's (now Mann's) Chinese Theater are impressed in cement hand and foot prints of the famous movie stars.

OVERLEAF: *First Church of Christ, Scientist, Berkeley, Calif. (1910). Bernard R. Maybeck, architect.* Constructed with the most modern industrial materials then available, the Christian Science church combines a Renaissance plan with hints of Gothic tracery, Romanesque columns, Byzantine decoration, and Japanese timberwork in great harmony.

County Courthouse, Santa Barbara, Calif. (1920). William Mooser, architect

Palace of Fine Arts, San Francisco, Calif. (1915; rebuilt 1967). Bernard R. Maybeck, architect

Ghirardelli Square, San Francisco, Calif. (1863 and 1893-1915; 1970). Wurster, Bernardi & Emmons, architects;
Lawrence Halprin & Associates, landscape designers

The Greater San Francisco Chamber of Commerce with federal aid recently made a survey of its old commercial buildings to determine their soundness for rehabilitation. Among others, the three projects here illustrated enrich the urban scene of the bay city. The most imaginative and most successful redevelopment, conceived before the survey, is the transformation of the four-story Ghirardelli chocolate factory of 1915 and a half dozen nondescript loft and residential structures into an engaging multilevel shopping, strolling, and dining center. A lively fountain by Ruth Asawa, landscaped terraces, cheerful lighting, and amusing shops all add to the pleasant experience of Ghirardelli Square. Near Fisherman's Wharf the three-story brick block of the Cannery, once owned by Del Monte, has been sandblasted to its original richness, an arcade placed on the upper floors, and a courtyard added at street level to entice customers into the new boutiques and bars. A glass-enclosed exterior elevator, an escalator, and a broad stairway tend to draw one within. The Ice Houses, two sizeable old cold storage facilities newly connected by an all-glass bridge, are now used as showrooms for the contract furniture and home furnishings trades.

OVERLEAF: *Auditorium Forecourt Fountain, Portland, Oreg. (1970). Lawrence Halprin & Associates, designers.* This block-square fountain, with its terraces and platforms, its cascades and still pools, its flat decks and secret caverns, serves as brilliant urban design and is one of the great attractions of the Portland city scene.

The Cannery, San Francisco, Calif. (1903; 1968).
Esherick, Homsey, Dodge, and Davis, architects

The Ice Houses, San Francisco, Calif. (1914; 1968).
Wurster, Bernardi & Emmons, architects

779

Marin County Government Center, San Rafael, Calif. (1962; 1969).
Frank Lloyd Wright, architect (1962); William Wesley Peters and
Taliesin Associated Architects, architects (1969)

The Marin County Government Center is Frank Lloyd Wright's largest creation and the most spectacular civic building in the country. Striding across the landscape for some seven hundred feet over hill and dale, increasing its depth in the valleys and cutting it on the ridges, with its tiers of arches it recalls the famous first-century B.C. Roman Pont du Gard in southern France. Wright's noted solicitude for the landscape has produced a fascinating sociability between structure and site. The building was basically conceived as a long, sky-lit spine lined with a double row of offices. Three tunnels for auto traffic pierce its base. A pylon (with boiler stack within) punctuates the mid-point of the complex.

The keenly designed and engineered Oakland-Alameda County Coliseum comprises a circular earth plinth on which rests a drum framed by thirty-two gigantic (fifty-seven-foot-high) X-members of reinforced concrete that were poured in place, topped by an eave-level compression ring, 420 feet in diameter. From this ring ninety-six cables are slung to the small tension ring at the center, and on this net of cables the roof is laid. A seventy-foot-high wall of gray glass next to the frame, but independent of that structure, encloses an inner area that accommodates as many as fifteen thousand spectators. The San Diego Stadium seats fifty-thousand spectators in armchair comfort and with good views of the proceedings. Facilities for vertical circulation—four cylinders of elevators for top-level seats, high-speed, reversible escalators, and six spiral ramps, each structurally independent—embrace the modified horseshoe arena.

Stadium, San Diego, Calif. (1967). Frank L. Hope & Associates, architects and engineers

Oakland-Alameda County Coliseum, Oakland, Calif. (1966). Skidmore, Owings & Merrill, architects

Sea Ranch, Calif. (1965-   ). Moore, Lyndon, Turnbull & Whitaker, architects of the condominium; Lawrence Halprin & Associates, planners

Situated a bit more than one hundred miles north of San Francisco, the Sea Ranch enterprise covers a ten-mile stretch of rolling, lovely land rising from the Pacific to meadows and wooded hills. Primarily an area for second homes, it is a remarkably well-planned development, undertaken only after considerable research into environmental problems and possibilities. To ensure maximum freedom of land, "clusters and commons" of houses were grouped together to leave the ground about them open to all property owners; the houses are angled so that none impede the view of those behind. Ten apartments, redwood town houses on a seagirt point, form a small hilltown condominium. After close study of wind patterns, angled or shed roof designs were planned to create tranquil lee-side shelter. The Kukui Garden project on Oahu is one of the finest housing developments undertaken by the Federal Housing Administration in any of the fifty states of the Union. This large complex, which accommodates 820 families, has been compactly but imaginatively planned. Six-story duplex units add variety to the basic three-story row houses. The latter combine a ground-floor flat with a duplex above reached by outside stairs. A community and recreational center acts as the focus of the development, with a fifteen-story tower at one corner reserved for the elderly. There are well-considered housing details, such as jalousie windows for protection from the sun, along with excellent apartment planning. The Portland Center project, with its three rental residence towers and adjacent shopping mall, garage, and related facilities, is a general model for middle- and upper-income urban housing. Located within easy walking distance of the central business district, only a block or so from the civic auditorium, and replacing the substandard structures that had previously stood on the site, this residential and commercial development has lured taxpaying citizens back from the suburbs.

Kukui Garden Housing, Honolulu, Oahu Island, Hawaii (1970). Daniel, Mann, Johnson & Mendenhall, architects

Portland Center, Portland, Oreg. (1968). Skidmore, Owings & Merrill, architects

Mauna Kea Beach Hotel, Mauna Kea Beach, Hawaii Island, Hawaii (1965). Skidmore, Owings & Merrill, architects

The main building of the Mauna Kea Beach Hotel contains three levels of bedrooms, half of them facing the ocean, half the mountains, each level stepping back as the structure rises to create tiers of privately screened balconies on both sides. These tiers do not meet at the top of the building, so its center is open to the sky. The planting is so deft that at times it is difficult to tell outside from in, which adds to the hotel's distinction. This unfolding and interweaving of spaces, both vertical and lateral, creates an extraordinary effect. With its roof open to the sun by day and the stars by night, with full-grown palms reaching towards the sky from the center of the building, and with the stepped-back levels that form the inner gallery corridors and overlook the garden courts, this architectural wonderland displays vitality at every turn.

State Capitol, Honolulu, Oahu Island, Hawaii (1969).
John Carl Warnecke & Associates and Belt, Lemmon & Lo, architects

The large central court of Honolulu's state capitol is also open to the sky, and with its sharply delineated contrast of lateral and vertical spaces develops potent architectural forces. This courtyard also imaginatively serves as a platform for viewing the two chambers for the Senate and the House of Representatives, which occupy lower levels on opposite sides and whose end walls are of glass enabling the public to watch proceedings. (There are, of course, interior spectator galleries.) The late Richard Neutra was a transplanted Viennese who added immeasurably to architectural developments in the United States, especially in California where he lived. His work includes some of the finest houses in the country. Among his larger commissions is the excellent Orange County Courthouse at Santa Ana.

Orange County Courthouse, Santa Ana, Calif. (1968). Richard and Dion Neutra
in collaboration with Ramberg & Lowrey, architects

Oakland Museum, Oakland, Calif. (1968). Kevin Roche, John Dinkeloo & Associates, architects; Dan Kiley, landscape architect

University Art Museum, University of California, Berkeley, Calif. (1970).
Mario J. Ciampi, architect; Richard Jorasch and Ronald Wagner, associates

The Oakland Museum—or museums, for there are three that are interconnected —is a highly imaginative architectural complex. Occupying four city blocks, the entire scheme comprises a series of landscaped terraces (some with works of art), museum wings, lawns, and gardens. All the outdoor promenades are in fact marked by luxuriant planting and the changes of level and of spatial relationships that make exploration of the area a dramatic experience. The several buildings provide exhibition spaces for art, cultural history, and natural science, each with its own identity but tied together in a manageable whole that can be easily recognized. At nearby Berkeley, the interior of the University Art Museum presents a galaxy of tantalizingly ramped and tiered spaces, all bathed in illumination from a central skylight. The building's concept is based on five double-decked platforms of exhibition space, lapped like cards in a fan formation, all pivoting on the central, catalyzing entry court which also serves for displays of art.

OVERLEAF: *Sculpture by Alexander J. Calder, University Art Museum, University of California, Berkeley, Calif. (1968).* A superb steel composition by Calder introduces the angled, stepped-back concrete walls of the Berkeley museum.

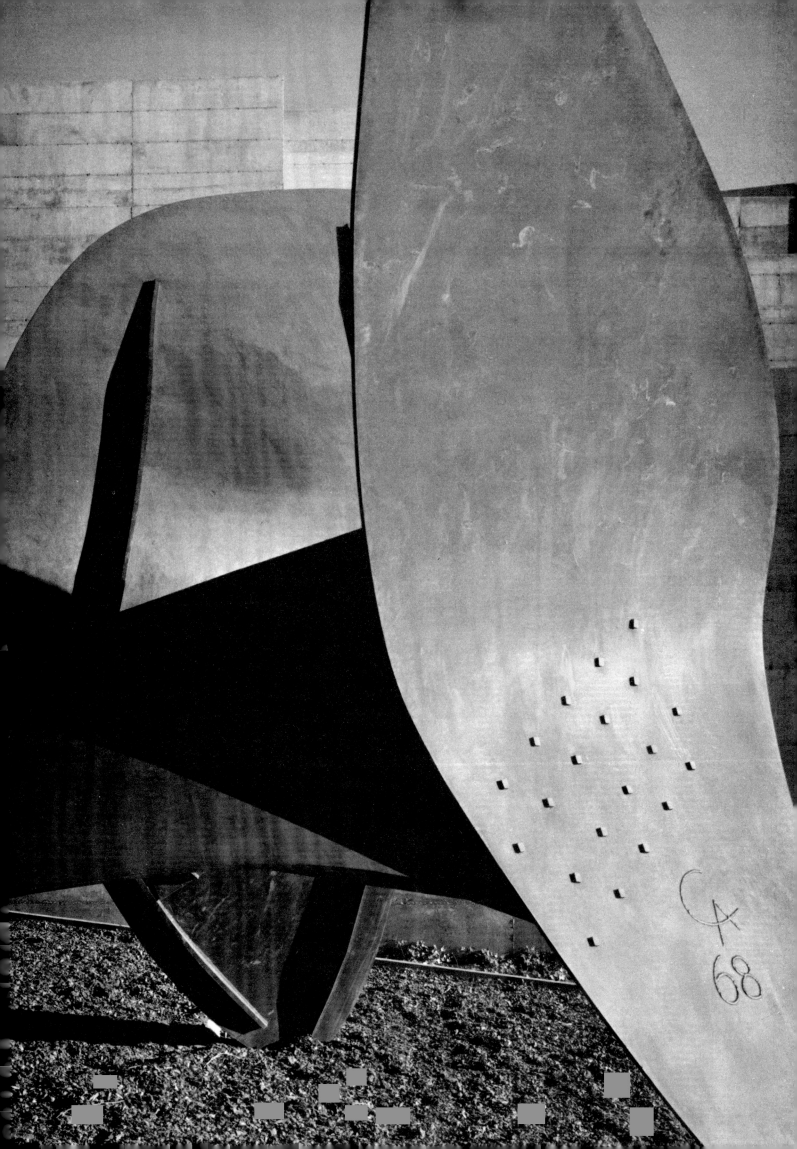

Foothills College, Los Altos Hills, Calif. (1961). Ernest J. Kump with Masten & Hurd, architects

Library, Mount Angel Abbey, St. Benedict, Oreg. (1970). Alvar Aalto, architect; DeMarks & Wells, associates

Washoe County Library, Reno, Nev. (1966). Hewitt C. Wells, architect; Mitchell J. Servan, landscape architect

The thirty-nine buildings of Foothills College epitomize the California pavilion approach, and the college has understandably exerted enormous influence on instructional building. In general appearance Foothills looks like a well-knit, one-story, educational village of vaguely Japanese ancestry, with friendly residential scale. The wide overhangs of all buildings serve as outdoor corridors (there are no inner ones) creating a continuity (plus some exposure during the brief rainy season). The Mount Angel Abbey library, which is used by the Benedictine abbey's high school, college, and seminary, is one story in height at the entry level, then, taking advantage of its hillside site, develops three and a half floors, two of stacks plus a mezzanine, with a basement dropped below on the north side of the building. It is difficult to know whether to classify the Washoe County Library as a space for the perusal of books and periodicals or as an inviting botanical garden. The luxurious planting and several small fountains set the stage, with projecting disc-shaped platforms, for reading perched among the greenery.

Administration Building, East-West Center, University of Hawaii, Honolulu, Oahu Island, Hawaii (1963).
I. M. Pei & Partners with Young & Henderson, architects

A two-story lounge, flanked on both long sides by six substantial piers with arched heads, constitutes the kernel of the Administration Building of the East-West Center (the Center for Cultural and Technical Interchange Between East and West). On these piers rest twin continuous beams which run the full length of the building. At right angles atop these beams are placed a series of lateral beams that span the width of the structure and are cantilevered fifteen feet beyond the long sides. On top, the inset offices are capped by a deep, fasciaed roof. In the rear a delightful oriental garden, its stream stocked with large goldfish, lures the stroller. The Evergreen State College seems to be carved out of its bosky site. An intimacy with nature and a close relationship of students with professors accord the school's informal philosophy. An airy library with a high bell tower dominates a central mall, which is loosely enclosed by this and other buildings.

Daniel Evans Library, The Evergreen State College, Olympia, Wash. (1972).
Durham, Anderson, Freed Company, architects and planners

Garden, East-West Center

Student Union, San Francisco State University, Calif. (1975). Paffard Keatinge Clay, architect

The Student Union at San Francisco State University presents an imaginative profile akin to sculpture as well as to architecture. The vista is dominated by the two buildings with shiplike prows extending skyward with, on one, a stepped roof doubling as a dramatic open-air amphitheater and sunning spot. Its angled geometry extends an enthusiastic welcome to the student. On a two-thousand-acre rolling site John Carl Warnecke has designed a master plan for the University of California at Santa Cruz comprised of a series of individual colleges, each with its own dormitories, dining and recreation rooms, together with classrooms and faculty offices. Kresge College, illustrated below, resembles a gigantic stage set nestled amongst the redwoods. The white wood frame and stucco buildings enlivened by bold color accents are angled along a spinal path to create a small village atmosphere. The resulting spatial intimacy imparts a sense of belonging to the students.

Kresge College, University of California, Santa Cruz, Calif. (1974). MLTW/Moore, Turnbull Associates, architects

Situated on Sitka's harbor overlooking a panorama of sea, islands, and distant snow-capped mountains, the Centennial Building serves as a community and convention center. The handsome structure of local stone base and wood sides is dominated by its roof of well-sculptured planes. Occupying its front section is a small regional museum under the direction of the Sitka Historical Society. A colorful Tlingit Indian ceremonial canoe in front provides an appropriate introduction to the exhibits within, which include a thoroughly researched model of Sitka as of 1867. In Washington, overlooking the Spokane River is an opera house-convention center, the permanent building of Spokane's Expo 74. The auditorium roof angles upward to the stage area at the west and is separated from the one-level convention center at the east by a covered mall. Both units are wrapped in smooth concrete panels with dark glass for contrast. At the far end of the entry there are steps leading down to the river, where outdoor concerts are given in the summertime. The performers take their places on floating platforms and the audience occupies the steps.

Centennial Building, Sitka, Alaska (1967). Allen McDonald, architect

Riverpark Center, Spokane, Wash. (1974). Walker, McGough, Foltz-Lyerla, architects

In the last decade several cities in California have provided commendable public architecture to house their civic functions. The winning design for the limited competition for the Los Gatos Civic Center placed the buildings for administration, police, and library on an elevated square plaza, with the council chamber on the lower level. The construction materials of the well-scaled buildings—concrete with red brick walls—are repeated in the design of the attractive plaza surrounded by landscaped terraces. The design for the bold new civic center in Thousand Oaks atop its hill site was selected in a national competition. The two one-story buildings, strongly stated in concrete with heavy parapets which shield the band of windows and hide the roof-top parking area, are barely visible from the residential community below. San Bernardino has combined a city hall and convention center in one bold structure of dark brown glass. A spacious entry porch resting on pilotis welcomes the visitor to the elevated civic offices and the convention center. The building is stepped in profile and chamfered on the corners and edges to relieve the geometric insistence of its tightly wrapped glass skin.

Civic Center, Thousand Oaks, Calif. (1973). Robert Mason Houvener, architect

Civic Center, Los Gatos, Calif. (1965). Charles D. Stickney & William R. Hull, architects

City Hall and Convention Center,
San Bernardino, Calif. (1972).
Gruen Associates, architects; Cesar Pelli, designer

*Seattle First National Bank, Seattle, Wash. (1969). Naramore, Bain,
Brady & Johanson, architects; Henry Moore, sculptor*

The personality of the fifty-two-story Bank of America
Building in San Francisco derives primarily from the unusual angled bays that frame all four sides and form the
varying-height setbacks at the upper levels. Single-pane
windows are flush with the granite facing of the structure.
The serrated façades recall the bay windows so familiar to
San Francisco domestic architecture. Seattle's outstanding
skyscraper is the fifty-story square shaft of the city's First
National Bank. Its floors are supported by the four gigantic
aluminum-clad steel corner columns and the concrete inner
elevator core, no inner columns being used in the tower
floors. Henry Moore's "Vertebrae," placed in front of the
structure, is one of America's finest examples of urban
sculpture. The building is topped by a heliport.

OVERLEAF: *The Strip, Las Vegas, Nev.* In utter contrast to the
formal structural organization of these handsome bank
buildings stands the Strip at Las Vegas, an orgy of contemporary American folk art in flamboyant neon lights.

*Bank of America, San Francisco, Calif. (1969). Wurster, Bernardi & Emmons with
Skidmore, Owings & Merrill, architects; Pietro Belluschi, consulting architect*

The Airport Business Center at Irvine, California, consists of twin sets of buildings—two rectangular one-story banks between two four-story office units. Solar bronze plate glass played against adroitly used weathering steel predominates in the construction. At San Rafael in California the Commerce Clearing House, a moderate-sized private office block, sensitively occupies its hillside site. A dining room has been angled out to provide a view of the Marin County hills. The Anchorage Natural Gas Building is one of the all-too-few meritorious structures in Alaska's first and largest city. A sculptured plaque, designed by Alex Duff Combs, an Alaskan artist, with semiabstract references to the state's wildlife and natural features, calls the attention of speeding motorists to this steel-frame building with its dark, anodized aluminum panels.

Airport Business Center, Irvine, Calif. (1969). Craig Ellwood Associates, architects

Commerce Clearing House Regional Headquarters, San Rafael, Calif. (1971).
Marquis & Stoller, architects

Anchorage Natural Gas Building, Anchorage, Alaska (1969).
Crittenden, Cassetta, Wirum & Cannon, architects

Salk Biological Research Institute, La Jolla, Calif. (1967). Louis I. Kahn, architect; Dr. August E. Komendant, structural engineer

The east-west-oriented court of the Salk Institute is lined with study towers, angled to face the ocean, that provide offices for thirty-six Fellows. These retreats are separated from two enormous blocks of laboratories by half-open, half-enclosed circulation "cloisters" where one encounters passages of sunshine and shadow, freedom and enclosure—an experience even more exciting than walking through the simple Italian cloisters which Dr. Salk (an eager client) initially had in mind.

OVERLEAF: *Court, Salk Biological Research Institute.* Hemmed by walls focusing on the immensity of the Pacific Ocean, the institute's court provides a brilliant formal setting on a gloriously informal site.

INDEX

Page numbers in italic indicate that the subject is illustrated.

Q

Queen Anne style, *757, 760-61*
Queen Emma's Summer Palace, Honolulu, Hawaii, *735*
Queens, N.Y., *262, 263*
Quincy, Josiah, Jr., 278

R

R. M. Gensert Associates: Blossom Music Center, near Akron, Ohio, *510*
Racine, Wis., *486-89*
Racquet and Tennis Club, New York, N.Y., *246, 247*
Raeder, Frederick: Sanger-Peper Building, St. Louis, Mo., *652*
Rague, John F.: Old State Capitol, Springfield, Ill., *449*
Raleigh, N.C., 352, *353, 404, 405*
Ramberg & Lowrey: Orange County Courthouse, Santa Ana, Calif., *790, 791*
Ranchos de Taos, N.M., *548-49*
Randall, Robert, 190
Rapson, Ralph R.: Tyrone Guthrie Theater, Minneapolis, Minn., *512*
Ravalli, Anthony, 639
Red Rocks Amphitheater, near Denver, Colo., *627, 678-79*
Redwood Library, Newport, R.I., *52*
Reed & Stem: Grand Central Station, New York, N.Y., 228, *229*
Regency style, *342*
Rehoboth Church, Union, W. Va., *328,* 329
Reid & Reid: Hotel del Coronado, Coronado, Calif., *708, 760-61*
Reinhart & Hofmeister: Rockefeller Center, New York, N.Y., *234-35*
Reliance Building, Chicago, Ill., *468,* 469
Reno, Nev., *797*
Renwick, James: St. Patrick's Cathedral, New York, N.Y., *198-99*; Smithsonian Institution, Washington, D.C., 204, *206-07*
Research Triangle Park, N.C., 412, *413-15*
Reserve, La., *572-73*
Reston, Va., *392-93*
Revere, Paul, 16, 39, 69
Reynolds, Smith & Hills: Tampa International Airport, Tampa, Fla., *400*
Reynolds Metals Building, Richmond, Va., *405*
Rhoades, William, 77
Rhyolite, Nev., 750, *752-53*
Richard Jackson House, Portsmouth, N.H., *37*
Richards, A. N.: Building, Philadelphia, Pa., *258-59*
Richards, Joseph B., 69
Richards House, Ideal Cement Corporation, Mobile, Ala., *274,* 369, *370-71*
Richardson, Henry Hobson, 18, 427, 467, 592, 625, 665, 777; Allegheny County Courthouse and Jail, Pittsburgh, Pa., *212-13*; Ames Monument, Sherman, Wyo., 668, *669*; Glessner House, Chicago, Ill., *466,* 467; Marshall Field Wholesale Store, Chicago, Ill., 427, 661; Trinity Church, Boston, Mass., 18, *94-95*
Richard Upjohn and Son: Greenwood Cemetery gates, Brooklyn, N.Y., *196-97*
Richmond, Vt., *77*
Richmond, Va., 332, 333, *373, 381-82,* 383-84, *385, 405*
Richmondtown Restoration, Staten Island, N.Y., *152-53*
Ridgely, Charles, 175
Ritchie, W. A.: Spokane County Courthouse, Spokane, Wash., 744, *745*
Riverdale, N.D., *698*
Riverpark Center, Spokane, Wash., 806, *807*

Robert Mills Historic House, Columbia, S.C., 338, *339*
Robert R. McMath Solar Telescope, Kitt Peak Observatory, Kitt Peak, Ariz., *617-19*
Robie House, Chicago, Ill., *483-85*
Roche, Kevin. *See* Kevin Roche, John Dinkeloo & Associates.
Rochester, N.Y., *259-61*
Rochester Institute of Technology, Rochester, N.Y., *260-61*
Rockefeller, John D., Jr., 294
Rockefeller Center, New York, N.Y., *234-35*
Rockingham, Vt., *44*
Rocky Hill Meetinghouse, Amesbury, Mass., 40, *42-44*
Rocky Mountain College, Billings, Mont., *690*
Rocky Mount Historic Shrine, near Johnson City, Tenn., *329*
Rodia, Simon: Rodia (Watts) Towers, Los Angeles, Calif., *776, 777*
Rodia (Watts) Towers, Los Angeles, Calif., *776, 777*
Roebling, John Augustus: bridge, Cincinnati, Ohio, *454-55*; Brooklyn Bridge, Brooklyn, N.Y., *200-201*; 10th Street Suspension Bridge, Wheeling, W.Va., *378*
Roebling, Washington: Brooklyn Bridge, Brooklyn, N.Y., *200-201*
Rogers, Cleo: Library, Columbus, Ind., *496*
Roi, Joseph, 434
Roi-Porlier-Tank House, Green Bay, Wis., 434, *435*
Romanesque style, *94-95, 204-05, 466-67, 666*
Roofless Church, New Harmony, Ind., 496, *498-99*
Rookery, The, Chicago, Ill., *469*
Roper, James W., 357
Rosalie, Natchez, Miss., *366*
Rose, Thomas: Stanton Hall, Natchez, Miss., *366*
Rosedown Plantation, St. Francisville, La., *567*
Rose Hill, Geneva, N.Y., *188*
Rosewall Hall, Va., 277
Roth, Emery. *See* Emery Roth & Sons.
Rothko, Mark, 612
Rothko Chapel, Houston, Tex., 612, *613*
Round Church, Richmond, Vt., *77*
Round Top, Tex., *584*
Rouse, William, 11
Rowan, John, 280
Row houses, Georgetown, Washington, D.C., *169*
Rudolph, Paul: Burroughs Wellcome Company, Research Triangle Park, N.C., 412, *413-15*; Earl W. Brydges Library, Niagara Falls, N.Y., *250*; Massachusetts State Service Center, Boston, Mass., 103, *104-05*; Orange County Government Center, Goshen, N.Y., 250, *251*; Southeastern Massachusetts University, North Dartmouth, Mass., *114-15*; Tuskegee Institute Chapel, Tuskegee, Ala., 390, *391*
Ruggles, Thomas: House, Columbia Falls, Maine, *66-67*
Rumbold, William: Old Courthouse, St. Louis, Mo., *662*
Rush & Endicott: Boston Avenue Methodist Church, Tulsa, Okla., 592, *593*
Russell, Nathaniel, 337; House, Charleston, S.C., *336-37*
Russian blockhouse, Sitka, Alaska, *737*
Rutledge, Edward, 138

S

S. C. Johnson Offices and Research and Development Tower, Racine, Wis., *486-89*
S. R. Crown Hall, Illinois Institute of Technology, Chicago, Ill., *520*

Saarinen, Eero, 242, 505. *See also* Eero Saarinen & Associates.
Saarinen, Eliel, 242; Christ Church Lutheran, Minneapolis, Minn., *490*
Sabbathday Lake, Maine, *60*
Sacramento, Calif., 706, 710, *754-55*
Sag Harbor, Long Island, N.Y., *216*
Sailors' Snug Harbor, Staten Island, N.Y., *190*
St. Augustine, Fla., 275, 283, *284-85,* 291, *292-93,* 383
St. Bartholomew's Church, New York, N.Y., 677
St. Benedict, Oreg., *796,* 797
Ste. Genevieve, Mo., *634-35*
St. Francis de Sales Church, Muskegon, Mich., *493*
St. Francisville, La., *567*
Saint-Gaudens, Augustus, 668
St. George, Utah, *644*
St. James Church, Goose Creek, S.C., *298-99*
St. John's Preparatory School, Collegeville, Minn., *502*
St. John's University, Collegeville, Minn., *492,* 502, 683
St. Jude Church, Grand Rapids, Mich., *490-91*
St. Louis, Mo., 623, *652, 654-55, 662-63,* 668, 669, *670-71, 674-75, 684-86,* 691, *700-701*
St. Louis Cathedral, New Orleans, La., *533*
St. Louis Cemetery #1, New Orleans, La., *576,* 577
St. Luke's Church, Smithfield, Va., *288-89*
St. Martinville, La., 533, *560,* 561
St. Michael's Episcopal Church, Charleston, S.C., *312-13*
St. Nicholas Orthodox Church, Juneau, Alaska, *739*
St. Patrick's Cathedral, New York, N.Y., *198-99*
St. Patrick's Church, Oklahoma City, Okla., *606-07*
St. Paul, Minn., *442, 451, 480-81, 490,* 623
St. Paul's Chapel, New York, N.Y., 170, *171*
St. Paul's Church, Ironton, Mo., 620, *647*
St. Paul's Episcopal Church, Edenton, N.C., *316*
St. Stephen's Church, St. Stephen, S.C., *322*
Salem, Mass., 12, 16, 62, *63-65*
Salem, Oreg., 746, *747*
Salk Biological Research Institute, La Jolla, Calif., *816-19*
Salmon, William, 14, 305
Salt Lake City, Utah, 624-25, 649, *650-52,* 664, 665
Samuel Paley Park, New York, N.Y., 270, *271*
Samuel Whitehorne House, Newport, R.I., *54*
San Antonio, Tex., 530, 532, 536, *552-55,* 558, 559, *594-95*
San Bernardino, City Hall and Convention Center, San Bernardino, Calif., 808, *809*
San Carlos de Borromeo Mission, Carmel, Calif., *715*
San Diego, Calif., 704, 709, *714,* 715, *785*
Sandwich, Mass., *23*
San Estévan del Rey, Ácoma, N.M., *550*
San Francisco, Calif., 702, 704, *706-09, 756-57, 766, 768-69, 772, 777-800,* 801, *810,* 811
San Francisco, Reserve, La., *572-73*
San Francisco de Asís, Ranchos de Taos, N.M., *548-49*
San Francisco State University, San Francisco, Calif., *800,* 801
San Gabriel Arcángel, San Gabriel, Calif., *716,* 717
Sanger-Peper Building, St. Louis, Mo., *652*
San Ildefonso Pueblo, N.M., *544-45*
San José de Gracia, Las Trampas, N.M., *555*
San José de Laguna, Laguna, N.M., *550,* 555
San José y San Miguel de Aguayo, San Antonio, Tex., 530, *552-53*